EDWARD MARTYN
AND THE
IRISH REVIVAL

BY
DENIS GWYNN

LEMMA PUBLISHING CORPORATION
NEW YORK
1974

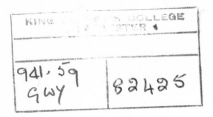
Published by
Lemma Publishing Corporation
509 Fifth Avenue
New York, N.Y. 10017

Manufactured in the U.S.A.

For sale and distribution only in the U.S.A.

LIBRARY OF CONGRESS
CATALOGING IN PUBLICATION DATA

Gwynn, Denis Rolleston, 1893-
   Edward Martyn and the Irish revival.

   Reprint of the 1930 ed. published by J. Cape,
London.
     1. Martyn, Edward, 1859-1923. 2. Ireland--
Intellectual life. 3. Dublin. Abbey Theatre. 4.
Church music--Ireland. I. Title.
DÃ952.M3G8 1973 914.15'03'90924 [B] 72-87977
ISBN 0-87696-046-8

Edward Martyn

From the painting by Miss Sara Purser, R.H.A. Reproduced by kind permission of the Municipal Gallery of Modern Art, Dublin.

EDWARD MARTYN
AND THE
IRISH REVIVAL

BY DENIS GWYNN

JONATHAN CAPE
THIRTY BEDFORD SQUARE
LONDON

FIRST PUBLISHED 1930

JONATHAN CAPE 30 BEDFORD SQUARE LONDON
& 91 WELLINGTON STREET WEST, TORONTO
JONATHAN CAPE & HARRISON SMITH
139 EAST 46TH STREET NEW YORK

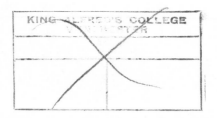

PRINTED IN GREAT BRITAIN BY
THE GARDEN CITY PRESS LTD.
LETCHWORTH

CONTENTS

LIST OF ILLUSTRATIONS

'THE IRISH REVIVAL'

Reproduced by kind permission of the artist, from the cover design drawn by Beatrice Elvery (Mrs. Gordon Campbell) for the late Miss Susan L. Mitchell's *Aids to the Immortality of Certain Persons in Ireland*. The portraits from left to right show: Edward Martyn, W. B. Yeats, George Moore, Lord MacDonnell of Swinford, Douglas Hyde, George Russell ('A. E.'), Sir Horace Plunkett, Sir Hugh Lane, Sir William Orpen, and Captain Frank Shawe-Taylor.

INTRODUCTION

INTRODUCTION

No other Irishman, in the various movements which together may be generally described as the 'Irish Revival' — between the eighteen-nineties and the establishment of the Irish Free State in 1921 — occupies the same prominent place as Edward Martyn as a connecting link between so many intellectual activities. He was in the peculiar position of being the only Irishman with large private means who was in full sympathy with almost every phase of the Irish Revival, and he was not only willing but eager to spend his money in promoting new enterprises that would give expression to the ideals of 'Irish Ireland.' But he was much more than the source of money which was indispensable for each new enterprise. He had already made a reputation among men of letters when Mr. W. B. Yeats was beginning to be known as a poet; and it was he who introduced Mr. Yeats to both Mr. George Moore and to Lady Gregory, and obtained their collaboration with him in founding the Irish Literary Theatre which afterwards developed into the Abbey Theatre. It was Edward Martyn who not only provided the money with which the first group of actors were got together, but who also wrote the first play which attracted favourable attention when it was acted in Dublin, and so made the subsequent development possible.

The creation of the Irish Literary Theatre always appeared to him as 'the most significant action' of his own life, and the theatre was always his chief interest.

But his activity in other directions had much wider results. When Arthur Griffith, as editor of the *United Irishman*, desired to republish the series of articles which he had written on the 'Hungarian policy,' as the model for what afterwards became the Sinn Féin movement, he turned to Edward Martyn, whom he scarcely knew as yet, for the financial assistance that was always so difficult to obtain in a country with few rich men of public spirit. Edward Martyn financed the pamphlet which was to be the political gospel of the next generation; and he became President for four years of the Sinn Féin organisation. To the revival of the Irish language, he was one of the few Irishmen who gave substantial subsidies. He was for years a member of the executive committee, or Coisde Gnótha, of the Gaelic League; and it was his enthusiasm for the language revival, and his desire to write plays in Irish, that stirred Mr. George Moore to wholly unexpected adventures and brought him to Dublin to assist in the foundation of the Irish Theatre, and afterwards to write his famous trilogy of Irish memories, *Ave*, *Salve*, and *Vale*.

While the Gaelic League would very probably have gone forward without Edward Martyn's assistance, it is to him more than anyone else that the revival of Irish music, which has made the annual Féis Ceóil (or musical festival) one of the most flourishing events in modern Ireland, is due. He could claim that he had been the first to discover traditional Irish singing, and to have saved a fast disappearing native tradition from extinction. And perhaps the most direct practical result of his life's work was the very definite improvement of ecclesiastical music and art which he inspired throughout Ireland.

His success in persuading the late Archbishop of Dublin
to reform the church music in the pro-Cathedral, by
introducing the Palestrina Choir, which Edward Martyn
handsomely endowed, seemed for many years to be little
more than an isolated achievement. But Edward Martyn,
in his enthusiasm for plain chant, was a pioneer in a
modern revival which has since swept Europe. He was
already negotiating with Archbishop Walsh before Pius
X, who undertook the systematic campaign to restore
plain chant throughout the Catholic Church, had yet
been elected Pope. And since Edward Martyn's death
there has arisen a concerted movement throughout the
whole Catholic Church which is rapidly restoring plain
chant in every country as an indispensable part of the
Church's liturgy.

Few men of his generation could claim to have achieved
so much by individual effort in assisting movements
which have all made a profound mark upon modern
times. Yet Ireland was the last place where any success
might have been looked for in the fulfilment of a young
landlord's intellectual ambitions, when he returned to his
feudal castle in County Galway after leaving Oxford at
the beginning of the 'eighties. No country could have
been more devoid of literature or art, and an utter indifference to all cultural movements was as characteristic
of his own social class as of all the rest. The whole
energies of the country were absorbed in political turmoil, with Parnell newly arrived as the leader of a
militant Nationalist movement, and the Land League
lately established and spreading like wild fire through
every county. For a young man who had none of the
ordinary country tastes, whose chief interest even in

B

literature was the theatre, and who had been born with an intense love of music, life in a remote castle in the west of Ireland seemed to offer less scope than almost anywhere in the world.

Yet before he had reached middle age, he was actively engaged in the promotion of flourishing artistic and literary movements in Ireland, which had already attracted attention everywhere and had produced in Ireland itself such an array of talent as a small country has very seldom contained. Mr. Yeats and George Russell, with the assistance of Mr. George Moore, whose paradoxical friendship with Edward Martyn swept him back to his own country for a time, had created a literary movement that before long brought to life a startling display of unsuspected talent. John M. Synge, introduced to an astonished world through the Irish Theatre, had died within a few years, when his name was just beginning to be known. Within a few years more, James Stephens, Lennox Robinson, St. John Ervine, had all made their reputations in an Ireland which, a generation before, would not have had either a theatre or a publisher that could have produced their work.

In art the revival was scarcely less astonishing. Sir William Orpen was still a student in the art schools in Dublin which Edward Martyn and his friends had lately got established, under the auspices of the comprehensive new Department of Agriculture and Technical Instruction. Hugh Lane, drawn into the same movement, as Lady Gregory's nephew, was still at the beginning of his fame as a discoverer of great painters ; and he, too, was to organise a wonderful exhibition of modern pictures in Dublin, to be followed a few years later by his own

princely gift of modern pictures, paintings and sculp-
tures, which formed the nucleus of a Municipal Gallery
of Modern Art that made Dublin familiar with the works
of Manet and Degas and Rodin, of Wilson Steer and
Augustus John and the new English Art Club long
before the Tate Gallery in London had awakened to
their existence. In sculpture there were two Irish artists
of outstanding distinction, Mr. Oliver Shepherd and
Mr. John Hughes. In architecture a new revival of the
early Celtic tradition was initiated by the brilliant work
of Professor W. A. Scott. In the applied arts, Miss Sara
Purser, with Edward Martyn's assistance, was to create
a stained glass industry which was to become famous on
both sides of the Atlantic. And in music, it was no small
achievement that Edward Martyn should have discovered John MacCormack among his choir boys at the
pro-Cathedral.

Much of the story and of the atmosphere of those
varied and fascinating movements has been told in the
three volumes of inimitable reminiscences, enlivened on
every page by the imaginative touches of a master of
fiction, in which Mr. George Moore has described his
own quixotic part amid so much intellectual activity. Mr.
Moore has, by common consent, achieved his place
among the immortal writers of imaginative confessions;
and in his three volumes of light memories, he has per-
petuated much of the spirit of those teeming years. To
those who have read his trilogy, the personality of
Edward Martyn probably lives as clearly as any character
in modern fiction; and his readers must have been vastly
entertained — as both Edward Martyn and George
Moore themselves were for so many years — by one of

the strangest friendships in literary history. It would be hard to imagine two characters more utterly contradictory than that pair of eccentric landlords from the west of Ireland, both sprung from old Catholic stock and linked by that kinship which exists in some degree between all the Catholic landowning families of the west. Both had been educated at Catholic schools in England; but whereas George Moore's wayward instincts had led him in endless pursuit of amorous adventures — whether real or imaginary — and of bohemian surroundings in Paris and in London, Edward Martyn had returned to live, under the stern care of his mother, in a modernised feudal castle in County Galway, a monk at heart, and hating all women with an instinctive, almost perverted antipathy. There was a difference of some six years between their ages, and Edward, as the younger of the two, had learned much in appreciation of modern paintings and modern literature from his unlikely friend, though their whole attitude towards life was quite antagonistic on most matters.

Both were to leave absurd portraits of each other in their writings, and in the end George Moore's malicious caricaturing of Edward in his trilogy was to estrange them completely. But so long as Mr. Moore's *Hail and Farewell* is read, the picture of 'dear Edward' will remain as he recurs through passage after passage — sometimes in affectionate glimpses as the most picturesque figure in all that gifted group of men who created the Irish revival, sometimes as the buffoon that Mr. Moore makes him appear, in those carefully polished conversations invented to show his own skill in scoring off his opponents in controversy. It was one of Mr. Moore's less conspicuous victims, who said of his volumes when they first appeared, that Mr. Moore had made a very valuable discovery in merely going round Dublin with a notebook recording all the clever things that other people said, instead of wasting his time in trying to write a clever book out of his own head. Another of his chief victims, who had been treated more unkindly, agreeing with that observant criticism, commented that Mr. Moore had really made a better discovery than that; for he went home with his notebook and attributed to himself all the clever things that he had heard other people say, and attributed to his friends all the silly things that he had said himself. 'For inventing such conversations after the event,' said this particular victim, 'Moore has an undeniable genius.'

Be that as it may — and it conveys the verdict of most of Mr. Moore's acquaintances during those years in Dublin — there is surely no other modern writer who can describe a man in his appearance and in his habits of life with the same delicate precision of detail. To those who know his famous trilogy, the name of Edward Martyn will always conjure up a picture of him as he is described in the opening paragraphs of *Ave*, when Mr. Moore used to spend his evenings with him in his garret in Pump Court in 1894, 'sure of finding him seated in his high canonical chair, sheltered by a screen reading his book, his glass of grog beside him, his long clay pipe in his hand; and we used to talk literature and drama until two or three in the morning.' It was on one such evening that Edward's announcement of his desire to write plays in Irish set Mr. Moore thinking of Ireland again after years of absence, and eventually brought him to Dublin to assist in founding the Irish Theatre. All through his recollections he haunts Mr. Moore; and towards the end of *Vale* he is driven to exclaiming:

'There is no doubt that I owe a great deal of my happiness to Edward; all my life long he has been exquisite entertainment.' How hard it was that Nature had made him so impossible a character to write a book about! 'A story would be necessary to bring Edward into literature, and it would be impossible to devise any action to which he should be a part. The sex of a woman is odious to him, and a man with two thousand a year does not rob nor steal, and he is so uninterested in his fellow-men that he has never an ill word to say about anybody.' And in another outburst: 'As I understand him, he is a temperament without a rudder; all he has to rely upon is his memory, which isn't a very good one, and so he often tumbles from one mistake into another. My God! it is a terrible thing to happen to one, to understand a man better than he understands himself, and to be powerless to help him.'

Edward's attitude towards their friendship, after Mr. Moore had written his trilogy, was that George Moore had 'constituted himself my Boswell.' Mr. Moore's attitude, clearly indicated throughout his books, was that Edward was his own Sancho Panza. There is immortal comedy in the repeated pictures of Moore's serenading his friend from the pavement outside his two rooms over the tobacconist's shop in Lincoln Place, just round the corner from Kildare Street Club. Edward's friends still chuckle at their own recollections of the plaintive notes of Mr. Moore's whistling rising from the street in the dusk of evenings, and of the smile on Edward's face when he would say: 'That's George outside. We'll make him do it again before we let him in.' Mr. Moore's own version of it is more romantic, and he explains that: 'It is necessary to whistle very loudly, for the trams make a great deal of noise, and Edward sometimes dozes on the sofa. On the other side is a public-house, and the serenading of Edward draws comments from the topers as they go away wiping their mouths. One has to choose a quiet moment between the trams; and when the serenade has been whistled twice, the light of Edward's candle appears, coming very slowly down the stairs, and there he is in the doorway, if anything larger than life, in the voluminous grey trousers, and over his shoulders a buff jacket which he wears in the evening. Two short flights of stairs, and we are in his room. It never changes — the same litter from day to day, from year to year, the same old and broken mahogany furniture, the same musty wall-paper, dusty manuscripts lying about in heaps, and many dusty books. If one likes a man one likes his habits, and never do I go into Edward's room without admiring the old prints that he tacks on the wall, or looking through the books on the great round table, or admiring the little sofa between the round table and the Japanese screen, which Edward bought for a few shillings down the quays — a torn, dusty, ragged screen, but serviceable enough: it keeps out the draught; and Edward is especially susceptible to draughts, the very slightest will give him a cold. Between the folds of the screen one will find a small harmonium of about three octaves, and on it a score of Palestrina. As well might one try to play the Mass upon a flute, and one can only think that it serves to give the key-note to a choir-boy. On the table is a candlestick

made out of white tin, designed probably by Edward
himself, for it holds four candles. He prefers candles
for reading, but he snuffs them when I enter and lights
the gas, offers me a cigar, refills his churchwarden, and
closes his book.'

In such descriptions of interiors Mr. Moore is quite
inimitable. As a chronicler of facts his imagination is
apt to play him false — if one may so speak of a literary
artist who has always proclaimed the necessity of remaining free from the restrictions of fidelity to fact. He is,
for instance, either wholly misinformed or else deliberately imaginative in his account of Edward's founding of
the Palestrina Choir. He makes the bold suggestion that
the endowment was made by Edward to appease his own
conscience after committing some sin — ('What sin can
he have committed?' asks Mr. Moore) — upon which he
had specially consulted Archbishop Healy. The revolt
of his tenants had caused him weeks of conscientious
anxiety, because they had fired at his bailiff on the high-
road to Gort; and as Mr. Moore puts it: 'If he had acted
wrongly he must make reparation before his sin would
be forgiven him.'

Whatever foundation (if any) there may be for his
reminiscence of Edward's early scruples, Mr. Moore is
quite hopelessly at sea in his account of the negotiations
with Archbishop Walsh for the foundation of the Palestrina Choir. Edward's chief interest in life consisted in
spending his money frugally on the promotion of the
artistic or literary enterprises which appealed to him,
and he must have derived vastly more satisfaction from
spending ten thousand pounds on endowing the Cathedral choir and on providing his most intimate friend,

Vincent O'Brien, with scope for his talent, than from any other expenditure in all his life. That he should have succeeded in persuading the Archbishop of Dublin to reform the music in the principal church in the Irish capital, and to accept Edward's own opinion as the principal authority on all musical matters — to say nothing of having induced him to make an endowment of equal amount — was vastly more than he could ever have hoped to accomplish. And the most curious feature of the story — as the correspondence of Archbishop Walsh which is published in this book will show — was that it was not Edward but the Archbishop himself who took endless pains to ensure for centuries to come against any possibility of the fund being diverted from the purpose which Edward had intended.

Mr. Moore's picture of his friend, of course, is a deliberate effort to make him appear foolish; and he has frequently insisted, in relation to painting, that scrupulous fidelity to nature imposes limitations which no artist should accept. 'There is nobody like him,' he writes of dear Edward, in a final effort, towards the close of *Vale*, to show him in this comic light. ' He is more wonderful than anything in literature. I prefer him to Sancho, who was untroubled with a conscience, and never thought of running to the Bishop of Toledo. Edward is not without the shrewdness of his ancestors and got the better of Archbishop Walsh, and for the last five years Vincent O'Brien has been beating time, and will beat it to the end of his life; and he will be succeeded by others, for Edward has, by deed, saved the Italian contrapuntalists till time everlasting from competition with modern composers. He certainly has gotten the

better of Walsh.' Accentuating his caricature, he tells
an absurd story of how 'the unrefined ears that weary of
erudite music left the Cathedral and sought instinctively modern tunes and women's voices,' with the
result that the big church at Westland Row became
crowded with poor people driven out from the Cathedral,
until 'the professional Catholics of Merrion Square'
were in their turn driven out of Westland Row by 'the
searching smells of dirty clothes,' and went to the University Church in Stephen's Green instead. And, piling
on his buffooneries, Mr. Moore breaks out again:
'There never was anybody so interesting as dear Edward, and there never will be anybody like him in literature. . . .'

Seldom indeed can a man of letters have spent so much
time and ingenuity in elaborating conversations intended
to represent him as scoring off one of his most intimate
friends. Yet there is a lingering affection even in these
acidulated descriptions of dear Edward, which is perhaps the only glimpse of human kindness in all Mr.
Moore's trilogy. 'He is original even in his candelabra,'
Mr. Moore exclaims, after describing another of many
visits to Edward's rooms. 'No one before him had ever
thought of candelabra in tin, and I fell to admiring his
appearance more carefully than perhaps I had ever done
before, so monumental did he seem lying on the little
sofa sheltered from draughts by a screen, a shawl about
his shoulders. His churchwarden was drawing famously,
and I noticed his great square hands with strong fingers
and square nails pared closely away, and as heretofore I
admired the curve of the great belly, the thickness of the
thighs, the length and breadth of his foot hanging over

the edge of the sofa, the apoplectic neck falling into great rolls of flesh, the humid eyes, the skull covered with short stubbly hair. I looked round the rooms and they seemed part of himself. The old green wall-paper on which he pins reproductions of the Italian masters, and I longed to peep once more into the bare bedroom into which he goes to fetch bottles of Apollinaris. Always original! Is there another man in this world whose income is two thousand a year, and who sleeps in a bare bedroom, without dressing-room, or bath-room, or servant in the house to brush his clothes? Only a maid of all work, so he has to go to the baker's for his breakfast. He has always said that he does not care for private life, only public life. One never knows exactly what he means. He seems to suspect private life, to be afraid of it.'

Edward's only retaliation at first, to the publication of *Hail and Farewell*, had been to announce, in filling up his next entry for *Who's Who*, that his recreation was 'Mr. George Augustus Moore,' knowing that Mr. Moore was always annoyed by the use of his second Christian name. But as Mr. Moore's provocation grew with the publication of the later volumes, Edward took the matter more seriously and wrote a play in which George Moore was held up to ridicule under the scarcely disguised name of George Augustus Moon. In *The Dream Physician* Edward showed that he had an undeniable gift for creating comic situations, and his talent as a writer of satire, which had produced his first book *Morgante the Lesser*, found new scope with a lighter subject. The idea of his play is really ingenious. He makes George Augustus Moon publish a book of poems

under a girl's name, and the hero of the play announces
that he has fallen in love with the writer of the poems,
though he has to confess that he has never even seen her.
His father, a highly respectable Colonel, is appalled at
the idea and exclaims: 'What! the grand-niece of your
funny old Mayo journalist! You would only be making
yourself and me ridiculous.' When the young man
protests, his father can only retort that 'by all accounts
she's as funny as her old grand-uncle. . . . She's a real
Mayo genius like her grand-uncle. Tell me, isn't she
called La Mayonaise?' That, the young man explains
proudly, is her *nom de plume;* and his sister, arriving on
the scenes, tries to persuade him that La Mayonaise is
'as authentic as the duels that George Augustus fought
in Paris.' Does he not know, she expostulates, that
George Augustus himself is universally believed to be
the author himself, and that 'he would have acknowledged
their authorship if the poems had not been considered so
absurd.'

Later in the play George Augustus Moon himself
appears, and Edward Martyn has his opportunity of
retaliation in describing George Moore's appearance.
'He is a little old man,' runs the stage direction, 'with a
plump body, short thick legs, very broad hips, very
sloping shoulders, a long neck and a pasty, almost feature-
less face, surmounted by what was once very red, but is
now sandy hair streaked with grey. He wears dark
clothes with trousers baggy at the knees, and has altogether a look of absent-mindedness and vacuity.' His
conversation gives Edward ample opportunities for caricature. The great author comes in babbling about the
exquisite vision he has just seen of little pigs — ('They are

the most beautiful things in the world. I never knew there were such things before as little pigs.') — and urging upon the Colonel the importance of breeding pigs on his estate. His presence is by no means welcomed, and to annoy him the other characters insist on addressing him as George Augustus. This irritates him so much that in a temper he leaves the room, vowing that he will never set foot in the place again. But a few minutes later the door opens and he returns, having thought out some sort of repartee. He then proceeds to read aloud some of his own recent writings, emphasising their literary quality and comparing himself to Swift — which provokes the retort that 'While Swift was a terror to his enemies, you are only a terror to your friends.' Edward can never have enjoyed anything more than writing these five acts, which bring in all his favourite jokes against Mr. Moore, even to calling him *mon ami Moon*. And having set out to be ruthlessly outspoken in reply to George Moore's own caricature of himself, he expresses his own feelings freely, making one of his characters exclaim: 'This genius for making the cad engaging is your chief claim to immortality,' in a scene which makes Mr. Moon talk grandiloquently about art in the most ludicrous setting of tomfoolery.

It had been a strange friendship, that caused as much embarrassment as amusement to Edward Martyn, who would never tolerate either blasphemy or indecorous conversation in other company, but who provoked Mr. Moore continually to both. 'Dear Edward's only indiscretion was George Moore,' was one of the epigrams of a witty Dublin lady who knew them both well. He had few really intimate friends, and he used to say that his

friends were all either Bohemians or priests. Many years
before his death he had lost the friendship that had
probably exercised most influence upon his youth, with
the death of his old neighbour in County Galway, the
French Comte de Basterot, who shared so many of his
own enthusiasms. A man of wide culture and a devout
Catholic, de Basterot had kept Edward in constant
touch with contemporary literature in France, through
his own intimacy with Maurice Barrès and de Maupassant
and their group. It was the old French Count, spending
each summer on his own estate in County Galway, who
had encouraged Edward most as a young man in writing
poems when he returned home from Oxford, who guided
him in the later development of his literary talent, and
who was able to restrain him in his frequent impulses to
make wild incursions into politics, after he had outgrown
the Conservative tradition in which he was reared, and
had become an uncompromising Nationalist.

After he had made his first incursions into Irish politics
during the Boer War, his natural obstinacy intensified,
and hostile criticism could only provoke him to further
outbursts. His sudden resignation of his commissions
as a magistrate and as a Deputy-Lieutenant for his
county had brought him into unexpected and sensational
prominence. But he was always aware at heart that
politics was not the field for his own talents, and in
Comte de Basterot he had a candid friend, who could still
influence him to refrain from such indiscretions. His
letters to the *Freeman's Journal* exhorting to demonstrations of public disaffection during the King's visit to
Ireland in 1903 caused intense pain to his old friend,
and the earnest reproof that de Basterot sent to him imme-

diately from Paris was probably effective in dissuading him from further interventions. 'I am about your oldest friend,' wrote the Comte. 'You must feel that I am very fond of you. I admire your literary talent, your artistic taste. I think I am free from the influence of what I was the first to call "shabby England" of clubmen, coteries, etc. Why do you rush wildly into print about politics that are not your line? *Ne forcez pas votre talent, vous ne ferez rien avec grâce.* La Fontaine was a good adviser. Literary talent and political insight do not seem to pull together. See what a sad figure Lamartine, Victor Hugo made in politics. Your two political letters in the *Freeman* have given me pain; the last of the 21st great pain. It is so scurrilous, and not even well put together. Who could believe it was written by the author of *The Enchanted Sea?* The harm is done, and you will say what is the use of this letter — to entreat of you not to be a catspaw of "parasites," to let the subject drop and to retire to the higher regions of poetry and art. It is there and not in "Home Rule" that you may serve Ireland.'

Nevertheless, the urge towards politics grew upon him with the years, colouring his whole outlook upon life. It had been his dream to encourage national art and national literature, and English customs and ideas had overlaid and stifled all that he was anxious to revive. As a young man he had soon outgrown the influences of his education in England. Travel, his own friendships, and most of all his intense Catholicism, had made him think in terms of a European tradition which had been lost in England since the Reformation; and English rule in Ireland had cut Ireland off from the older civilisation

of Europe, introducing false standards that had no relation to the ideas or the religion of Irish people. He had
been a Unionist like all his neighbours in Galway, as a
young man; and he had loathed Gladstonian Liberalism
as English demagogy. But his interest in the national
revival made him more and more anti-English, and when
he began to read Irish history, the influence of Lecky—
although that earnest historian was a staunch Unionist
himself—increased his hostility to England, and made
him an extreme Nationalist. The bitterness of Irish
politics grew upon him, and in the later years, when the
fastidious de Basterot was no longer there to restrain his
outbursts, his political writings became more frequent
and more scurrilous.

Always a lonely man, it was Edward Martyn's tragedy
that his whole ambitions were concerned with public
life, yet his natural shyness and his eccentricity made him
unfitted for it. On various occasions he was invited with
great urgency to stand for Parliament, as one of the very
few landlords with popular sympathies who would have
made an admirable representative for his own county;
but a sound instinct made him always refuse. In each of
his most important ventures he dropped out, after the
movement that he had originated had gathered momen-
tum; yet he was sensitive that his own part in the bringing
of so many schemes to life should be ignored. In his last
years, when infirmity confined him to his castle at Tulira,
and he was left without friends, he collected a number of
papers that he had contributed over some thirty years to
various newspapers and reviews, and wished to publish
them as a record of his own ideas and achievements. He
gave the projected volume the title *Paragraphs for the*

Perverse, and he wrote an introduction for it, summaris-
ing his own reflections upon what he had seen and done
and attempted. The essays are too laboured to be suitable for publication as he left them, and only extracts
from them have been included in this memoir.

In his introduction to the collection, he explained that
he intended it to serve 'as a condensed record of a very
determined fight for some of the improvements in civilisation actually brought to pass amongst us. As the articles
were mostly directed against the perverse of the past, I
now offer them in a distilled form to the perverse of the
present, whose minds the continued blessings of English
government and education have the more distorted and
hardened to dislike of all intellectuality and good taste.'
Prolonged infirmity and the loneliness of his later years
had made his attitude more bitter and his style more
crabbed. 'I am one of those,' he continued, 'who walk
the thorny path of the reformer, a path everyone knows
is as thorny as that of the venerable female of our rather
eccentric patriotic device. Perhaps it is because we have
chosen a decrepit old woman as the symbol of our
country struggling for her rights, and called those who
follow her "wild geese," that we may be more difficult
material for the reformer than other peoples. Be that as
it may, our history would seem to show beyond doubt
that we excel most nations, and probably all humanity,
in the curious propensity of wanting to turn things to
uses for which they were never intended. An immortal
example of this is related in *Handy Andy* where the little
electioneering agent asks the hero, who is for the time
"Boots" at an inn, for a boot-jack. Andy brings him one
with a broken crook, and to the guest's remonstrances

c

explains that it had been reduced to that condition by the cook using it for "batin' the cock." Frightened by the little man's indignation at such Irish savagery to a weak domestic fowl, he hastens to add that he did not mean the "hin cock," only the cock of the porter barrel which he was hammering in with the boot-jack.

'I am sure that "batin' the cock" with a boot-jack instead of a hammer may stand as a symbol for things done in other lands as well as in Ireland. The only difference is that these things are done far oftener in Ireland, and are doubtless the cause of our morbid propensity to resist the most obvious reforms as cranks of the abnormal, in which of course a normal country would merely see reasonableness and necessity. We have many clever, brave and consistent people, the best I have ever known in any country, but we have not enough of them. The vast bulk of our countrymen of all classes, politics and denominations are just a conglomeration of Handy Andys, and the reason why the able plans and organisations of our great men, which begin so well, often end in failure is that as they develop they must necessarily sweep in the Handy Andys, who produce confusion, jobbery and collapse.'

Even in the end he was aware that his own writing tended too much to rancour; and at the conclusion of his introduction he attempts to justify himself. 'I need scarcely say I hope that my readers may not look upon me as one of those animals that seem to infest Ireland, that are known by the delightful name of soreheads, and that write books in order to show the ingratitude of our countrymen for not at once swallowing their nostrums. The proof I am not so is that although my reforms are resisted as much as ever, I am more ardent than ever in reform. In fact opposition only adds fuel to my ardour; and I should despise myself if, like the soreheads who when resisted veer round to opposite ideas and disgusted leave the country, I were to cede before triumphant Handy Andyism. By such action I would consider myself no better than the Handy Andys themselves, whose thick heads on the contrary I hope I shall never cease to pound, until the intelligent and well informed prevail in the affairs of our country.

'I am even stimulated by the perversity of that Donnybrook Fair type of Irishman, Mr. George Augustus Moore, who by constituting himself my Boswell has, like his prototype, obtained a notoriety of mean vanity, if not for the unique fidelity of the portraiture, an immortality which assuredly none of his other works could bring him. *Mon ami Moore* yearns to be *le génie de l'amitié*, but unfortunately he can never be looked upon as a friend. For he suffers from an incurable complaint which manifests itself in the form of a catarrh or looseness of the brain which causes a perennial condition of mental diarrhoea. This must be shot somewhere at once, and necessarily over those nearest to him, his friends. Then, in order to hide his infirmity, he pretends he has done something very clever, and like the infant Morgante, when he misbehaves himself, clapping his little hands he laughingly shouts: "I did this because I knew it would annoy you." But it does not annoy somehow, I suppose because it is *mon ami Moore*.'

It was not often that his good nature failed him so far as to write such bitter words of anyone. But he had suffered extreme provocation from Mr. Moore, who had ridiculed his personal appearance with such minute detail; emphasising everything that could serve a comic purpose. And the fact that even while the volumes were going to the printers, Mr. Moore continued to write him occasional letters of literary criticism, was no atonement for such gross and unprovoked insults. Their friendship had for many years been one-sided. 'It is I who go to him,' says Mr. Moore in a page of unguarded frankness in his memoirs. And Edward, the most good-natured of men, would never refuse to meet an old friend who called at his rooms. For years they had been a source of continual amusement to each other. Edward had long ago adopted the habit of calling him '*mon ami Moore*' in allusion to an old joke they had together, which Edward told so often that Mr. Moore is driven to giving his own version of it on a page of *Salve:* 'His face became grave again and he muttered "*Mon ami Moore, mon ami Moore.*" Old friends have always their own jokes, and this joke has tickled Edward in his sense of humour for the last twenty years or more. It appears that in a moment of intense boredom I had asked a very dignified old lady in a solemn salon in the Faubourg St. Germain "*si elle jouait aux cartes, si elle aimait le jeu,*" and on receiving an answer in the negative, I had replied: "*Vous aimez sans doute bien mieux, madame, le petit jeu d'amour.*" The old lady appealed to her husband, and explanations had ensued, and my friend Marshall, of the "Confessions," had to explain "*que son ami Moore n'a pas voulu*" — what, history does not relate. The story has no other point except that it has tickled Edward in all his fat for twenty years, and that he regaled Gill with it that afternoon, shaking with laughter all the while, and repeating the phrase "*vous aimez sans doute, madame, le petit jeu d'amour*," until at last, to stop him, I had to say: "My dear Edward, I am ashamed to find you indulging in improper conversation.'"

How remote from these undignified exchanges were the happy years when Edward had made Tulira Castle a place of noble hospitality for Irishmen of all classes who were interested in the arts or in literature or in the economic revival. They had been welcome there at all times of the year, and frequently when he was not there himself, he would urge his friends who needed a holiday to treat it as their own. But there was a tragic loneliness about his later years, when he had grown estranged from those who had helped him to found the Irish Theatre, and his own friends in the neighbourhood had gradually disappeared. George Moore had never lived at Moore Hall in Mayo, after he inherited it on his father's death, and his own excursions to the west had usually been centred at Tulira. But there had been a remarkable group living in Edward's neighbourhood. Lady Gregory's house at Coole, where so much of Mr. Yeats's work was written, was only a few miles away. Lord Killanin, another public-spirited landlord, who became Chairman of the Galway County Council, was a kindred soul, who lived entirely among his books, in one of the most attractive country places in Ireland. And as he was also a Catholic, he and Edward had many interests in common, and he was deeply grateful to Edward for having introduced him to the architect Professor Scott who designed the charming Celtic church he built for the parish of Spiddal. And quite close to Tulira was the home of one of his oldest friends, Lord Gough, who had seen much of the world in the diplomatic service and who shared Edward's artistic and philanthropic enthusiasms.

As the years passed, the circle of his friends had dwindled, and he could only watch from outside the progress of so many movements with which he had once been so closely connected in the beginnings. In Dublin he had lived a hermit's life in the two stuffy rooms over a tobacconist's shop, going for all his meals to the Kildare Street Club, which had formerly expelled him from its membership, because of his advanced Nationalist politics, but had been obliged to reinstate him when he won his fantastic lawsuit against them. There, his days were still devoted chiefly to reading and to music and to his untiring efforts to revive the Literary Theatre, with a company of his own which would not be exclusively devoted to the production of peasant plays. He had few really intimate friends left in Dublin; and the conductor of his Palestrina Choir, Mr. Vincent O'Brien, was the chief solace of a lonely life. But his intensely religious nature gave a deeper meaning to his love of music, and he was drawn closer to one of his oldest friends from County Galway, Father Cyril Ryan, now living with the Carmelites at Clarendon Street. To him he finally bequeathed his whole library and his unpublished papers, which have been used as the material for the present memoir. Among the papers, besides a vast quantity of articles and essays, are various unfinished plays, but this memoir will make no attempt to treat of him as a dramatist. So much has already been written concerning the Abbey Theatre and the modern Irish Drama that Edward Martyn's own plays are already sufficiently known, and it would be affectation to claim that, with the exception

Father Cyril Ryan, O.D.C.
From the drawing by Patrick Tuohy, R.H.A.

of the earlier plays, they demand more elaborate attention than they have already received. The only one of his published works which will be discussed or quoted in any detail is his early satire *Morgante the Lesser*, which is very little known and gives a very faithful exposition of his attitude towards life.

The present memoir is no more than an attempt to describe, largely with the help of extracts from his own writings, Edward Martyn's very vital and indispensable contribution to the public life of Ireland in a period of intense activity and revival. Incidentally, it may present him as one of the most original and vigorous characters of his generation: a landlord who welcomed the downfall of his own class; an aristocrat who fought the battles of the people; the inheritor of great possessions who gave lavishly all that he had to give in the education and improvement of his country; an eccentric misogynist with an unsatisfied gift for friendship, and a magnificent generosity towards all who shared his ideals; one who never escaped from the conviction that he belonged by right to the middle ages, and whose deepest admiration was for the cloistered life, so that — having elected to live like a hermit always, whether in a garret within the tower of his own ancestral castle in Galway, or in his two miserable rooms in Dublin — he left it as the strictest injunction in his will that his body was to be taken to the dissecting rooms of Dublin Hospital, to which he left one of his many large bequests, and that his remains should be buried in an unnamed pauper's grave. 'I am too unlike other people ever to be a success,' he had confided in a friend soon after he left Oxford. Yet his work was more fruitful than that of almost any other Irishman of his time. Above all, in a country where moral courage and independence of judgment were almost unknown in his own generation, he set an example that was to have an immense influence, by always forming and proclaiming his own views with absolute independence, and by being completely free from either snobbishness or fear.

I

LANDLORDS AND LITERATURE

LANDLORDS AND LITERATURE

Tulira Castle, with its solid Norman tower, was already older by many centuries than any records that survived at the time, when Cromwell set about ordering all Irish Papists to Hell or to Connacht. Beyond the banks of the Shannon he did not attempt to pursue them, and there were many feudal strongholds like Tulira where Catholic landowners managed to preserve their power as well as their property. But before the seventeenth century closed the Dutch King William had succeeded, by the Treaty of Limerick, in persuading the Catholic landowners to lay down their arms; and a swift repudiation of the Treaty immediately afterwards left them helplessly at his mercy. The penal code against Catholic landowners was elaborated and enforced in all its ruthless and logical severity during the years that followed, and nearly all the Catholic estates in Ireland passed into Protestant hands.

The Martyns had for long been one of the most famous and widely distributed families in County Galway. They were generally believed to trace their descent from an Oliver Martin who had come to Ireland with Strongbow. The head of Edward's branch of the family during the violent years of the seventeenth century was, apparently, a man of pacific disposition who took no active part in the Irish resistance. For his attitude he was rewarded by the passing of a special Act of Parliament, the 8th of Anne, c. 3, which was designed to

amend in his particular favour the Act to prevent the
further growth of Popery. The Act recited that Oliver
Martin of Tulliry, County Galway, was during the
rebellion a person who behaved himself with great
moderation and was remarkably kind to numbers of
Protestants in distress, many of whom he supported in
his family, and by his charity and goodness saved their
lives. In recognition of those services it was accordingly
enacted by a special statute in his favour that he might
enjoy his estate to him and his heirs, and settle and dispose of the same to his eldest son and his heirs male.
'This solitary instance of their legislative justice,' declares
Hardiman, the historian of Galway, 'is particularly conspicuous because it stands alone and surrounded by the
most unjust and ferocious enactments that ever disgraced
the code of any civilised country.'

It meant in practice that the Martyns of Tulira were
thus exempted from the barbarous law which offered a
constant inducement to any dissolute younger son to
claim, and to obtain, the entire estates of his family by
the simple expedient of declaring himself a Protestant.
So the Catholic tradition of the Martyns remained unbroken, and they did not suffer, as so many of the old
Catholic families had suffered, a drastic and increasing
curtailment of their estates through the operation of the
penal laws. They remained in the happy position of
being a wealthy landowning family, with estates in
County Roscommon as well as County Galway, and with
house property even in Galway city, where the Catholics
had been expressly prohibited from owning real estate
for fear they might make it a centre of Catholic
industry. John Martyn, the father of the subject

of this memoir, married a Miss Smith of Masonbrook in the same county, whose father belonged
to a much more humble stock than the Martyns,
but had amassed a large fortune by buying up
properties that came on the market through the operation of the Encumbered Estates Act, and was able to
provide his daughter with a dowry of ten thousand
pounds. They had two sons, of whom the younger died
in early manhood, soon after having obtained his commission in the Army. The elder son, who had been born
in 1859, and christened Edward Joseph, thus became
the only surviving Martyn in his own generation; and as
most of his relatives died without leaving any offspring,
he was to grow up profoundly conscious of his own
isolated position as the last survivor of the Martyn family
in the county which had once been full of them. His
father, who as the owner of Tulira and the inheritor of a
great family tradition, had been one of the leading men
in the county, had died when Edward was a small child,
so that Edward had no recollection of him. His mother,
a devout Catholic and a stern disciplinarian, settled down
to an austere widowhood, with her whole thoughts for
the remainder of her life centred upon the career of
her eldest son, and the preparation for his marriage
and her own posterity.

When he was old enough to be sent to a preparatory
school, she established herself in a spacious Georgian
house in Dublin, having decided to entrust the education
of her son to the Jesuits. From them he received his first
schooling as a day-boy at Belvedere College, which was
housed in one of the most magnificent of those old
Georgian houses built in the time of Grattan's Parliament,

when Dublin was one of the most luxurious capitals in
Europe. The Irish landowners of those days used to come
to Dublin for half the year to make laws and to obtain as
many lucrative sinecures as possible for their relations,
before returning to their estates to hunt and shoot and
drink during the remainder of the year; and the reckless
competition in extravagance had begun among them
which has left its monuments in many noble streets and
squares, now converted into dilapidated tenements,
where magnificent staircases and panelled walls, and
highly decorated mantelpieces or ceilings, the work of
Italian craftsmen imported at the time, still mock the
squalid poverty of casual labourers and their half-starved
families who sleep on bare boards with cold winds blowing
pitilessly in through broken window panes. The house
that had eventually been bought for a song by the Jesuits,
and by them converted into Belvedere College, had been
one of the most sumptuous of all these lordly mansions
when the north side of Dublin was still — less than sixty
years before Edward's birth — the centre of a madly
extravagant fashionable world. And as a small boy,
learning his lessons from his Jesuit teachers in their black
gowns and Roman collars, Edward Martyn had ample
opportunity to study the riotous stucco decorations of the
classroom ceilings, and the ornate mantelpieces that
were to be reproduced with devout care afterwards as
illustrations to the monumental volumes of the Dublin
Georgian Society.

No Catholic school in Ireland, however, was in those
days regarded as offering suitable social conditions for
the education of a wealthy landowner; and Edward
Martyn's mother had decided that he should follow the

same road as nearly every other family of the Catholic aristocracy, and receive his serious schooling in England. At Beaumont College, near Windsor, the English Jesuits had established, not many years before, a school of the more expensive kind where some of the old Catholic families and many of the most famous titled families in Spain and France and Poland found it possible to give their sons the sort of Catholic education they required in England. To Beaumont Edward was accordingly sent from Belvedere, and he found there a few other Irish boys of famous families who had come there, like himself, to acquire the proper education of an English gentleman. Edward's mother shared the attitude that was universal among Irish landlords in the Victorian era, in regarding England as the one civilised country in the world. She had not reckoned with the eccentric tendencies of her son, who obeyed her with such unquestioning docility, and whose mediocre progress at his school gave no hint of the independence of character that was to lead him into many unexpected courses in his life. The one strong propensity he showed clearly from his early childhood was a passion for music; and no religious congregation was less likely than the Jesuits to encourage him in that pursuit. Had he been taught by the Benedictines he would have revelled in the beauty of their elaborate ritual, and he might in all probability have found a vocation for the priesthood, in some Abbey where scholars and musicians consecrate their whole lives to developing their natural gifts in the service of their Church. But the Jesuit system, with its deliberate indifference to liturgy, its short Masses, and its systematic standardisation of all human talents, was utterly uncongenial to Edward Martyn's mystical and independent temperament.

The presence of a very large proportion of foreign boys and masters in the college also introduced an element of strict supervision that Edward intensely resented, and before long, he and a few high-spirited friends had formed a group who were in constant revolt against the Jesuit system as practised in Beaumont at the time. One restriction which exasperated him and his friends especially was the locking of the dormitory doors by day, which on occasions caused an immediate practical inconvenience by making it impossible for two boys who had been fighting to obtain a clean handkerchief with which to wipe their bleeding noses. A day came when Edward and his particular friends became directly aware of this inconvenience, and on an impulse of exasperation they decided to take the law into their own hands. Edward's most intimate ally at school was the future Duke de Stackpoole, the son of another Catholic landowning family in County Galway, which had been ennobled with a Papal title. There was another Irish boy of specially high spirits, the son of a Dublin doctor called Hayden, who planned the direct action by which they were to express their feelings; and he, with Edward Martyn and George de Stackpoole, set out deliberately to blow up Beaumont as an act of protest. The conspiracy was somehow discovered before any damage had been done. Hayden as the ringleader was immediately sent home; and the Duke de Stackpoole and Mrs. Martyn were both requested to remove their sons. The expulsion was not carried out, in deference to the parents' entreaties, but Edward's days at Beaumont were already nearly at an end.

He had been an undistinguished pupil throughout his time at the school, and being naturally an unhappy boy, he had found the atmosphere of a Jesuit school completely unsympathetic. But they had taught him far more than he would yet have admitted, and he left school for Oxford with a solid grounding in Classics, which was to provide him with real inspiration when he went up to Christ Church. Contact with the young aristocracy of Catholic countries on the Continent had also given him a much wider outlook than was common among undergraduates at Oxford in the later 'seventies; and he arrived at Oxford as a young Irishman with a decided interest in literature and art, who soon discovered how extremely isolated was the position of a Catholic student in the older English Universities. Many more years were to pass before the young men from the old Catholic aristocracy in England were to be allowed to enter the Universities without being denounced for so doing by the Bishops. Newman, after the failure of his hopeless attempt to create a Catholic University for both English and Irish Catholics in Dublin, had desisted from his efforts for a time, but he was still known to sympathise strongly with the idea of founding some sort of Catholic centre at Oxford. Cardinal Manning's fierce antipathy towards all Newman's schemes, however, had produced a renewed prohibition by all the English bishops; and it was not until after Manning's death that the policy of prohibition was finally reversed.

So it was that, after his arrival at Christ Church, Edward Martyn, now grown into a bulky young man

D

with a passion for music and a real enthusiasm for art, soon discovered himself to be very nearly the only Catholic undergraduate in the University. To his obstinate nature, such isolation was a direct incentive to revolt against the conventions. Having been all but expelled from Beaumont, he now found himself in the position of being a solitary champion of the Faith that the Jesuits had impressed upon him as the most sacred possession of his large inheritance. And in a generation of students that were profoundly influenced by the æsthetic teaching of Walter Pater, which led many of them to a cult of the Catholic liturgy, he was in the wholly unexpected situation of belonging to a Church which was gradually attracting a very large number of converts among the intelligentsia. They were much happier years than which he had spent at school, and he made several close friends at the University. He travelled extensively during the long vacations, discovered new enthusiasms for painting and architecture and sculpture, and returned with the intoxication of a born musician from the first of many visits to the Wagner festival at Bayreuth. Oxford had done much for him, though he left no mark upon the life of the University. It had stimulated his natural bent towards criticism, and had awakened in him the desire to be a literary satirist. It had made him take his classical studies so seriously that he went on a tour of Greece, and wrote solemn essays about his visits to the Acropolis and to Delphi. And after leaving the University, with a life of unbounded leisure before him as the future owner of Tulira Castle, he entered upon a serious effort to make himself a name in literature through composing an elaborate classical poem.

More pressing than any literary pursuits, however, were the problems of Tulira Castle itself, where Edward's mother had made so many plans for his own future. He was devoted to her, and he accepted without demur the continuance of her stern discipline in the ordering of his life when he left Oxford. She was determined that he should take his place as one of the principal landlords of the county, in a time when the whole life of the country-side — from the control of the highways or of sanitation to the administration of justice by the grand juries — was exclusively in the hands of the gentry. Edward was well aware of her ambitions on his behalf, and already full of apprehension at her immediate determination to make a suitable marriage for her son. And partly to give her pleasure, partly to distract her attentions from matrimonial schemes, he yielded to her exhortation to modernise the uncomfortable old house that was attached to the feudal castle. His own interests in life were wholly concentrated already in his library and music, and his chief personal concern with the new structure was the organ which was to provide him with an occupation for much of his life. But he threw himself into the plans for rebuilding, got one of the best-known Gothic architects in London to draw up the designs, and deliberately committed himself to an outlay of twenty thousand pounds, the whole amount that had accumulated from the annual income during his long minority. The result was one of the most spacious modern mansions in all Ireland. Its completion only increased the impatience of Edward's mother to find him a suitable wife who would bring a new generation of Martyns into the world. Only by degrees did she discover what an uncompromising and incorrigible misogynist her own son was; and that his decision to have his own bedroom in the old feudal tower, bare of furniture with whitewashed walls and a stone-flagged floor, was an idiosyncrasy that no amount of persuasion could overcome.

A friend who requested him to invite ladies to Tulira, even some years before Mrs. Martyn's death, received the following most discouraging reply:

'My dear T——,

' I received your letter of the 26th inst. in which you ask me to invite Mrs. and Miss L. to meet you at Tillyra for some unexplained reason. I was upon the point of asking you when you could come to see me over there, and hope that you will do so as soon as I return myself. Nothing also would give me greater pleasure than if the L's. would pay me a visit if they should happen to go to Ireland: but do you not yourself see that it would be a most marked thing if I were not also to mention in the invitation Mr. L. whom I have always found interesting and civil to me?

'However, there is one thing which I clearly see would be most unwise, as it might possibly lead to misunderstandings, and would certainly make me ridiculous, and that is, that I should ask you and the L's. to meet each other. Never having had a love-affair myself, and not being a marrying man, it would be affectation on my part, if I were to say that I took a very lively interest in the love affairs of others. My enemies, if I have any, will even allow that I have a certain sense of the absurdity of certain things; and that a person of my modes of life or oddities, whichever

people may please to term them, should turn his
philosophic abode into a temple of Hymen, would be
an absurdity, seems to me to admit of no doubt. I hope
you do not mind my writing frankly to you. You are
a near relation and a dear old friend, and you will prove
that you are the latter by coming over to meet Stenbock
and Bond in the course of a fortnight or so.

'Ever yours affectionately,
'Edward Martyn.'

Among all the papers he preserved, only one woman's
letters appear in any number — from his cousin, a nun at
the Benedictine Convent at Stanbrook in Worcestershire.
She wrote to him at intervals over many years, discussing
many religious questions and telling of the peace of her
own religious life, and the progress of her Order and its
work. The first letter of a long series that continued at
intervals over many years was written on St. Edward's
Day, 1894, when she was a young nun, not long established at the Convent, and she wrote to ask his advice
concerning the armorial bearings of a royal Irish saint
whose life was being included in an elaborately illustrated
copy of the Convent's Holy Rule. 'An opportunity of
writing to you presents itself to me,' she wrote, 'which I
gladly accept, for all that I have heard of my monkish
cousin has interested me exceedingly and made me
desire to know more. These reports induced me to visit
Tillyra in thought, and thus I have wandered through
the hall perhaps at a moment when you were seated in
state in your abbatial chair, smoking your curious pipe,
a relic doubtless of some commendatory Abbot!!! Then
I found my way to what particularly took my fancy, i.e.,

the tower with its secret passage and sanctum. As I listened to this and that about you, my interest increased, and it seemed to me that you, like we nuns, belonged to those dear middle ages, and I wondered where you got your monastic tastes from; perhaps from the Saint so dear to all Benedictines whose feast we keep to-day, and whose name you bear? or from St. Gerard d'Aurillac? an ancestor of our present revered Lady Abbess, also honoured to-day. He longed to become a monk, but was prevented by his spiritual advisers, who saw how his presence in the world was needed for the good of God's church. So, though obliged by his position to keep up a court, he lived the life of a monk in the world, as far as this could be done. You seem to have inherited some of his spirit.'

It had been difficult enough to induce him to take any part in the ordinary social life of the county and even to show any enthusiasm for country pursuits. But he had set himself deliberately to become a passably good horseman, and for a man of his large bulk and weight, he was able to acquit himself remarkably on occasion. Colonel Maurice Moore, who had been absent from Ireland for some years soldiering, has a clear recollection of him when he returned to find the great modern Gothic house all built, and Edward installed there as a country gentle-man with several good hunters. 'He was not a finished horseman, but could ride well enough,' writes Colonel Moore. 'His hands were heavy, and I don't think he would have done much with untrained horses.' But the Colonel remembers seeing him 'when we were all held up in Galway by a high stone-and-mortar coped wall, take his horse a little to the right, face him at it, and

clear it finely.' 'No one followed,' he adds; and it may be
assumed that there were no ladies present, for Edward had
a deep-rooted repugnance to doing anything that might
attract the attention of women to himself.

Public life had as yet no interest for him, and his whole
attention, apart from his books and his music, was
absorbed in his estate and the old castle, where he had
chosen his own monastic retreat from the unending
sequence of eligible young ladies whom his devoted
mother was for ever inviting to stay at Tulira. He had
refused to sanction any further expenditure upon the
house itself, and he vetoed on grounds of unnecessary
expense a proposal of his mother's to have high roofs
added to the turrets. He declined even to undertake the
compromise that was suggested, of raising the height of
the battlement. The only effort he made to add further
to his own property was an offer to buy from his neighbour Lord Clanmorris a piece of land which Clanmorris
readily admitted 'looks as if it ought to belong to you,
and not to me, and quite spoils your square of demesne,
cutting in in that most provoking fashion.' But the en-
tanglements of Irish property in land were beyond the
power of man to unravel, and Lord Clanmorris had to
explain regretfully that 'your father, *on several hundred
occasions*, my mother tells me, did all he could to buy it
from my father, in fact every time they met, they had
some jokes and talk about it, but I fear I *cannot dispose of
it*, as it is unfortunately coupled with Creg Clare demesne,
in jointures, mortgages and younger children's portions;
otherwise you should have it and welcome.'

So the place remained very much as it had been in his
father's time; and the rise of the Land League, after the

desperately bad harvest of 1879, which produced conditions bordering upon famine, made for so much agrarian
unrest that landlords had little inclination to undertake
new developments. Evictions and strikes against payment
of rent became more and more frequent, as the Land
League spread through the west; and before long,
Edward and his mother were to have the bitter experience
of having their land-agent shot at near Tulira. There
were times when the young landlord must have wished
that he were back again in England among his friends in
Oxford and in London. All his correspondents in England wrote in a strain of condolence about the agrarian
unrest, and the resulting troubles of Irish landowners.
And Mgr. Parkinson, of St. Aloysius' Church at Oxford,
wrote in an apologetic strain to inform Edward Martyn
that they had now managed to obtain an organ for the
church, and that Edward's promised contribution of ten
pounds must accordingly be collected; though he knew
that the Irish landlords were not in a position to be
generous at the time. 'The church has been otherwise
improved a little,' he wrote, 'so that we are always
advancing, however slowly.'

Within a week, needless to say, Edward had sent the
requested donation; and a grateful reply informed him
that 'the organ is now in full swing, and the services have
improved wonderfully, what with its backing and the
careful painstaking of F. Jones.' 'God grant that the Land
Bill may work good to poor ould Ireland,' Mgr. Parkinson
went on. 'I fear a spirit has been raised of an ugly kind,
that will not speedily be laid. Have you seen Mat
Arnold's edition of Burke's Letters on Ireland? I have
only seen a notice of them, but I should say that

they are well worth reading. Wishing you well through the storms, and do not forget that kindness is an impenetrable shield with your countrymen. *Crede experto.*'

They were ugly times for landowners, and the Land League made no distinction between Catholic and Protestant landlords. 'In the past five months since I returned here,' wrote one of his Catholic neighbours, 'I have never been outside the gates except to Mass and one trip to the income-tax people in Galway last March! So I see and hear nothing about anyone. There have been such terrible things happening all around, I thought it necessary to be always on the spot. The past year has certainly been a sad one for everybody. Both houses near us, Corgary and Vermount, were burnt in January. They carried away during the winter a good part of Corgary woods, also mine. The lawlessness is very great. Most people appear to have become thieves.' In such circumstances, consultations between the neighbouring landowners became more intimate than usual. 'I told you I would let you know the result of my dealings with the tenants,' wrote Sir William Gregory from Gort. ' They came down yesterday in a body to meet my agent, and said they would pay their rents if they were *fairly* dealt with. I told them I would give them ten per cent. now and ten per cent. in May. They refused the offer, and went off hinting at Griffiths' valuation or twenty per cent. I asked them if they thought the rents too high or that times were bad, but they did not make these excuses. They said they would not be allowed to pay, which is not the case, as I have reason to know. I am going to give them notice that after the 12th of November I withdraw all reduction and must go to law. I am pretty sure that if we landlords all stand together in this neighbourhood, the tenants will pay readily. My brother-in-law, A. Persse, has been collecting, and has been paid *in full* without a grumble.' Edward Martyn himself responded to such appeals with a sense of absolute loyalty to his own class — so much so that one of his Nationalist friends in later years, Mr. R. J. Kelly, K.C., was to write long afterwards that 'in his early years he was most extreme in his landlord views, and no man on the Galway Grand Jury — which he regularly attended, always wearing his hat in the room — was more severe, strict and hard on the popular class, in measuring out compensation for malicious injuries.'

Personal experience as a landlord made him vehemently hostile towards the Land League, and his strongly anti-democratic instincts, and the philosophy of politics which he had acquired at Beaumont and at Oxford made him regard Gladstone as a dangerous demagogue, and his followers as corrupt agitators. One of his closest friends, and also an Irish Catholic, was his cousin, Mr. Woulfe Flanagan of *The Times*, who about this time wrote the famous series of articles on 'Parnellism and Crime,' which resulted in Parnell's historic libel action. But Edward's position as a Catholic landowner and his friendship with the clergy could not fail to give him some instinctive sympathy with the popular side. Even at the end of 1887, however — long after the worst agrarian fever had died down — when an incident arose to test his political sympathies, he refused to commit himself to any public association with Home Rulers. Lord Ripon, as a convert to Catholicism, had obvious claims to his regard,

and John Morley's austere and fastidious scholarship
raised him far above the ordinary level of politicians.
There could be no doubt that Morley was sincerely
anxious to improve conditions in Ireland as Chief Secretary, and he and Lord Ripon were to visit Dublin together
at the beginning of 1888. Just before Christmas, Edward
Martyn received a letter from Sir Christopher Redington
at Oranmore, asking if he would join the reception committee which was being formed to do them honour. The
MacDermott, head of one of the principal families of
the west, was organising the committee, and Redington
wrote on his behalf to invite Martyn to join. 'Lord
Hartington's late utterances,' he wrote, 'seem to mark
an utter breach between him and those who are in favour
of some kind of self-government for Ireland — or even of
an improved local government in Irish counties. I don't
see what parties there are, therefore, in existence save
the Tory "no surrender" one and the Gladstonian
"conciliation and concession" one. And among Glad-
stonians, no one has spoken more justly or fairly on the
Irish Land Question than J. Morley. I hope you will
favourably consider the propriety of openly adhering to
the latter party. In any case, pray keep this communication strictly secret.'

Edward Martyn replied at once with a letter which
reveals how far he still was — as a young landlord, now
nearly thirty years of age — from the popular sympathies
that he developed rapidly afterwards:

'My dear Redington,

    'On this morning I received your letter asking me to
act on the committee of reception in connection with

the visit to Dublin of Lord Ripon and J. Morley.
There is no influence that would persuade me so
quickly as yours to take action in such cases in general,
albeit I feel myself utterly unfitted to mingle in politics, for which I have consequently rather a distaste.
But by filling the position to which you now invite
me, I would be going against all my ideas of political and moral right, although at the same time
I am fully cognisant of the insignificance of the
importance of my ideas to everybody except myself.
I am therefore obliged to refuse you with sincere
regret.

'This is not the place to argue upon the merits or
demerits of Home Rule. I will only say that I do not
believe that the people of Ireland really desire it; and
that any attempt to rally the forces of the so-called
National Party after the severe blow which they have
received over here by the more or less efficient carrying
out of the law, and in England by the success of the
Hartington and Goschen meetings at Dublin, seems to
me so mischievous that if I were to help on such an
attempt in ever so small a way, I should always consider
myself more or less responsible for the inevitable
result of boycotting and murder which are certain
to ensue upon the restoration of the League to its
former vigour.

'I will, of course, keep your communication strictly
private and hope you will excuse my being so outspoken to one who is older and of infinitely better
judgment. However, I feel this to be a case where a
man must judge for himself if he is ever to judge at
all. I am no politician and belong to no party—only

I believe in Hartington and Goschen more than in Ripon and Morley.

> 'Yours very sincerely,
> 'E. Martyn.'

His mind, through these early years, was still centred almost exclusively on literature, and he kept in touch constantly with his friends in England who shared his interests. George Moore and his brothers had been close friends since his earliest memories, and Augustus Moore had been at school with him at Beaumont. For a time Mrs. Martyn had moved to London, in the earliest years of his childhood, and had taken a house in Onslow Square while the Moores lived in Alfred Place. As small boys they had scandalised the respectable residents of Onslow Square by attempting to have a croquet party on a Sunday morning, and the attempt had been severely crushed by a converging top-hatted attack advancing upon the children from all corners of the Square. The two families had remained close friends always, and George Moore's successful adventures in literature had encouraged Edward particularly in his own instinct to write. They had seen much of each other at intervals, especially when Edward took rooms in London after leaving Oxford, sharing rooms in Pump Court with a young baronet from Kent who had been at Christ Church with him and had since started life as a young barrister.

The young baronet was one of his most enthusiastic visitors at Tulira, and a letter from him after one of his visits gives a pleasant glimpse of Edward's early hospitality: 'It was perfectly delightful,' he wrote, 'every luxury of civilisation with the ease of bachelor life. I cherish much the clinging memory of *tout ensemblè*, of everything to gratify every intellectual and bodily pleasure, the delightful soft Irish atmosphere, the stroll over the park, down to watch, through circles of cawing rooks, the sun setting over Galway Bay, and those wild rides in the heather-covered mountains with the views over the level green plain dotted here and there with slate-coloured masses of demesne woods, the easy placid morning over fire and books: and then again, I am ever harping on the wicked luxury of, after a day's hunt, the champagne rolling down one's gullet lovingly, and the skin tight with wine and meat, lying on the hearth, listening to the organ wailing out some mediæval chant of grief and triumph. I enjoyed it even more than my previous visits to you. And you must know all my people agree that it has improved me physically, and I think morally. If ever I reform, and I am getting better, you will be, just as you have been, confessor and preacher, etc. But allow that all the time I was with you, I never even tried to tell one dirty story.

'I fear you will be greatly grieved,' his old College friend continued, 'to hear of a sudden, terrible and permanent catastrophe that has fallen on a friend of ours, F. R.; a sad and solemn event; he has become *engaged*, to a young lady. I have seen her photo, large. He is very much in love. I have seen him several times in a state I can only compare to drunkenness.' And prattling on, by the fireside at Pump Court which Edward shared when he came to London from Tulira, his friend told him of another country house where he had lately been staying with some '60,000 acres of good land outside the demesne,' whose owner had been far from living up to Edward's standards of hospitality. 'The wine was pigwash, the claret made me a total abstainer.' 'George's book is out; I read a review in the *Globe*,' he continued, and then follows a recent anecdote of Oscar Wilde. 'In mixed company, the talk fell on Rome. Oscar Wilde had not been there, and wanted to get rid of the subject, so he said, very bored, "Oh, don't talk of Rome. It's the Whiteley of Art," at which all gaped and were silent. *We* thought that it should have been answered: "Quite true, for at Rome, just as at Whiteley's, they give no credit to impostors." ' And as a final piece of gossip, he concluded, 'Barnett has again disappeared, leaving as a legacy to the *Court and Society Review* a libel action from a writing of his therein.'

The young Englishman's enthusiasm stirred Edward to attempts to write of his own home; and a short story, re-written several times and never published, survives among his papers, in which he records his own vivid impressions of the magnificence of the Irish country mansions and of the loveliness of his own surroundings. The plot was evidently based upon a true story, of an old Galway landlord being robbed and finally dispossessed by a dishonest agent. The narrative gives the impression of a young Englishman arriving to spend a holiday with a college friend at his home in County Galway. The house, which is called Crofton Court in the story, is evidently an idealised vision of Tulira, the ornate mantel-pieces and the splendid pictures (except for those of the French Impressionists, which were his own) being borrowed from other houses with which everyone in the county was familiar. In the conversations between the two young men, the Irish Gerald Crofton expresses many opinions which appear in Edward's own early writings:

'Here the surrounding country looked less desolate than the other parts of the West of Ireland through which I had just passed,' says the young Englishman. 'The few houses had a comparative air of prosperity and the rich green fields were fenced with neat walls. We passed almost immediately under a very ancient and beautiful arched gateway, draped with just enough ivy to enhance its delicate charms, and entered a small park furnished with huge old ash trees and spreading beech. In a few minutes we were at the house. While Gerald was giving directions to the groom, I had leisure to notice its peculiar aspect. It was a square structure two stories high, built of a grey stone which age had encrusted with mellow orange-toned lichen. Sashes, curved like thin mullions, were fixed in its pointed windows. The roof, which had an ornamental border of wood, rose steep and concave, like that of a Chinese pagoda, and was surmounted by a timber balustrade. A flight of steps led to the hall door, over which was carved a coat of arms and the following inscription:—"*Welcome to all, for this is the house of liberty.*"

'As we walked into an exquisite hall, all panelled in old dark oak, a great Irish wolf-dog advanced to welcome us. To the right was a high chimney-piece, supported by two Atlantes, masterpieces of seventeenth-century wood-carving. Curious weapons and rare china hung upon the walls. At the end, opposite to the entrance, I noticed a small organ, on either side of which rose two superb oak staircases.

'Mounting one of these, we turned on a landing, and continued our ascent by a single flight, equally richly carved, to the first story. My bedroom, commanding a fine view of the park, contained a stately old four-post bed and some curious furniture.

'When I again descended, I found a door open in the hall, through which I walked to another oak room with seats in the window recesses. This must have been a drawing-room once; but now it had more the appearance of a library, as there were shelves along the walls filled with books. There were also a few pictures of the Modern French School, of which I knew my friend was an admirer. Among others, I recognised an Autumn river scene in oils, by Claude Monet, and a wonderfully vigorous pastel representing two circus girls, by Degas. The chimney-piece was of white marble, light and beautifully proportioned, and inlaid in imitation of flowers with other marbles. I have since heard that these chimney-pieces are rather common in old houses throughout Ireland, and were executed by Italians who settled in the country at the end of the last century.

'Presently Gerald appeared at a door leading to the dining-room, and bade me to lunch. This room was in its way equally charming. A soft red paper with a flower pattern, blended harmoniously with the family portraits that hung upon the walls. These consisted of one or two "beauties" by Lely, a fresh young girl in a white dress by Romney, a young man holding a gun in a sylvan scene full of observation and character, by the magic brush of Gainsborough; a sentimental wasp-waisted damsel, carrying a basket of flowers, by Angelica Kauff-mann, and some mediocre pictures of other ancestors

E

by unknown artists. The ceiling was painted in a rich design of Tudor roses. The mantelpiece of stucco had garlands and baskets of fruit exquisitely modelled over its front, the whole being tastefully touched with faint colours. Against the opposite wall stood a spindle-legged Sheraton sideboard, bearing two beautifully inlaid knife-holders and a quantity of rare Irish plate; and the quaint Chippendale chairs had still their hair seats uninjured.

' "What a charming old house you have, Gerald!" I said, as I sat down. "It is unique. I never saw anything like it before."

' "Yes, it is one of the few genuine old houses in Ireland, and of its kind hard to beat. It was built about two hundred years ago by that determined-looking personage there over the chimney-piece in judge's robes, who before he was made a Justice of the King's Bench in Ireland by James II, acted for a short time as his minister at The Hague. A great deal of wood-carving was done in the Low Countries; and the staircase is almost an exact copy of the celebrated one in the Picture Gallery of that city. This house will soon, I fear, be all that will be left to me, if times don't mend for us land-lords. The people have been thoroughly aroused, and now hunger for the land."

'This led to a discussion upon the state of the country. He told me that not long ago a landlord and a dragoon, acting as his protection, while driving in a trap quite close to Crofton Court, were both shot dead in broad daylight by a volley fired upon them through a loop-holed wall; that a locally notorious nobleman's agent and his driver were killed in the same manner.

' "However," he said with a laugh, I suppose perceiving my uneasiness, "you or I might walk all over the land day or night and not be molested."

'When I had finished my lunch we both lit cigars and strolled across the hall into the study. This, and the room opening from my friend's bedroom, were also all of dark oak. The study was lined round with splendid book-cases crammed with books. There were a few small casts from the antique scattered about, and on a pedestal in a corner stood a bronze replica of the celebrated dancing faun from Pompeii, cast in a mould so perfect as to equal the original in every respect.

' "Look at this," he said, pointing over the fireplace to a small picture representing a river scene with trees in the fore and a town in the background. "It is by Corot. What a poetry in the sweep of those trees! What silvery light from the pale blue sky falls through the clouds, like April rain upon the river, and lifts the sombre shadows beneath the leaves. The objects are little more than indications; but what indications! What absolute mastery in conveying the intended impression!"

'Puffing at my cigar, I wandered round the book-cases, examining the books and answering him from time to time, while he continued to æstheticise. Their titles declared the breadth of his interests; and a glance through the pages of several, where pencil marks noted passages for reference, showed how carefully they were read. Among the classical authors I noticed Pollux and Apuleius. There were a few theological books, the works of St. Augustine, the sermons of St. John Chrysostom, St. Basil's Homilies, and a liturgy of the Greek Church. Of course, all the great English writers were represented, and many of the French likewise; and among the Germans Winckelmann and Goethe were conspicuous. There were some philosophical books, too — Plato, Schopenhauer and an English translation of Rosmini's *Nuovo Saggio*. Then several publications on Classical Archæology were ranged along the shelves or piled on chairs; the *Journal of Hellenic Studies*, the report of the German Government upon the excavations at Olympia, etc., while portfolios were filled with photographs direct from the originals, of the great pictures and statuary in every gallery of Europe. Upon the table lay a superb volume with coloured plates illustrating Byzantine Architecture; and some sheets of manuscript were scattered over a broad desk.

' "This is certainly an interesting collection of books," I remarked, "but you do not seem to have a single Italian book — not even a Dante."

' "For the very good reason that I cannot read them, at least, very badly; nor do I want to learn. I take no interest in the Italian language."

'He was a Catholic, and, I knew, hated the Italian Revolution; but I was not prepared to hear such sweeping opinions, even from him.

' "But, surely, the world admires Dante, Petrarca, Tasso?"

' "That may be. To me Dante is incomprehensible, even in a translation — Petrarca, the little I have read, milk and water. In fact, the Italian language appears to me to be as great a caricature of the Latin as the modern native of Italy is of the ancient Roman citizen."

'I felt rather irritated. But he was in one of his satirical humours, and I was sure to argue with him would only act as a stimulant, so I said nothing; and he, somewhat disappointed, continued:

' "Of course, the newspapers and the spouters cry up Italy as a great, rising nation. Great nation, indeed! By Jove! that is too good! A people whose real genius consists in the drilling of ballet-girls and the manufacture of *bonbons*! Hurried along by her fustian Bismarck Crispi, she may make a brave show in prosperous times; but the stamina is not there. Nations are welded and tempered by men of genius to greatness with iron and blood in spite of all opposition, as Prussia in the last century, while well nigh the whole continent was in arms against her. On the contrary, Italy was nursed into her present condition by a conglomeration of blackguards from all countries, while foreign Powers opposed to the Church looked on and applauded. I have no doubt that a general collapse will follow upon the first serious reverse. Meanwhile, the glorious democracy of the Garden of Europe is working wonders everywhere."

'His voice grew soft. "I visited Rome long ago with my parents, when I was a child. I remember the exquisite old city, then comparatively small, with its picturesque streets, its churches, many as the days of the year. Truly a venerable and awe-inspiring Capital of Christ's divine Empire on earth. What a charm it had for strangers! How even those outside the Fold loved to gather within the shelter of its ancient walls. I went there again last Spring; and, oh! what a change! what a change! They have turned it into a huge modern city with glaring acres of abominable new buildings. Never was there such an opening for an architect of genius! Never had the decadence of Italy exhibited such impotence! They talk now of abolishing the beautiful old bridge of St. Angelo, and of replacing it by an iron monstrosity! The proposition has made the Roman municipality famous, and has aroused a world-wide disgust at such brutish stupidity. But by this stupidity these civic Yahoos have defeated their ends. They have driven strangers from Rome. Their new houses remain unlet; and if they have not sufficient intelligence to feel shame for such barbarities, their sense must soon receive the rude shock of impending bankruptcy.

' "The truth is" — here he smiled maliciously — "the modern Italians are vain, verbose, degenerate, and utterly wanting in sentiment for art and beautiful things. A fine tree or a revered building seems to vex them. 'Let us destroy the horrible thing,' I can imagine them saying to themselves, 'let us replace it with something beautiful!' Then, when they accomplish a work like the iron bridge at St. Angelo, they wave their hands and, embracing each other, exclaim '*Stupendo lavoro!*' The young men usually amuse themselves by making love. Well, I suppose this profitable occupation is not altogether unknown to young men in other countries. Those of maturer years amuse themselves by flattering each other in the most exaggerated and ridiculous manner. You hear two middle-aged men of a status perfectly obscure, address each other as *illustrissimo professore, chiarissimo dottore*, etc. When I was leaving Turin some months ago for Paris, a number of these puerile elders entered the carriage of the train in which I had taken my place. From their conversation I gathered that they had just come from some wretched old flower show in that city. Immediately the patriotic tomfoolery and mutual admiration began; and amid hand-wringing and gesticulations, I heard *ad nauseam* such phrases as *questa magnifica e stupenda esibizione, gloria di Patria nostra. Dottissimo avvocato, mirifico magistrato, espertissimo notaio*, and so on. Can you imagine any people, great, or with the possibility of greatness, conducting themselves in such an imbecile a fashion?" '

Edward was trying, in this early effort, to utilise the short story as the medium to convey his own ideas on all sorts of matters. It is curious to find among his early papers the draft of an indignant letter addressed to *The Times*, protesting against the vandalism of modern Roman architecture, which is in substance and in many of its phrases identical with this dissertation of Gerald Crofton's. From it, the story proceeds with a further digression to include a description of the typical scenery around Edward's home. The young Englishman is to be shown his host's stables on the first day, before going out for a cub hunt on the day after, and after that he is to sail to the Aran Islands with his friend 'to examine and report upon the state of the ruins there for the Society of Antiquaries.' 'I beg you will accompany me,' says his polite host. 'These remains are among the most ancient and curious in North Europe and well deserving a visit.' Here and there on the margins of the typescript are indications that Edward's short story has been subjected to severe criticism by someone, to whom he showed it as an early effort. The writing bears a strong resemblance to Mr. George Moore's, and it is not surprising to find among these marginal outbursts one crude comment which asks: 'Did ever people talk to each other like this?'

Nevertheless, Edward was already acquiring a distinct

power of descriptive writing, and some of the subsequent passages show how strong was the instinctive feeling for the country and its life which was later to find expression in his plays, when he had attempted to learn Ibsen's technique and he originated the Irish Literary Theatre. 'Leaving the house,' the story continues, 'we turned to the right and passed into a bright Dutch garden, fenced from the Park by a ha-ha and stone balustrade, upon which, at each angle, rested a bronze urn faintly discoloured with age. Beautiful old-fashioned flowers lit up the beds bordered with neat box amid the quaint labyrinth of party-hued walks, and in the centre on a pedestal stood a marble copy of the Apollino with his arm cast gracefully over his head, as he dreamt beneath the afternoon sun. Beyond this, we came to a walled-in garden, which appeared stocked with all kinds of fruit trees and vegetables, and contained two good-sized glass houses.

'We then left by an opposite gate, and walked through a large wood intersected by many winding paths. Here the larch and the fir grew in primeval wildness, while occasionally an old beech extended its giant branches over the varied greens of the laurel or the holly; and from between rocks clothed in moss sprouted forth underwood of box and soft young ash. It was a delightful place. The smell of the pines acted upon me like a tonic, after my long sojourn in London amid the stifling air of the dead season. I opened my mouth wide and inhaled the delicious odours over and over again.

' "I always feel like that," said Gerald, "when I come into this wood after having been a long time in town. That is why I brought you here to-day. After you are in the country a short time you lose the sense of the aroma.

Here is where we shall cub-hunt. The earths are behind those rocks, and the wood covers about five hundred acres."

'Taking one of the by-paths we came after a while to a wicket opening into some walled paddocks, in which were some brood mares with foals at foot and some calves. Beyond, in a very large field, a few cows grazed among several young horses of different ages.

'That evening, after dinner, we sat over our wine, talking of mutual friends and past events with interest ever new, and discussing each other's divers occupations and projects. According to the old fashion, the cloth was removed from the round table, disclosing a dark mahogany leaf that shone like a mirror, whereon stood wedgwood dishes containing dessert, some beautiful Venetian glasses, and in the centre a huge silver goblet filled with a profusion of bright flowers. Wax candles in silver branch-candlesticks, softened the shadows in corners the most distant from the cheerful glare of the log fire on the hearth. The door leading to the hall, as also those of the drawing-room and study, were open. All the rooms were lit with the same pure lights fixed in silver sconces.

' "You have the house illuminated, as if for a ball," I remarked.

' "Yes; it is always so every night I am at home. I like to walk from one room to the other."

'He was in a communicative mood and, putting a few questions, I easily drew him to talk about his way of life.

' "I am able," he said, "to make something by the horses — not much, but still I do not lose. Last year, after deducting all expenses, I was £200 to the good. The dealers like the sort I turn out. They often come here and give me a very decent price. I am thus saved the endless bother of fairs, shows, etc. Of course, it is not much of a money-making business; but it amuses me, for I am very fond of horses."

' "How many have you?"

' "Well, just at present thirty, including all kinds. However, I shall sell three or four very soon." '

The germ of his future political philosophy as an Irish Nationalist emerges in a further passage soon after, when the two young men begin to discuss absentee landlords. ' "I always have had the greatest dislike and contempt for absentees," declares Gerald Crofton. "The absentee landlord has the soul of a flunkey. Dissatisfied with the country that produced him, and from which he draws his sustenance, he seeks the society of English folk, who in turn despise him, and whose insolence only seems to attach him to them the more. And what, after all, is this mess of pottage for which he exchanges his birthright? I don't pretend to be a society man, as you know. Still, I have seen a little of London drawing-rooms; and for the life of me I can discover no greater interest in them than in those this side of the silver streak. Plenty of art jargon, no doubt; but never an idea. And if a man of genius happens, perchance, to stray in, like a lost child, he is immediately frozen up by his surroundings. I have heard many ideas among men in the free play of talk over clay pipes and grog, but never in a drawing-room. And so the cockney Irishman drags on his despicable existence. The cockney Irishman, the would-be Briton, who abuses everything in his native land; only a trifle more absurd than the cockney Irishman, the would-be Nationalist,

who repeats often-refuted arguments at tea-parties.
Both are very careful to keep away from Ireland,
since they have grown to feel so out of touch with their
countrymen."

' "I should think, old fellow," I said, "that all
this denunciation comes rather funny from you, who
are always wandering about, and so often in
London."

' "Quite so! but I know my own country better than
any other place, and I live here longer than elsewhere;
and I am more in touch with my countrymen than with
others. It is a poor thing to be a stranger in one's
country."

' "You are right. Indeed, you ought to be happy –
apparently able to do what you like."

' "No; I am not!" he answered, with a quick look full
of the most painful meaning. "I am *never* able to do
what I like." '

The short story was one of his very few early attempts
to write about Ireland. For years he had been working
with conscientious patience upon the long classical poem
that had been inspired by his visit to Greece. He had
spent day after day in polishing the laboured verses, and
he had dreamed of literary fame through their publication.
But strange qualms of conscience had come over him, as
the intensity of his preoccupation with religious matters
grew upon him; and he had begun to ask himself with
increasing earnestness, that devastating question of St.
Ignatius: *quid hoc ad æternitatem?* The conviction that
service of the Catholic Church was the only purpose
worth considering in life had grown enormously stronger
since he had escaped from the irksome tutelage of his

early Jesuit masters, whose influence had left an indelible
impression on his soul. And as he contemplated the long
poem that had occupied all his labour and his ambitions
for years, he had been smitten with a guilty feeling that
his cult of the ancient classics was in reality not only
waste of effort but unworthy of anyone who realised the
prime necessity of glorifying God and His Church.
Publication of the poem would not only be a confession
that he had squandered his own time and his literary gifts
upon vanities. It might distract others, and even encourage them also to similar distractions from the real
purpose of life. And after months of doubt and heart-
burning and hesitation, the voice of that uneasy conscience
had quite suddenly prevailed. Edward decided ruthlessly
to destroy the whole cherished labour of his youth, and
he wrote to the friends with whom he had so often discussed it while he was engaged upon it, to announce that
he had burned the entire manuscript.

Among the very few papers surviving from this early
period of his life, he preserved two letters of sympathy
and genuine distress. One of them, written on New
Year's Eve, 1885, was from Henry Barnett, the editor
of the *Court and Society Review*, who had just arranged
for the serial publication of Mr. George Moore's next
book. He found the editorship an exacting position —
'the cash is minute — at present; the cigars — well, I
smoke a few; and as for Fleet Street and the Strand, they
see me very little, for I am at work from morn till night,
and sometimes far on to the next. The whole weight of
the concern is on my shoulders, and it is heavy. But,
thank goodness, the paper has already begun to move —
upwards! and there is every chance of success.' From his

labours as the editor of a struggling review, Barnett made time to send a word of real sympathy with Martyn in his self-denying ordnance. 'You have made a great sacrifice,' he wrote, 'and one which I cannot think is altogether wise or justifiable. Yet I do respect you for it. There are few men who would have done as you have done; and however much I must regret the results of it, I admire your fortitude and conscientiousness.'

There was no accounting for the eccentricities of this monastic young aspirant for literary fame; who, not content with destroying his own work of years because of religious scruples, was now threatening to stop his subscription to the *Court and Society Review* if George Moore's new novel, in its serial form, were to contain any offence against either faith or morals. 'That concerns me a good deal what you say about Moore's book,' Barnett wrote, appalled at the possibility of losing one of the small number of subscribers upon whom he had relied as a nucleus for the future prosperity of his review. 'I don't know that there is any specific attack on Christianity *per se*, in it. If there is: out it goes. Any way I should be sorry if anything that he or I shall say in the paper will compel you to discontinue reading it. Whatever you may think of the opinions of the paper on sectarian matters — I know, of course, that we are not of your party — yet you must admit that it is on the side of decency and reverence: and on those points I may say (*between ourselves*) that I have power to edit Moore. There is a special clause in the agreement to that effect. I hope, therefore, you will think better of your intention to reject the paper when his tale begins.'

The news of George Moore being Bowdlerised must

have brought a gleam of humour into a melancholy period in Edward's life. A few weeks earlier, a still more agitated letter had reached him from the young baronet in Pump Court, who wrote to tell him that the decorators had now finished with his room, and that he hoped for his early return. In the meantime, though it was too late to save the precious manuscript from destruction at its author's hands, he covered pages of notepaper with earnest expostulation. It was useless now to argue, but his replies to Edward's arguments reveal the uncompromising attitude of Edward's own mind at the time. 'Your reasons,' he wrote, 'you state are—

'(1) The subject and philosophy are not compatible with your belief as a Christian and a Catholic.

'(2) That in future you wish to write "only what is conducive to the glory of God rather than to the poor gratification of personal vanity."

'Now I am not a Catholic, but I do believe in the existence of a God, and I furthermore write as your friend. I hope, therefore, that you will do me the fairness to consider what I subjoin, not in any spirit of opposition (and perchance you may think it a test of right-doing, that the course of action you adopt is contrary to your own wishes). . . .

'As to (1) Whether any particular writing is or is not incompatible with a Christian's belief is just a question of fact. Now I would never advocate publishing anything directly contrary to Christianity, nor would I do so myself. So if you are thoroughly convinced that what you have written is directly prejudicial, your duty is not to wait, not to ask anyone's advice, but to put it in the fire at once.

'As a matter of fact I perceived nothing whatever incompatible in your poems as far as I read; how could there be in the Pheidias and Pericles?

'If there is a *bona fide* doubt whether or not a writing is compatible, etc., whether or not it may have some remote tendency and whether that remote possible tendency is a ground for destroying (and I fear in such a balancing scale you might through over-conscientiousness decide against yourself) is it not a direct principle of Catholicism to submit your conscience to that of the Priest? Now it is a very subtle question whether remote and unforeseen consequences need be considered if all is meant right; and why, in such a subtle question, should you set yourself up as judge, why not consult some eminent theologian of your Church thereon? This at all events is what Pascal did. He had given up writing for reasons like you, but during insomnia, having thought out some problem in geometry and written it, he showed it to a friend of great piety, who told him to publish.'

The young baronet certainly showed an unusual knowledge of the theological mind — which is still more apparent in the shrewd advice that followed: 'If you think that an eminent theologian would not give up the time, say you will, on his considering and writing, pay so much to cathedral, church, or charity; so the theologian would read it as a work of charity.

'So much on the mere question of fact as to any particular writing, but as to (2) you would *only* write what is conducive to the Glory of God and not to gratification of personal vanity — that is a broad assertion, it would stop all poetry by Catholics as you.

'Now, of course, you must not write what is adverse, but may one not busy one's self on matters indifferent, poetry, painting, mathematics, novels? If your proposition were universally applied, how would the world progress? Or are you going to leave its progress to be conducted by atheists? Further, is it not a little *presumptuous* to consider that anything you or the uninspired man would write would conduce to the Glory of God? Let a man improve the talents with which God has endowed him, and if it pleases God to make use of the result as an instrument for good, will it not be reckoned for the advantage of the instrument on the last day?

'I do not think your talent lies in the way of hymns or theology, but rather for poetry. Now in your poetry you have no irreligious and anti-Christian intention; all your object is to write poetry to the best of your ability. You write it is as poetry, not as theology, in which you are not an expert.

'Pascal showed the Voltairians and the Encyclopædists of the eighteenth century that a man could be an exquisite reasoner and a good Catholic. Do you show the nineteenth that a man can be an exquisite modern poet, without a taint of infidelity. Would not that in itself conduce to the Glory of God and of Catholicism? Poetry is indifferent in itself so long as there is no anti-Christian intention. You are not bound to force religion into things indifferent. If I had forced my Protestantism into your will, I should have so made it that the bequest for masses should be void.

'There is a good old cavalry maxim: "Commit your

soul to God and charge home." Do you, leading a Christian life, and having told your rosary, then sit down to put together rhymes and reason — surely a most innocent employment.

'I trust you will pardon this long argument,' G——— concluded, 'but it seemed to me somewhat monstrous that you should cut yourself off from a harmless interest in life on account of a proposition which I can hardly consider to be theology, viz., that every man is bound to write nothing but that which he considers in his own mind will be directly conducive to the Glory of God in the mind of any reader.'

But Edward was deaf to all such pleading, and his scruples drove him like a haunted spirit. They intensified after the destruction of his own poems, and he considered it to be his duty to express disapproval in unmistakable terms whenever he felt that improprieties were finding their way into print. He had already made Barnett uneasy by his threat to discontinue taking the *Court and Society Review* if George Moore's novel proved to contain obnoxious matter. Two years later George Moore's friend Dujardin was to receive a more definite protest, and the final withdrawal of his subscription for having published an article by Huysmans. The following letter speaks for itself:

'Dear Sir,

'I have only this day read in the October number of the *Revue Indepéndante* an article by M. J. K. Huysmans, entitled "Le tableau de Bianchi au Louvre."

'I am much surprised at your giving publication to such sentiments in the Review, which I must ask you

F

in future not to send to me, as I have decided to discontinue subscribing to it.

'I remain,
'Yours faithfully,
'E. Martyn.'

At the end of 1888 he even took a step which very few
Catholics who have any ground for regarding themselves
as students ever feel it necessary to take. He applied to
his bishop with a formal request for an individual permission to read books that have been condemned and
placed on the Index Expurgatorius. Even among the
most devout Catholics, it is usually taken for granted that
the prohibition against reading books on the Index is
intended rather as a warning against being influenced by
ideas contained in them. It is assumed in practice that
any student or scholarly person whose studies require
that he should be widely read, may read anything if his
motive for reading forbidden books is not dishonest.
But as his scrupulousness intensified, Edward Martyn
was no longer willing to take any liberties with the strict
discipline laid down by the Church. And in writing to
Bishop McCormack he conveyed clearly that he regarded
the request as one which might very reasonably be
refused:

'My Dear Dr. McCormack,

'I fear you may consider the request, which I make
in this letter, somewhat unusual. It is this. Would
you be good enough to exempt me from the prohibition
against the keeping and reading of books on the Index
or otherwise condemned by the Church? If you have

not the power to grant this, would you kindly inform
me how and to whom I should apply for such permission?

'My Confessor advised me to seek an exemption.
He said they were given and that he himself had one
from Rome. I hope you will not think that I ask this
favour with a view of abusing the great privilege.

'Trusting you will excuse my thus troubling you,
            'I remain,
                'My dear Dr. McCormack,
                    'Yours very sincerely,
                        'Edward J. Martyn.'

Bishop McCormack did in fact take a serious view of
the situation. He was one of the old school of Irish
bishops, who believed absolutely in the necessity of
keeping a strict control over the faith as well as the morals
of their people. Was it not he whom Mr. George Moore
describes (in his *Memoirs of My Dead Life*) as the 'dear old
Bishop McCormack,' who used to preach sermons denouncing 'that degrading passion called loave.' The
request that Edward Martyn had formally made to him
was apparently something beyond the bounds of any
previous experience in his diocese. Cultured men who
read widely, before Edward Martyn's disconcerting conscience had made itself felt, were presumably content to
leave the question to their own consciences, being happily
ignorant (as the vast majority of educated Catholics are
in every country) of which books or authors have or have
not been formally condemned by the Sacred Congregation.
Edward Martyn's humility and conscientiousness had
produced a baffling problem for the saintly old bishop at

Mount St. Mary's. Having made the best inquiries he could among his theologians and in the text-books, he was obliged to write back that he was 'not competent to give an exemption from the prohibition referred to in your letter, except in favour of priests, and on a limited scale.' All that his lordship could suggest was that his young friend should apply to the Holy See, through the Most Rev. Dr. Kirby, Rector of the Irish College in Rome. 'I don't know any other way in which you can obtain the concession,' he confessed. 'Should you decide upon addressing your application to the Holy See, it may be of some use to have a line from your bishop testifying to your character as a good Catholic, and this I shall be glad to supply.'

By return of post Edward Martyn replied with a request for the introduction to Dr. Kirby; and on receiving it he wrote the following letter, from the Kildare Street Club in Dublin:

'Most Rev. dear Sir,

'The enclosed introduction from the Bishop of the diocese in which I live explains the nature of my request. I am advised by my Confessor to seek this concession, as I have recently read of the serious consequences attending the reading of books on the Index by a Catholic in countries, as in Ireland, where the prohibition is in force. In England, I understand, there is no such prohibition. I have also been told that books which were otherwise harmless have been condemned for a single passage.

'Now I have in my library books of general literature, philosophy, etc., a few of which I have heard were on the Index, although whether they are still or not I do not know, as I understand that the censure is often removed from works.

'It would, therefore, be an immense relief to my mind if I were to obtain an exemption from the rules of the Index.

'I would then ask you to be kind enough to seek from the Holy See in my behalf.

'I have some misgivings as to the presumption of a private individual like myself making such a request, but my conscience compels me to do so. Moreover, I understand from my Confessor that such concessions are granted and that he has one himself.

'I am in my thirtieth year.

'Hoping you will excuse my causing you this trouble,

'I remain,

'Your Lordship's most obedient Servant,

'Edward Martyn.'

'At all events, I feel perfect confidence in placing my case in your hands, as I am certain that whatever may be the result, it will be in the end for my welfare.'

With so much to provide all the conditions for a singularly happy life—unfettered liberty and ample private means, a wide range of friendships and great enthusiasm for literature and art, and a still stronger passion for music—it was difficult to imagine that a young man should be so unhappy as Edward Martyn certainly was in those earlier years. Those who knew him intimately must often have wondered why he did not enter the religious life, but he was under no illusion about having a vocation to the priesthood. His friends were all aware of how much he suffered from his mother's constant efforts to induce him to marry, and many of them were urged by her to add their own influence to assist her efforts. But they knew how strong was his curious repugnance towards all women. One very intimate friend, a priest who was implored by Mrs. Martyn to impress him with his duty to perpetuate the Martyn family, asked him quite frankly whether, if he had to choose the lesser of two evils, he would prefer to marry or to become a cloistered monk. Edward's reply was unhesitating — that he would infinitely prefer to become a monk, 'and you,' he added, 'know well how much I would hate to be one.'

But the most acute crisis of his youth passed, when he had destroyed the poem upon which he had built so many hopes of the literary reputation that he desired with a pathetic craving; and when he had obtained, without the smallest difficulty, the permission he sought for reading books that were prohibited by the Index, his scruples troubled him less, and he was able to face life with an easier conscience. His brother's death, as a young officer in an Irish regiment, had made Mrs. Martyn still more dependent upon him; but he felt less burdened by his own peculiar scruples as he turned his face against romantic literature, and settled down to the management of his own estates. He had evolved a more definite philosophy of life, and his early idea of writing satire revived and offered him new scope in a happier frame of mind. He decided that he would write a complete book of satire upon the decadence of modern morals and society, and with solid determination he set himself to an enormous task. His friends soon became aware of what he had in contemplation, and they realised that this ambitious book, which made no secret of its debt both to Rabelais and to Jonathan Swift, was to give expression to his whole attitude towards life.

In the spring of 1890 the long-expected satire made its appearance, being published anonymously by Swan Sonnenschein, with the title, *Morgante the Lesser, his Notorious Life and Wonderful Deeds, arranged and narrated for the first time by Sirius.* On the title-page were two lines of quotation — the first from the *Persæ* of Æschylus, and the second being Baudelaire's line 'Enorme et laid comme le Monde.' It opened with an elaborately satirical preface, explaining the author's diffidence at undertaking so important a work, which was followed by a still more elaborate Dedicatory Address to His Majesty the Illustrious and Ancient Genius of Error. These introductory pages were followed by yet another pair of quotations — this time from Carlyle's *Sartor Resartus*, the first being 'Vanity (which is your clearest phasis of the Devil, in these times),' and the second, 'It is the night of the world, and still long till it be day; we wander amid the glimmer of smoking ruins, and the sun and the stars of Heaven are as if blotted out for a season; and two immeasurable Phantoms, *Hypocrisy* and *Atheism*, with the Gowl *Sensuality*, stalk abroad over the Earth and call it theirs.'

With these formidable preliminaries the book opens with a first chapter on the great Morgante's genealogy. The parody of Rabelais is unconcealed, and with a tremendous parade of superlatives and exaggerated

images the book explains the antiquity of his hero's
ancestry, which is traced from the first labours of 'one
Arashdolt' who 'was very assiduous in his exertions at the
construction of that most useful edifice the Tower of
Babel,' through the successive generations of heretical
philosophers, including 'the next celebrated ancestor
settled in Rome, in the person of a poet named Lie-
screechius.' The trend of his satire becomes plain when
he continues: 'Having now triumphantly poisoned and
exterminated all ancient philosophy, this useful family
set about seeing what it could accomplish in the same way
against the life of Christianity, which now began to grow
into great vigour throughout the world. With what success it engaged in this most profitable work we shall see
in the following brief narration of the actions of its most
notorious members, culminating in the all-important
history of its last, most notorious member, to wit, the
prodigious, the flatulent, yea, the most notorious Morgante.

'For many ages from this time forth, the family appears
to have abandoned its traditions of materialism, and to
have been amply satisfied if only it could start and keep
alive sufficiently important errors of any kind, which
might tend to weaken the Christian Church. In truth,
the promulgation of a materialist philosophy was as yet
premature. Later on, when the way had been paved by
centuries of heresy in almost every conceivable shape, it
will be seen how this elevating and dormant principle
stalked forth again into the light. Therefore, it is only
necessary to mention just the names of the chief scions of
this illustrious house during the early and middle ages,
until we arrive at the period of that great error which has
borne such wonderful fruit in our time.'

The list comprises most of the famous leaders of heresies, up to the arrival in the world of Martin Luther, 'whose teaching, as we shall see, has proved of such exceptional value to mankind. The sixteenth century will ever be remarkable for that widespread and most useful movement, actively promoted by Luther, Calvin, Melanchthon, and other ancestors of Morgante, viz., the Reformation, so called because it laboured to free the human mind from the trammels of authority; to make every man his own theologian, and consequently of importance to his own particular self; to foster irresponsible speculations; and generally to disorganise the forces and discipline of the Christian Church. This wonderful movement is particularly memorable, because, unlike other heresies, which died out gradually, their members returning again to the Church, it seems early to have developed a spirit of antagonism to Christianity altogether. For the notorious family, now for the first time after centuries of laudable activity and preparation, feels that it may safely return to its ancient traditions of materialism, scepticism, etc.'

For several pages, in this scarcely disguised ironical commentary, the narrative proceeds, including most of the pioneers of agnosticism in English and French literature — most of the names being altered only in their first letter. 'After him,' it continues, 'there arose in France one Auguste Baron, the inventor of the system of evolution. This man was a most respectable atheist, and has succeeded in founding a school of very superior persons, who are justly proud of themselves and of each other, in that they claimed to set the *ton* in culture, taste, and disbelief.'

Here at last his gift of extravagant fantasy comes into play, and in particular his instinctive hostility towards all women finds expression. Auguste Baron 'had a son born in England named Fitz Ego, who is chiefly renowned for being the father of the most notorious Morgante.' Having discharged his burden of serious criticism, he finds scope at last in a graphic description of Morgante's father. 'In outward appearance, he was tall and thin. His legs were weak and very much bent inward at the knees. His shoulders were slanting. His neck was long, and balanced most deftly at its summit a remarkably capital head, which towered up prodigiously at its rear. His nose was short and turned up. His mouth had an indescribable air of superciliousness. His eyes were very close set, yet at the same time almost twisted outward on to the sides of his head, because the latter was marvellously narrow. In fine, as he walked, springing high on his toes, down the street, his demeanour was very strikingly refined; for he had stamped upon him most indelibly the much coveted characteristic of being indeed a superior person. So much for his exterior. His interior or mental gifts, as well as his natural disposition, were equally attractive and remarkable. His intellect, if not very profound, was well balanced and serene. His memory, if not large, was tenacious of what it could hold. His will, if vacillating, veered about for his own satisfaction. His disposition, if cold to many, was monstrously affectionate and affable to the few who praised him to his face. If he was no statesman, he was a good housekeeper. If he was unfitted for the navy or army, he could tie papers neatly in red tape. If he had no literary talent, he was an able journalist. If he propounded nothing new in philosophy, he was advanced in his disbelief. If he was no artist, he was a good actor. If he was ignorant of law, he was learned in etiquette. If he knew nothing of physic, he was a loud champion of patent medicines. If he was no sportsman, he was most keen and skilful at catching fleas. Lastly, if he was a dull companion among men, he was naturally domestic and generally liked by women.

'Such, then, was the man, about whose greater gifts — nay, about whose very existence — history is silent, but to whose sterling worth we are thus compelled to do tardy justice. A bachelor, he lived the well-balanced rational life of a superior person, until he arrived at about the age of five-and-thirty, when he bethought himself of not deferring any longer the important step, marriage, which he naturally considered the crowning business of a complete existence. And as he considered the matter, the more he became convinced that such a step should by no means be taken in a hurry. He therefore deliberated long, and consulted exhaustively his various and numerous acquaintances concerning the *pros* and *cons* of the matrimonial state before he decided in a general way that he would marry. Next, he set about to search for a superior person with means, who might prove suitable for a wife. He was likewise convinced of the advisability, when he should have found such a person, of not marrying the same in haste, but determined still to wait a further considerable time, so that he might become thoroughly acquainted with the lady's disposition and temper. So commendable a resolution could only have been formed by a person who would surely have the power to carry it out. It was a considerable time before he discovered the person of his choice. Among the spinsters of his acquaintance he knew

of none who approached altogether to his ideal of woman-
hood. He was enormously fastidious because he was such
a monstrously superior person. There were but a few
females whom he thought good enough for him. Not
that he was a misogynist, in whose sight every feminine
charm or coquetry appears inexpressibly ludicrous and
despicable — far from it. No one was so impressionable
as the gentle, superior Fitz Ego. He was only extremely
particular in his choice.'

The descriptive gift of such writing is unmistakable,
and a still stronger gift of grotesque imagination is revealed in his description — which conveys his own
repugnance towards the idea of marriage — of Morgante's
mother, as Fitz Ego found her first.

'In this state of search and indecision, then, he hovered
about seeking introductions here, avoiding parties there,
and meeting with disappointments everywhere, until well-
nigh despairing of ever being able to suit himself, he
almost resolved to relinquish the pursuit. Then, all of
a sudden, he met his fate in the shape of the person
who was to be his consort. It was at a fancy ball
that this incident, so momentous for mankind, took
place.

'On that occasion Fitz Ego, yellow-stockinged and
cross-gartered, impersonated the famous Steward Mal-
volio. The character eminently suited his style; and as he
slowly, on springing toes, paraded the brilliant saloon,
and smiled in a manner unspeakably bewitching, he
looked the perfection of superior refinement and grace.
While thus stalking and smiling, he became magnetically
aware of the presence and fascination of another in a
costume as strange and characteristic as his own. This

other was a female, who represented Ophelia in the mad
scene — an impersonation which evidently came most
natural to her genius; for, arrayed in a shapeless white
robe, her glassy eyes wandering, her blood-red hair
wildly dishevelled, from which straws stuck out and
waved with each motion of her proud head, she seemed
the very incarnation of vehemence and derange-
ment. Their mutual attachment was instantaneous and
complete.

'She threw herself at his feet. He raised her and bowed.
It was impossible for the company to restrain their
emotions! He inquired of her her name — who was her
father? who was her mother? She told him that she was
called Amentia, that her parents came from the same stock
as his own, that she adored him, because he was superior
to all the superior persons whom she had ever met. He
could not resist the appeal, and although he had only just
made her acquaintance, and she had naught to speak of
for dowry, he married her by special licence on the following day.

'After his marriage, Fitz Ego retired with Amentia to
live on a considerable estate which belonged to him in an
out-of-the-way part of England. There he took out the
Commission of the Peace, made himself very busy at the
neighbouring Poor Law Board, of which he was a member, and by judicious management of the Custos Rutu-
lorum, caused himself to be elevated to the exalted and
coveted dignity of Deputy-Lieutenant.

'One of his first pleasant surprises of matrimony was
the discovery in his wife of an altogether ferocious temper.
Yet he loved her, and was very — very happy; she sneered
at him before his visitors, and barged him before the

servants; yet still he was very — very happy; she knocked
off his hat before the labourers, and kicked it about the
fields, yet still he was very — very happy; she banged him
about whenever the caprice entered her head, yet still he
was very — very happy. Finally, she ruled him most
absolutely, and he was ever very — very happy.

'She was unquestionably a woman of genius. She never
troubled about the management of anything inside or
outside of the mansion, making her husband attend to
the housekeeping as well as to all other work. Her principal business in life was the reading of romances, from
which she occasionally sought relaxation by writing long
letters to her female acquaintances, and by singing to
the banjo, whereon she thrummed hardily. The romances
which she devoured were full of the most unnatural and
absurd invention, such as, for instance, the *Arabian
Nights' Entertainment*, *Amadis of Gaul*, the novels of
Émile Zola, Spanish Legends of Chivalry, Icelandic Sagas,
The Adventures of Baron Munchausen, *Jack the Giant
Killer*, etc. However, the work in which she took
most delight was the *Morgante Maggiore* of Pulci,
which she read and re-read, until her brain reeled with
the fantastic visions it excited in her sympathetic
imagination.

'The deeds of giants were her especial diversion. She
never tired of fancying the world peopled by a race of
such glorious beings, who might rove about knocking
down ordinary mortals and changing existing institutions.'

Still more exuberant is the account of Morgante's
eventual arrival in the world:

'After a time it got wind throughout the land that she
was what is conventionally termed in an interesting con-

dition, which blew up a veritable flutter of interest in each feminine heart. To the inquiries of the anxious and the curious, Fitz Ego solemnly shook his head, and Amentia smirked as she said that the event, to use a colloquialism, would take place at such and such a period hence. But lo! the promised time arrived and passed away, and nothing came of it; and a good deal more time passed.

'Meanwhile, Amentia indulged more and more her caprice, dreamt the strangest of dreams, and became subject to the most transcendent hallucinations. She insisted upon the doors being taken from their hinges and the sashes from the windows, in order that the air might have free play throughout the house. She would daily run, dance, and leap, showing feats of activity of which none would have heretofore believed her capable. She would ride off to the meets of the neighbouring foxhounds, and then, although never accustomed to the saddle before, would lead the hunt over the highest and strongest fence and gates, and across the broadest and deepest brooks, to the wonderment of all beholders. Descending on one occasion the gorgeous front staircase of her house, she bounded in her impatience over the balustrade from a height of at least twenty feet into the hall beneath, where she landed as lightly as a child's toy bladder in the presence of her surprised and terrified lord.

'When he recovered his stupefaction he endeavoured to remonstrate with her for this and other imprudences; but she met his remonstrances with such paroxysms of rage and such volleys of vituperation, that he deemed it wiser to thwart her wishes no more, especially as she never seemed the worse for her numerous strange performances.

'Her dreams were many and truly marvellous. She dreamt of giants and of cities and of caves, and of pinnacles and of towers and of cocks and of bulls and of tubs. She dreamt of "posthumous activity" among innumerable atheists; of how she could "live for others in life" and "live in others after death." She dreamt of the future notoriety of that son whom she was soon to bring forth. She dreamt of his prodigious labours, of his wisdom and of his popularity. Lastly, she dreamt that she was delivered of a balloon, which, rising swiftly high into the air, burst and disappeared. . . .

'Thus three years (an impossible time, we grant, under any circumstances less exceptional) passed away in agreeable anticipation for Fitz Ego. He was very—very happy. While in bachelor days, he had had his ambitions like most men; but these ambitions now were dissipated and scattered to the winds in the plentitude of his adoration for this beautiful and accomplished woman—an undeniable proof of their reality and strength. Indeed, he was very—very happy. In the evenings both would sit on either side of the broad fire-place in the large drawing-room, the furniture heaped up and safely covered from the action of the elements, which had free play through the demolished windows and doorless thresholds. Their conversation, when unbroken by hours of silence and meditation, would turn upon subjects profound and diverse. And one evening they sat as usual, while a violent gale of wind, sweeping over the park and through the dismantled house, threatened every moment to lift the roof from the wall-plates. She extended her arms in an ecstasy of delight and awe at the ravages of the tempest. He, in a faded Scotch cap, an old ulster, and a particoloured plaid, sought shelter behind a heavy screen, which was with every gust blown violently down upon him. Under such circumstances, it was difficult for them to speak so that they might each hear the other. They, therefore, as was their wont in rough weather, addressed to each other all observations through large speaking-trumpets, such as are commonly used by ship-captains for giving orders to their crew. Their conversation on this occasion was more interesting and significant than heretofore. They began, as was their wont, with remarks upon the weather. She burst forth into exclamations of joy when she saw the havoc which the storm was making. He answered, adding with tender solicitude his inquiries, whether she did not feel chilly, clothed as she was in such light garments. She replied that she did not; that the cooling effects of wind were beneficial both to the outer and inner person. Hereupon she swallowed a huge gulp of air. Whereat her husband mildly remonstrated, declaring that wind impaired the digestive organs, and was productive of inward pains. She retaliated by proving, on the contrary, its truly benevolent action, and in confirmation of her assertion cited the opinions of grave physicians. He returned to the charge with a list on his side of opinions culled from equally eminent authorities. The argument waxed hot and brilliant, because of the splendid learning, logic, and rhetoric displayed by both parties.

'At last Amentia, feeling that she was getting worsted in the war of words, lost all control over her temper, and with a defiant wave of her trumpet at Fitz Ego, began out of sheer perversity to swallow mouthful after mouthful of air as fast as she possibly could. Wherefore her head

G

visibly began to distend before the eyes of her terrified husband, until it became well-nigh as large as a waste-paper basket. At last she ceased swallowing wind, for the obvious reason that she was utterly unable to contain any more; and as she arose from her chair, her demeanour was verily appalling and sublime. There was a moment of ominous silence. Then, with tightly closed eye-lids, she began to gesticulate vehemently, all the while bellowing like a cow. Distracted, Fitz Ego summoned the domestics for assistance. They came and helped to quiet her distemper. In apoplectic accents she asked for her handkerchief. They brought her a huge one of red cotton. Then did she blow her nose ten times with such deafening noise as shook the walls of the house and brought down the rain from the sky; and at each blow her head gradually became less, until it almost returned to its normal size. A pale fear flitted across the mind of Fitz Ego.

' "Gracious," cried he, "is the result of all this inconvenience to be nothing but wind?"

'He was happily mistaken; for at the eleventh blow, which was louder and more terrible than any of the preceding, Amentia triumphantly held forth in the handkerchief an exceedingly small male infant, that had the appearance for all the world of a well-grown toad.

'When the first stupefaction of intense surprise had gradually passed, Fitz Ego and the domestics pressed round in order to inspect the babe. He was doubtless very small, and somewhat unusual in shape and limb. His hips were enormously large and broad for his size, and his belly unproportionately capacious and deep. On the other hand he had a very small chest with shoulders that were so narrow and sloping that they merged altogether into his long neck, at the extremity of which was an apology for a head, consisting of a mouth, a nose, two ears, and two wide-open eyes; but there was no trace of a cranium. His legs and arms, which were all about the same length, were thick and sturdy for the noble babe that he was.'

The elaborate satire, which is much too long to admit of further quotation, is concerned with the exploits of this grotesque creature, who meets with unbounded popular success as the author of a new philosophy. He is sent to Oxford as an undergraduate, and his exploits there give Edward full opportunity for making fun of his own University. Morgante propounds new theories concerning 'the Use and Advantages of the Abdomen as a vehicle for Emotions,' which are received with ecstatic admiration by innumerable disciples, who call themselves 'Enterists' in enthusiasm for their new master. Morgante, accompanied by a still more grotesque figure called Bucco, proceeds to captivate society in London and in Paris, and after a time he visits Hell, where Voltaire, as a forlorn inhabitant of Hell, explains to him the life and customs of the place. The chapters describing Hell are much the most powerful part of the book, and show Edward's real originality as a young man, both in his gift of writing and as a thinker: while they reveal still more emphatically his fierce detestation of all womankind.

On his return from Hell Morgante found that his former prestige had been forgotten by his faithless disciples, and that upstarts had taken his place. He succeeded, however, in restoring his own position until he was confronted, at one of his public meetings, by an interrupter named Theophilus, who in the course of a long chapter outlines Edward Martyn's own ideals of society and politics by a description of conditions in the island city-state of Agathopolis. This chapter is much less vigorous than the rest of the book, but it is noteworthy as evidence of its author's intense dislike for democracy and of his belief in monastic discipline as the essential condition of good government. A dictatorship is set up, to save the country from the disastrous mismanagement of corrupt politicians, and the dictator is an Admiral with autocratic powers. Cultivation of the arts and of literature plays a large part in his civic duties; there are elaborate descriptions of the trend of literature and painting and music in the ideally governed State; and its dictator is described in terms of august reverence that suggest a Pope much more than a King. 'For our eyes have been opened,' declares Theophilus, 'to foreknowledge of the spiritual joys of heaven; and we see in dissolution nought but a hopeful passing to a more perfect paradise without end. Therefore do we so dispose ourselves in life that we shall have no irregular or overmastering affections which might cause us in leaving it regret, and that we shall, as far as we are able, hold ourselves ever in readiness to encounter death, for which the chief aim of our deeds is, as it were, a preparation.'

'This, my valiant and fair Enterists,' Theophilus explains, 'is, in no small degree, the secret of the unexampled felicity radiating with blinding lustre from Agios Joannes — that majestic iceberg which soars aloft in its cold purity amid the abominable seas of the world: this is the deep treasured wisdom of Agathopolis, the beautiful city, the ideal commonwealth for uncloistered monks of all time.'

The last chapter of the book, with the ironical title 'Apotheosis,' describes the destruction of a discredited Morgante by internal combustion, while addressing a meeting of his disciples in Trafalgar Square, and the triumph of the excellent Theophilus.

Such, in its curious form of presentation, was the whole philosophy of Edward Martyn — the last survivor of a famous Irish clan, inheritor of ancient estates, and formed in his ideas about the modern world by an English education and by much travel in Europe. Its publication was at least the fulfilment of a dream. 'You will publish a book and become famous,' says one of his own characters in a later play. For years Edward had been consumed with that desire, and the destruction of his own poem had seemed to convict him of futility. Henceforward, however, he would at least be regarded among his own class in Ireland as an author — though there was little likelihood that many of them would read his book. Nevertheless, there were a few Irish landowners, and especially among his own neighbours, who would read it and be able to discuss his ideas with him. 'You have written a very clever book,' Sir William Gregory wrote kindly to him, after receiving a presentation copy — 'which not one in a thousand will read, and not one in a hundred of those who do read it will understand. Still, it is a very clever book, and has surprised me. I did not know you had inhaled so much of the spirit of Rabelais.'

But the criticism which probably weighed with him most was the carefully considered letter sent to him from Rome by his friend and neighbour old Comte de Basterot.

'I was at once struck with the good vigorous English,'
wrote this remarkable Frenchman, who had been spending the winter months with his friends Maurice Barrès
and Guy de Maupassant and other literary celebrities,
'and a strong vein of humour, and now I think I can
affirm that the book is a good one, far above mere clever-
ness. I have reflected on this judgment, and do not think
I am biassed by my affection for you.' Some parts of the
book he had found greatly superior to other parts — 'the
city of Hell' for instance was, he thought, really powerful.
But some of the more fantastic parts were less convincing,
and in regard to the idealised description of Agathopolis
he could not refrain from real censure. 'There is an
exaggeration in your treatment of women,' he wrote, 'and
something lame, for Agathopolis is not a convent, and
people must breed in the island. Your treatment of
womenkind wants moderation.' What would be the fate
of the book? speculated this cultured French aristocrat.
'A whole volume of satire is a *tour de force*. I think you
have succeeded in keeping up the interest, but of course
it cannot be called easy reading, and you trample on the
pet corns of the crowd, and you will have the women
against you. What I can say is that *Morgante* ought to be
read and discussed.'

One result of the successful publication of *Morgante*
was that Edward, regarding himself with greater self-
confidence henceforward, decided to take steps to have
himself nominated as a magistrate for the county. He had
doubts owing to some past trouble or other, as to whether
objection might not be taken to his nomination; but Sir
William Gregory was able to reassure him, after consulting the proper authority, who told him that no difficulty

existed. 'Will you write a line to Dillon signifying your
wish for the Commission of the Peace,' wrote Gregory in
a friendly note, 'and the matter will be settled at once.'
The passing of the Local Government Act had not yet
changed the whole administrative system of the country;
but even in the years since he came to manhood he could
realise what a fundamental transformation was taking
place. The old Grand Juries, of which he now became a
member, still had the whole local government of the
country in their hands, but they were soon to be swept
away; and local administration, instead of being the
hobby of a privileged landowning class who could still
feel that it gave them certain public responsibilities while
the old system endured, was soon admitted to be the
concern of the people themselves. Under the new conditions, every vestige of public responsibility was to be
taken out of the hands of the landlord class, and only a
few like Mr. Horace Plunkett or Lord Killanin or Lord
Monteagle and some others, were uneasily conscious that
they enjoyed privileges and powers for which they gave
no return. The publication of Horace Plunkett's generous appeal to his own class under the title *Noblesse Oblige*
fell upon deaf ears in most places. But County Galway
possessed an exceptionally good proportion of public-
spirited landowners, and among them Edward Martyn,
as one of the new magistrates, and before long as Deputy-
Lieutenant for his county, was soon a prominent and
active figure.

In a social world where fox-hunting was the principal
business of life, he was certainly exceptional. But he was
a regular supporter of the County Galway Hunt, and
Frank Shawe Taylor could write with full confidence in

appealing to him for a supplementary subscription to
assist in paying off a deficit — 'as you have always acted so
generously to us and taken such an interest in the noble
sport of fox-hunting, which I know you wish should
always live and *flourish* in Galway.' But Edward's indifference to shooting rights was a continual worry to the
owners of adjacent properties, and he needed frequent
reminders that he was spoiling sport. 'Your kind mother,'
wrote his friend Lord Gough, 'during your minority gave
me the preservation and shooting of the townland Inche-
boy until you were of age. Would you kindly continue
it to me now? I am sorry to say there is no game on it —
but it lies between my properties, and if not mine, is made
an excuse for poachers coming down on mine. They burnt
all the mountain two or three years ago — I believe
accidentally — so that there has been no grouse on it; there
used to be generally a pack — but it is growing again, and
I dare say will in a few years hold a few birds, and I have
to cross it to go from one of my hills to the other. Of
course, if you wish to preserve it yourself I am *quite* as
well pleased, but my object is that it may be preserved
strictly.'

From Lord Gough, too, a few years later, was to come
another kindly remonstrance, which was attached to the
expression of his warm congratulation on the 'immense
success of your first play which I hope will be succeeded
by many another triumph.' But Lord Gough was far
from his own estates at the time, being employed at the
British Embassy in Berlin, and at that distance was more
actively interested in a matter which loomed much larger
in his eyes as a landowner in County Galway. 'You have
deserved well of the country in one important respect,' he

wrote; but he turned to more serious matters when he
pointed out that 'in another respect I submit for your
consideration that her partridges, etc., require encouragement.' Edward had committed the appalling error — long
in advance of legislation which let such things go by
default — of handing over the shooting rights of his
property to his tenants. 'Whether you or I individually
shoot is of no importance,' Lord Gough remonstrated,
'but I would have suggested your keeping all your shooting rights and not giving them up gratis. They are of no
use whatever to the small holders of individual plots.
Thus a property (game) is abandoned to destruction and
no one profits.' The reproach was well founded, and
many a landlord — including those who had supported
the popular movement — was to repent bitterly in the later
years of a sacrifice that did great injury to the country's
shooting. Meanwhile, Edward's indifference at Tulira
had created a position which his neighbour now sought
to retrieve, at his own expense, if it were not already
hopelessly too late. He was willing to pay one year's purchase to Edward's tenants if they could be induced to
surrender a right that had been conferred upon them;
but he feared that the situation could no longer be
remedied.

But Edward had begun to develop other much more
absorbing interests of his own. *Morgante* had been widely
reviewed and brought him real reputation, which gave
him a new self-confidence in meeting his own literary
friends in London. He began to feel that his own instincts
for writing would yet make his name famous; and with
the discovery of Ibsen in the 'nineties, it dawned upon
him that he might even find a new field for literary ex-

pression by writing plays of Irish life, that would require
no original or exciting plot to justify their production, but
that might yet win him a hearing as a truthful exponent
of Irish life and character. The story of his efforts to
create an Irish drama, and of the very remarkable intellectual revival that accompanied it, belongs to a later
chapter. But before he had yet entered upon his own
active career as the pioneer of so many Irish movements,
his mother, who had been so bitterly disappointed by his
refusal to marry and found a family, and who would have
rejoiced in his rapid achievement of literary fame, had
died in the great Gothic mansion he had built to please
her.

Her death in the summer of 1898 brought a great
change to his life in Galway, and left him sadly bereaved.
He had been devotedly attached to her, in spite of their
profound disagreement about his not marrying, and his
most intimate friends realised how much the loss must
mean to him. From Mr. Arthur Symons in London he
received a particularly charming letter of sympathy:

'My dear Martyn,

'I heard yesterday of your irreparable loss, the one
absolutely irreparable loss that one can have in a lifetime. I have suffered it, as you know; and I have never
felt myself or things about me to be quite the same
since. That is why I do not write to you to say any of
the consoling things we sometimes try to say to each
other in our troubles. There is no consolation for
this; only, in some degree, the very slow medicine of
time. But I want to say, if you will let me, that I
sorrow with you through my own memory of my own

sorrow, and I beg you to believe me, now more than ever, always your friend,

'Arthur Symons.'

Her death had spared her at any rate one most painful duty which would have been imposed upon her by Edward's early will, if he should have died before her. It was not the first will that he had made, for it revoked all preceding wills; but it still bequeathed to his mother, 'for her own use and benefit absolutely,' all his real estate and all his residuary personal estate after providing for a number of separate legacies, of which the majority were intended to benefit either certain churches and religious institutions, or else his own tenantry. But the will, which appointed his mother as his executrix on the assumption that he would die first, contained two remarkable provisos. The first concerned the possibility of his being either 'murdered, maimed, or injured in my person' by any 'crime of the nature commonly known as agrarian, or arising out of any unlawful association,' or by any of his own tenants. Should that happen, he directed that none of the provisions in his will directed towards remission of rent or the relief of the poor on his estate should be effective.

The second proviso was purely personal and involved a duty which he must have known well would cause infinite pain to his mother. But it reflected an obsession that had haunted him all through his life, and that found expression in the chapter of *Morgante* which described his own notions of the ideal State. 'I commend my soul,' the will said, 'to the divine mercy of our Lord and beg humbly His forgiveness of my sins; and I implore the

intercession of His blessed Mother. I desire that my·
executrix should within seven days after my death cause
my body to be anatomically examined by two competent
practising medical men who, having taken proper means
to be fully certain that I am really dead so that by their
operations they may not kill me, if I should by any chance
not really be dead, shall dissect my body in order that the
cause of my death shall be ascertained and certified in
writing by the two medical men, to whom I direct my
executrix to pay proper fees.' To compel his mother to
order the dissection of his body after death was, he knew,
to impose an unnatural obligation. But he expressly
stated, after arranging for the disposal of his body, that
'if my said mother shall refuse or neglect within seven
days after my death to cause my body to be so examined
and dissected as hereinbefore mentioned and provided
for, then I revoke the said residuary devise and bequest
to my said mother hereinbefore contained, and I further
revoke all the other legacies bequeathed by this my will
(except the two legacies of £100 each to the Superior of
the Carmelite Priory, Loughrea, which I direct to be
paid in any event) and in lieu thereof. . . .'

She was spared that gruesome discovery in Edward's
will; and indeed there was much to cause her grief in his
later years if she had·lived to witness his development.
Whether he would have developed, as he did in fact
through his participation in the Irish Literary Theatre,
may indeed be doubted; for even after her death, the
memory of her stern upbringing exercised a constantly
restraining influence upon him. It was not until her
dominating presence had disappeared from Tulira that
Edward began in fact to emerge from his monastic

seclusion, and that his strong instinct towards public life began to assert itself. His activities in the intellectual revival aroused him to a new interest in the history of his own country, and reading Irish history soon converted him from the traditional Unionist politics in which he had grown up to a sternly logical adoption of Nationalist ideas which was to be far more uncompromising than that of most Nationalists. Mr. George Moore has given a highly-coloured picture, in his trilogy, of how the mere fact of engaging in an Irish Literary movement created in himself a fierce antipathy towards English ideas and English politics. The main influence upon him was, of course, Edward Martyn's; and Edward himself had become so anti-English by the time of the Boer War that he sided instinctively with the Boers.

The matter was to have a practical bearing upon Edward's life, and to draw him into the full limelight of Irish politics with an unexpected blaze of publicity. In association with Mr. Yeats and Miss Maud Gonne and others, he had taken part in Nationalist demonstrations to celebrate the centenary of the rebellion of 1798; and with them and the more advanced Nationalists, he had expressed his personal objection to the singing of 'God Save the King.' It happened that during his absence from Dublin a concert was held at Tulira by the local Glee Club, of which he was a generous supporter. Some of the gentry who attended it took exception to the absence of the National Anthem from the programme, and the matter was raised publicly as indicating a disloyal attitude on the part of Edward as a magistrate and a Deputy-Lieutenant for his county. He had already incurred the strong disapproval of his neighbours for his participations in Nationalist gatherings, and they were delighted for an opportunity to force his hand. Lord Clonbrock, as Her Majesty's Lieutenant for the county, challenged him directly to explain or justify what had happened.

Edward accepted the challenge at once, and announced publicly that he had resigned his commissions, both as a magistrate and as a Deputy-Lieutenant. It was the first of several occasions on which he was to become the exponent of a considered doctrine of revolt against the commonly accepted notions of loyalty and disloyalty towards the King, whom he refused to consider otherwise than as the head of a political administration in Ireland which he held, as a staunch Home Ruler, to be a usurpation of popular rights. But he was a very isolated figure indeed as the champion of such views among the Irish aristocracy. There were very few of them who would even have supported the attitude of the local Protestant rector at Ardrahan, who wrote to him at once, upon reading the announcement that he had resigned his commissions, to protest — as any Englishman would have felt in the circumstances — that Edward was at least entitled to decide what music should or should not be played in his own house. 'I hope this is not so,' wrote the rector, after alluding to 'that unfortunate concert'; 'but if it is, it is really I who am to blame, as the compiler of the programme, and I intend to write to-morrow to the paper to assume that responsibility. I did not put the National Anthem on the programme (although I will yield to no one in loyalty to our Sovereign) nor did I ask you to have permission to sing it, and I was the more determined not to interfere or suggest it, when I saw others fussing about the matter at the concert. If, owing to that incident, the authorities have placed you in such a position as that you have felt it necessary to resign the commissions, I think it is very unfair on their part. And I feel exceedingly grieved that the Glee Club which you so generously supported, and with which I was personally identified, should be the means of leading you into all this " annoyance." Surely a man ought to have a right to sing or not to sing what he likes in his own house.'

II

THE IRISH LITERARY THEATRE

II

THE IRISH LITERARY THEATRE

THE Literary Movement which had its beginnings in the Irish Literary Theatre that was founded by Edward Martyn, Mr. W. B. Yeats, and George Moore, reached its apotheosis in that curious scene in the Hall of the Swedish Academy on an afternoon of December 1923, when, in the presence of the King of Sweden, the Nobel Prize for Literature was solemnly awarded, with its diploma and medal, to the Irish poet and dramatist, Senator William Butler Yeats. The brilliant ceremony has been described by Mr. Yeats himself in the little volume printed by his sisters at the Cuala Press, which includes his own address, delivered to the Swedish Royal Academy, in which he tells the story of the Irish Dramatic Movement. In the course of it he explains how he 'had told Lady Gregory that I saw no likelihood of getting money for a theatre and so must put away that hope, and she promised to find the money among her friends. Her neighbour, Mr. Edward Martyn paid for our first performances; and our first players came from England; but presently we began our real work with a company of Irish amateurs. Somebody had asked me at a lecture "Where will you get your actors?" and I had said, "I will go into some crowded room, put the name of everybody in it on a different piece of paper, put all those pieces of paper into a hat and draw out the first twelve." I have often wondered at that prophecy, for though it was spoken probably to confound and confuse a questioner, it was very nearly fulfilled. Our two best men actors were not indeed chosen by chance, for one was a stage-struck solicitor's clerk, and the other a working man who had toured Ireland in a theatrical company managed by a negro.'

In a postscript note to the same lecture, Mr. Yeats elaborates, not altogether graciously, this rather casual reference to the colleague whose collaboration and financial support had made possible the first production of his own play. 'Our first performances were paid for,' he explains, 'by Mr. Edward Martyn, a Galway land-owner with a house, part fourteenth century, part a pre-tentious modern Gothic, once dear to Catholic families. He had a great hall, adorned with repeating patterns by that dreary decorator Grace, where he played Palestrina upon an organ, and a study with pictures of the poets in poor stained glass, where he read Ibsen and the Fathers of the Church and nothing else. A sensible, friendly man, with intelligence, strength of purpose, and a charming manner, he shrank from women like a mediæval monk, and between him and all experience came one overwhelm-ing terror — "if I do such and such a thing or read such and such a book I may lose my soul." My *Countess Cathleen* and a play of his own were our first perform-ances. My play's heroine, having sold her soul to the devil, gets it back again because "God only sees the motive, not the deed," and her motive had been to save a starving people from selling their souls for their bodies' sake. When all our announcements had been made, Martyn withdrew his support because a priest told him that the play was heretical. I got two priests to say that it was not, and he was satisfied, for we all have democratic ideals. He withdrew permanently, however, after a few months, foreseeing further peril to his soul. He died a couple of months ago, and with him died a family founded in the twelfth century: an unhappy, childless, unfinished, laborious man, typical of an Ireland that is passing away.'

Mr. Yeats gives amusing details of the birth of the Abbey Theatre, but there is no further allusion to Edward Martyn in his book. His version of the story is, to say the least of it, incomplete. The Irish Literary Theatre, and the Abbey Theatre which arose from its early beginnings, would never have come into existence if it had not been for the public spirit and the enthusiasm of Edward Martyn, who is dismissed with this melancholy gesture of condescension. And although quite a number of large books have been written concerning the modern Irish drama, the story remains curiously unconvincing without any full record of Edward Martyn's own part in bringing it to life. For Edward Martyn not only originated the idea of having Irish literary plays produced in an Irish theatre, and when the time came provided the money needed for the experiment and found the first group of actors; he actually wrote one of the first two plays that were acted in the theatre, and he met with considerably greater success for his own play than was accorded to the other play by Mr. Yeats. In the present chapter some new light may be thrown upon the story from the papers left by Edward Martyn to his literary executor.

Lady Gregory's account, in *Our Irish Theatre*, which was published in 1914, gives a detailed record of the experiment when it was about to develop on more permanent lines. But even her account begins the story considerably after the first stages. Her book opens with an extract from her own diary at the time, in which she records how she had met Mr. Yeats in London early in 1898, and of how he had talked to her of 'taking or building a little theatre somewhere in the suburbs to produce romantic drama, his own plays, Edward Martyn's, one of Bridges', and he is trying to stir up Standish O'Grady to write some. He believes there will be a reaction after the realism of Ibsen, and romance will have its turn.' The last sentence is noteworthy, for it was in fact Edward Martyn's cult of Ibsen that brought the Irish theatre to life. He probably did not realise for a long time that, in associating with Mr. Yeats in the enterprise he had in view, his own ideas were to be completely ousted, by the unexpected combination of Mr. Yeats and of his neighbour, Lady Gregory, in managing the new theatre. Later in the same year, Lady Gregory continues, she was staying with their French neighbour, the old Comte de Basterot, for a few days at his place overlooking Galway Bay. 'On one of those days at Duras in 1898,' she writes, 'Mr. Edward Martyn, my neighbour, came to see the Count, bringing with him Mr. Yeats,[1] whom I did not then know very well, though I cared for his work very much and had already, through his directions, been gathering folk-lore. They had lunch with us, but it was a wet day, and we could not go out. After awhile, I thought the Count wanted to talk to Mr. Martyn alone; so I took Mr. Yeats to the office where the steward used to come to talk — less about business, I think, than of the Land War or the state of the country, or the last year's deaths and marriages from Kinavara to

[1]Throughout this passage the impression left (unintentionally of course) is that Edward Martyn was just a neighbour making a call, there being no indication of the fact that Comte de Basterot was Edward's cousin and most ntimate friend.

the headland of Aughanish. We sat there through the wet afternoon, and, though I had never been at all interested in theatres, our talk turned on plays. Mr. Martyn had written two, *The Heather Field* and *Maeve*. They had been offered to London managers, and now he thought of trying to have them produced in Germany, where there seemed to be more room for new drama than in England. I said it was a pity we had no Irish theatre where such plays could be given. Mr. Yeats said that had always been a dream of his, but he had of late thought it an impossible one, for it could not at first pay its way, and there was no money to be found for such a thing in Ireland. We went on talking about it, and things seemed to grow possible as we talked, and before the end of the afternoon we had made our plan. We said we could collect money, or rather ask to have a certain sum of money guaranteed. We would take a Dublin theatre and give a performance of Mr. Martyn's *Heather Field*, and one of Mr. Yeats's own plays, the *Countess Cathleen*. I offered the first guarantee of £25. A few days after that I was back at Coole and Mr. Yeats came over from Mr. Martyn's home Tulira, and we wrote a formal letter to send out.'

The sequel is so well known that it needs no detailed repetition. Lady Gregory, with a newly acquired typewriter, sent out the letters appealing for guarantees. The replies from all manner of people make amusing reading in the light of after events; but, as Lady Gregory points out, the guarantees were never called upon, as Edward Martyn 'generously paid for the whole performances.' That matter may be so trivial as to be beneath controversy, but the ideas and the influence of Edward Martyn in the beginnings of the Irish Theatre were so individual and so important that no account of the modern Irish drama can be accurate which ignores them. The beginnings of the experiment went much farther back than the meeting which Lady Gregory recalls in her early diary. Edward Martyn turned his attentions to writing plays very soon after the successful publication of *Morgante* in 1890. In the months when he had shared rooms with his young friend at Pump Court, he had been a constant theatre-goer, mixing with many of the dramatic critics in London. It was as far back as 1894 that he had suggested to George Moore that he wished to write plays in Irish instead of English, but that dream had never materialised.

With exemplary industry, he had set himself to become a disciple of Ibsen, and after much concentration and sustained effort he had produced a play of his own, *The Heather Field*. It was much the best play he ever wrote, and it not only showed great courage and originality as one of the first attempts to write a play of ideas for the modern stage, but came nearer than any of his later plays to expressing his whole philosophy of life. The scene was the West of Ireland, and the main character was an Irish landlord who devotes all his resources to reclaiming a great tract of mountain which had been over-run with wild heather. His friends, especially his wife — who symbolises Edward's own conception of all womankind — urge him desperately to cease squandering his money on a scheme that cannot succeed; and when he raises a new mortgage that cripples the estate, in a final effort to extend his reclamation on a bigger scale, his wife tries to have him certified as a madman. Overwhelmed with the anxiety and the obsession of his great plans, he does lose his reason, and at the end of the play the little child comes in with a bunch of wild heather buds which show that the wild heather has broken out again on the mountain in spite of all his labours. Carden Tyrrell is unable to understand what has happened, and is completely happy, having lost all comprehension of his surroundings and gained liberty to live entirely in his dream.

It was scarcely the sort of plot that would appeal to London theatrical producers in the 'nineties, when Oscar Wilde's and Pinero's smart comedies of elegant society were the nearest approximation to literary drama that any manager would even consider. But Edward's friends were so impressed by the novelty and the surprising artistic perfection of what he had written, that he began to form a definite ambition of getting *The Heather Field* produced. George Moore had returned from Paris, and was exciting much attention by his controversies with the leading dramatic critics; and he had decided to stake his own reputation on winning recognition for Edward Martyn as the exponent of a new school of literary drama. Through Edward, he had been introduced to Mr. W. B. Yeats, and Yeats also had been writing plays in verse which were even more unsuitable for the ordinary London theatres than Edward's *Heather Field*. But Ibsen had begun to dawn upon the intelligentsia of London, and the first performances of Maeterlinck's *Pelleas and Melisande* had been a still more unlikely innovation. The Stage Society and the enthusiasts for the more exotic forms of modern drama, were beginning to have a real influence in the literary reviews, and it began to appear even remotely possible that Edward's play might yet be produced.

Mr. George Alexander had been approached about it by George Moore, and declined the play at once. Mr. Forbes Robertson wrote a polite letter of refusal. It was quite obvious that none of the London theatres would consider it; but the rapid rise of Mr. Yeats's reputation as a poet gave considerable possibilities of eventual success somewhere, if his *Countess Cathleen* and *The Heather Field* were to be put on together. Edward himself was emboldened after a time to make inquiries in Dublin, but the result there was no more encouraging. A friend approached the owner of one of the Dublin theatres on his behalf and wrote at once to report to Edward. 'You must forgive me for telling you plainly,' he wrote, that the theatre-owner, having read the plays and seen Mr. Yeats, 'does not consider that they would "take on" in their present shape. He thinks the "stories" are pretty, but, as plays, are wanting in dramatic power, and he says that "for your own sakes they should be thoroughly revised by a competent dramatist." He thinks they might be made more effective as operettas, or at all events as musical plays. He would not on any account produce the plays as they are, himself, and if you do so, it must be entirely on your own responsibility.' In that case he would be prepared to provide the theatre and all accessories, except stage scenery, for £200 for one week. But the intermediary added by way of friendly caution: 'I tell you *frankly*, I don't think he is at all keen about the plays, and I am sure you will think it much more friendly of me to tell you this frankly than to be beating about the bush.'

Matters had reached this stage in the autumn of 1897, and it was fairly evident that no theatre, whether in Ireland or in England, was at all likely to consider the plays

George Moore

on their own merits. But Edward had gone so far, and had received so much encouragement from his friends, that he began to consider seriously the possibility of hiring a small theatre on his own account, and if necessary undertaking the expenses of collecting the actors for the plays. In the meantime, he decided to have his own two plays published in book form. For he had by this time written the short play, *Maeve*, as well. In plot and in treatment it was even less likely than *The Heather Field* to attract a commercial producer. He founded his second play also on a mystical love of the country in western Ireland; the heroine in this case being a girl called Maeve who is being obliged to marry a rich man against her will, but is spirited away on the night before her wedding by the legendary Queen Maeve. The writing of it had interested Mr. Yeats much more than *The Heather Field*, with its Ibsenesque group of characters in an Irish land-lord's house. He had already begun to spend much of his time in Galway, either with Edward at Tulira, or at Coole, where Lady Gregory used to take him out for walks to discuss folk-lore with the old peasants, to distract him from overwork. In a letter to Edward Martyn at the time, Mr. Yeats sends some particulars he has been able to gather concerning local visions of the legendary queen. 'I have found an old woman,' he wrote, 'who has seen her and says that when she thinks of "the ladies" now after thinking of her "they seem like children who are not able to put their clothes on right. It is ladies I would not call them women." Maeve, as she describes her, is a tall, beautiful amazon kind of woman in a white tunic that leaves her arms and legs bare. She has both sword and dagger. This woman saw her coming from the place of her tomb on Knocknarea. She says the pilots often see her go by.' Such authentic glimpses had been gaily incorporated by Edward in his own little play, and the result was a fine piece of poetic imagery. It had been improved further by being submitted for close criticism to his friend Arthur Symons, who had re-written many passages. 'The vision I have given particular care to,' wrote Mr. Symons after a fortnight's close study. 'I have tried to get a sort of exalted chant into the rhymes, and to distinguish between the mortal ecstasy of Maeve and the immortal peace of Queen Maeve. I feel certain you will agree with what I have done.'

In the same letter Mr. Symons reported that George Moore had seized upon the re-written copy of the typescript, and had carried it off to write the introduction with which he proposed to present Edward Martyn to the discriminating public. The two plays, *The Heather Field* and *Maeve*, were published in one volume in the following year, which was dedicated by Edward to his three closest friends and associates at the time, George Moore, W. B. Yeats, and Arthur Symons. Mr. Moore, in his long introduction to the volume, expressed his own vigorously critical views of contemporary drama in England, with special attention to the shortcomings of Mr. William Archer as a dramatic critic. 'It was open to Mr. Archer, Miss Robins and Mr. Massingham to have produced this divine play,' he wrote in his introduction, after several pages of lyrical eulogy of Yeats's *Countess Cathleen*; 'or, if they had wanted a prose play, they might have produced *The Heather Field*, which will now be performed by the Irish Literary Theatre on alternate nights with Mr. Yeats's play.' He explains how

he had sent Edward Martyn's *Heather Field* to Mr.
Archer, who had seen in it even less than George Alexander had seen in it; 'nor did discussion help him to
understand that it was the first play written in English
inspired by the examples of Ibsen.' Mr. Archer had
replied scornfully that Mr. Moore might, if he chose,
prefer a piece of rude original sculpture to a piece of
academic work. Mr. Moore's considered retort, as given
in the introduction, was a commendation of Edward's
play more vigorous than Edward could ever have hoped
to receive. 'A play that possesses qualities of balance,
design, sequence, is a work of art, and will hold its own
in any company,' declared Mr. Moore; 'and although
The Heather Field will seem small by the side of *The Wild
Duck*, it will hold its own by the side of *The Wild Duck*, or
Macbeth or *Hamlet*, just as a housewife by Peter de Hoogh
will hold its own by the "Marriage Feast" by Veronese,
or "The Entombment of Christ" by Titian, or "The
Last Judgment" by Michael Angelo.'

Dealing with the play in some detail, Mr. Moore went
on to assert boldly that 'the hero of *The Heather Field*,
Carden Tyrrell, is the first appearance of humanity in the
English prose drama of to-day — of the eternal instinctive
humanities, and not the ephemeral differences which
divide the grocer from the baronet. It were surely impossible to point to a scene in the English prose drama of
the present century so essentially human as the scene in
which Carden Tyrrell speaks to his brother Miles of the
days when they sailed their skiff to Lorlie, and Carden,
who is the elder brother, tells Miles, who was then a boy,
the legends of the Rhine. This scene is certainly a
beautiful and pathetic expression of that passionate

wistfulness which rises up in the heart and brain when we
look back on the days of our early youth, those days fresh
and fugitive as the days of early spring, when the buds are
breaking into tiny leaf and the daffodils star the grass.
In a moment we are in the midst of the emotion which
Mr. Martyn has expressed in this scene, an emotion
known to all over thirty, to the hind as well as the king.
Expression of it has hitherto been sought by bringing
together an elderly spinster and an elderly bachelor who
did not marry, and who fear that it is now too late, the
assumption being that if they had married they would
have been happy. But Mr. Martyn probes deeper than
the ephemeral griefs which circumstances create, and in
the scene between Carden Tyrrell and Miles Tyrrell we
are face to face with that primal melancholy which is at
the root of human existence, we look into its eyes, infinite
as the sky, and are absorbed in pity for all things that
live, and we feel in our soul the truth that man was not
intended to be happy.'

After continuing in this strain of high eulogy concerning *The Heather Field*, Mr. Moore passes to the second
play *Maeve*, in which he finds a different expression of the
same thought; and in the 'power to re-tell the same story
in a different form' he acclaims 'the sign of a true artist.'
Summing up his own feelings concerning Edward's two
plays, Mr. Moore proclaimed openly that 'to triumph
thus over common instincts and infect the reader with
sympathies and longings which lie beyond the world, is
surely to succeed where hitherto no modern English
dramatist has even dreamed that drama was to be found.'
More than that, he claimed that the two plays were
'perfectly constructed; they could be acted as they are

written, without curtailment; they were composed with
strict regard for the stage, though perhaps not with a view
to representation on the stage. Mr. Martyn was not
innocent enough to think that a play, in which human
emotion is the whole of the play, would be tolerated in a
theatre of the present day. He wrote them with strict
regard for the stage, because it is impossible to write
good plays without the actors and the actresses, who will
never interpret them, being before your eyes. It is as
impossible to compose literary plays that do not act as it
is to compose sonnets in fifteen lines; but by some strange
irony it has come to pass that the plays which lend themselves to interpretation are the plays which are neglected
on the stage and cherished in the study.'

Having won this immensely enthusiastic commendation from Mr. Moore, it is not surprising that Edward,
as a young man of considerable private means, should be
encouraged to make the bold experiment of producing
his own play in association with Mr. Yeats. His plans
had been thrown back for a time by the personal tragedy
of his mother's death, while his book was still in the
publisher's hands. Her death had been the heaviest blow
of his life, and he had counted much upon giving her the
joy of witnessing his own success as a dramatist. In his
loneliness, he returned to his work with greater intensity
than ever, and the plans for finding a suitable theatre in
Dublin were pressed forward with renewed energy.
The new Local Government Act had just been carried
through Parliament, and Yeats and Edward had succeeded, by lobbying the Irish M.P.'s of all parties, in
securing the insertion of a clause which would enable
them to obtain a licence for theatrical performances. All

possibilities were explored, and the final decision was to
apply to the municipal authorities of Dublin for permission to give the proposed performances in the Ancient
Concert Rooms. Edward's letter to the Town Clerk
and the Town Clerk's reply are both preserved among his
papers. 'The National Literary Society,' he wrote,
'desire in the month of May next to hold a literary
dramatic entertainment in the Great Hall of the building
known as the Ancient Concert Room, No. 42½, Great
Brunswick Street, Dublin; the proceeds of such entertainment to be devoted exclusively to literary purposes.
The plays proposed to be acted are of a more literary
nature than are usually acted in theatres, and are not
expected to appeal to a popular audience. For the purpose of such representation the Literary Society requires
an occasional licence under the 89 Sec. of the Local
Government Act, 1898. I, on behalf of the said Society,
and by their instructions, request the Council for the
County Borough of Dublin either to make the necessary
application to the Lord Lieutenant for an occasional
licence, limited to the month of May next in the above-
named room, or, should the County Council desire me to
take that course, I would make an application direct to
the Lord Lieutenant upon the fiat of the Council. There
are two plays proposed to be acted, namely a play by Mr.
W. B. Yeats called *The Countess Cathleen*, and a play by
Mr. Edward Martyn called *The Heather Field*, both being
exemplifications of Irish life, and copies of the plays,
which are published works, can, if desired, be submitted
to you or to any person named on behalf of the Council.
Also it is possible that there may be a short dialogue in
the Irish language. The room, being a public room,

already I believe inspected by the Corporation, has attached thereto all proper sanitary and other appointments. Any further information you desire I shall be happy to afford, and I would request a reply at as speedy a date as possible.' The reply came within a few weeks, announcing that the required licence would be granted; and the way was now open for Edward to get his company of actors together.

All sorts of suggestions were forthcoming from the many enthusiasts who were interested in the new schemes. One of the most curious was sent to Edward Martyn from A. E., who was still engaged for a good deal of the year bicycling to remote parts of the country to organise co-operative creameries, but always returning to Dublin, where he was the centre of so many interests. His work for Plunkett's Irish Agricultural Organisation Society had taught him the supreme necessity of considering economy. 'Many thanks for yours enclosing cheque for I.A.O.S.,' he wrote in one letter to Edward. 'I think we will keep on our legs for some time anyhow. The I.A.O.S. manages to work marvellously on very little, and though we get face to face with bankruptcy about once in every three months, the gods provide, and good friends to the country, like yourself, help it when it is not self-supporting.' He was well aware of the big expenses that Edward was likely to be incurring with his new theatrical venture, and he submitted 'rather timidly as I know nothing about stage mechanism' an idea which had flashed across his mind that might be useful to Edward in saving expense. 'The scene painting must be a large item in the expense of production,' he wrote. 'Would it not be possible to get over this difficulty by the use of coloured photos of

I

scenery, the castle at Gort, etc. used as magic lantern slides and flung from behind upon a thin hanging? It would be infinitely more illusive in its effect than any painting. The same could be done for most of the scenes in Yeats's *Countess Cathleen*. In fact the idea seems so simple that I imagine it must have been used already. I think it would be worth while thinking it over anyhow. If not capable of use just now, the idea may be of value at another time. It would be also very easy to change one scene to another. If you thought it worth while to ascertain the possibility of this, I imagine it would be well to write to some of the popular entertainers who use limelight views or the instrument makers. They would know to what extent the views could be enlarged.'

In May, the great venture was at last undertaken. Mr. George Moore has made an epic of the story, and readers of his trilogy need no reminding of the strenuous weeks of rehearsal, of how Mr. Moore came on the scenes when Edward and Yeats had collected their own actors, insulted the actors till one of them threw chairs at his head, persuaded Edward to pay them to go away, and replaced them with others of his own choosing. He has described that ludicrous scene in the Ancient Concert Rooms. — 'I had never seen such gloom anywhere, except in Sickert's pictures,' was his first impression when he arrived in haste from London — when the furies were let loose against Yeats's play for its travesty of the Irish peasants, whom it represented as selling their souls to proselytisers, whereas their fidelity to their religion had always been their proudest tradition. It was no wonder indeed that Edward, as a fiercely scrupulous Catholic, should feel uneasy about the storm that Yeats's play had provoked. He had foreseen trouble before, but Yeats, with his unfailing resource-fulness, had mobilised literary theologians to allay Edward's scruples, just as he had mobilised Horace Plunkett and Tim Healy to insert the clause in the new Local Government Act which had enabled them to obtain a licence for their experiment. But the storm of indignation that burst on their heads might well have shaken the confidence of the most intrepid; and Mr. George Moore's unceasing jibes at Catholicism must have made Edward feel that he was keeping strange company, for so zealous a Catholic. 'He runs after his soul,' exclaimed George Moore, in a brilliant afterthought, 'like a dog after his tail, and lets it go when he catches it.'

Edward found moral support, however, in the collaboration of Lionel Johnson, as fervent a Catholic as himself, who had written the prologue that was spoken at each performance. And the pamphlet *Souls for Gold*, which was rushed out in denunciation of Mr. Yeats's play, was so hysterical that they could both disregard it. Canon William Barry's approval of the play, when it had been submitted for his opinion as a theologian, had been unhesitatingly favourable. He had even said expressly: 'I would give the play first and explanations afterwards,' besides providing the apposite text from one of St. Paul's epistles which Mr. Moore was to quote against Edward at hourly intervals while the controversy raged. And even when Cardinal Logue fulminated against Yeats's *Countess Cathleen*, his admission that he had not read the play, but was only scandalised by what he had heard of it, left Edward free to ignore his objections as being admittedly based upon hearsay.

In any case, Edward's own bishop, Dr. Healy, showed

no sign of disapproval. He wrote at once to congratulate
Edward on 'the universal favour with which *The Heather
Field* was received by the Dublin Press. I had read both
it and *Maeve* and liked them very much for their beauty
and simplicity,' he wrote. 'There is, I think, even more
poetry in *Maeve* than there is in the other, but I suppose
that took my fancy most on account of the spirit of Celtic
romance which it breathes in every line. I should like
to see it acted' he said; and he even alluded to the delicate
question of Yeats's *Countess Cathleen*, saying, 'I think
your friend, Mr. Yeats, has been rather severely handled
by the theologians, but as I have not yet read *The Countess
Cathleen* and can only judge from the extracts, I would
not venture to offer a definite opinion. I most sincerely
congratulate you on the success of your work.' Such
praise from his own bishop was all that Edward could
have desired. He had been prepared already for angry
criticism from the more prejudiced, and he was well
aware that his own association with George Moore made
him suspect among many devout Catholics. For though
few people in Ireland even knew the names of Mr.
Moore's novels or were aware of the erotic indiscretions
of his *Confessions of a Young Man*, Mr. Moore had made
his own name anathema in Nationalist and Catholic
Ireland by publishing *Parnell and his Island* a few years
before. A friend on the staff of the *Nation* had written to
Edward to apologise for being unable to review his volume of plays. 'I'm so very sorry,' he wrote, 'that *The
Heather Field* was not sent direct to me instead of to the
Nation office. The editor got hold of it, and, just as I
feared, was frightened by the preface. The very name of
George Moore was enough to rouse the worst suspicions in

his breast; and the Théâtre Libre and Independent Theatre suggested all sorts of dreadful things to him. I suppose when he is quite satisfied that there is nothing "contrary to faith and morals" in the book, that he will review it in some sort of fashion. If only I had got hold of it first, I should have run in the review all right without any difficulty.'

The truth was that Edward Martyn's religious scruples had nothing whatever to say to his severance from the Literary Theatre. He was so delighted with the undoubted literary success of their first efforts, and with the high praise given by the dramatic critics — including Max Beerbohm and A. B. Walkley, who were sent over to Dublin when the riots at the theatre had caused a public sensation — that he began negotiations almost immediately for a much more ambitious plan of taking the Gaiety Theatre next time. 'Lady Gregory informs me that you are thinking of closing with the Gaiety's offer for the Irish Literary Theatre,' wrote a friend in Trinity College, who had personal experience with the theatre in producing plays for the University Dramatic Society. 'I am not sure you can improve on the terms. You might hold out to pay them only 50 per cent., but I should like you not to mention the University Dramatic Society's arrangement as it is a secret, and I got the information in private. If you hold out, insist that the Irish Literary Theatre would help to popularise the Gaiety with the people of Dublin, as this, I believe, is the great object of the new management into whose hands the theatre has only lately passed.'

That letter came from one of the ablest of the young men whom Mr. T. P. Gill had collected on the staff of

the *Dublin Daily Express*, which, under his editorship,
was rapidly changing from the organ of Diehard Unionism into a national newspaper that provided a platform
for every progressive movement in Ireland. For some
time its literary page on Saturdays had contained an
astonishing amount of good writing, supplied by all the
rising figures in the literary movement. Sir Horace
Plunkett, with whom Mr. Gill had been collaborating
since his retirement from Parliament, had acquired,
through financial backers in London, sufficient control
in the paper to enable him, with Mr. Gill as editor, to run
it on their own lines; and Mr. Gill had displayed extraordinary gifts as an editor. The newspaper, when he
assumed charge, had been almost derelict. Its machinery
and type were scarcely more decrepit and obsolete than
its whole editorial and managerial staff; and Mr. Gill,
with his rare capacity and enthusiasm as an organiser,
had undertaken to modernise the whole paper and make
it the organ of every constructive movement in Ireland.
He had a real genius for collecting men of talent to co-
operate in his schemes, and he had sufficient journalistic
experience in his youth to have acquired all the necessary
technical knowledge, besides having a clear conception
of all that a vigorously conducted daily newspaper, in
capable hands, could accomplish as an instrument for
promoting national unity. With him as editor, and
Horace Plunkett as the principal controller of its financial
management, it began to make very remarkable headway.
The Local Government Bill, which swept away the Grand
Juries and introduced popular control of local administration all over Ireland, owed much to its shrewd and influential criticism of details; and the creation of Horace

Plunkett's comprehensive Department of Agriculture and Technical Instruction was almost an embodiment of its practical policy for economic development in Ireland. It had done more than any other influence to foster the literary revival, and it acclaimed Edward Martyn's venture in producing the first plays of the National Literary Theatre as an epoch-making event. During the week of the performances Mr. Gill organised a banquet at the Shelburne Hotel to celebrate the occasion, at which all the leading figures in the various phases of the Irish revival were present. That banquet has given Mr. George Moore the subject for the most memorable chapter in his *Ave,* where he introduces and describes all the principal personages of his own saga of modern Ireland. Had Mr. Gill's bold venture been allowed to continue, the whole trend of Irish politics in the following fruitful years might well have been profoundly altered.

But the difficulties were too great even for so accomplished a diplomatist as Mr. Gill. The ultimate financial control of the paper still remained in the hands of the Diehard Unionists; and as they watched with resentful apprehension the evolution of a policy which was obviously drawing Horace Plunkett continually nearer to a modified support of Home Rule, they decided to approach Lord Ardilaun. He, after a little suitable argument, was easily scared into believing that the safety of the British Constitution in Ireland was being undermined through the *Daily Express.* He came to the rescue gallantly, by buying enough shares to outvote the Plunkett interest, so that both Plunkett and Gill had to withdraw immediately, after unavailing protests, from the paper. Reformers and literary enthusiasts alike learned with

consternation that their platform had been taken from
them. Hopes rose among the few who knew that Plunkett
and Gill, encouraged by their undeniable success and
their still greater possibilities, if they had been allowed
to carry on, had actually obtained from their previous
financial supporters the necessary backing to organise an
entirely new newspaper. But the new Department of
Agriculture and Technical Instruction, with its all-
embracing programme, came into being and absorbed
the entire energies of Plunkett, as its Vice-President or
responsible Minister, and T. P. Gill as its organising
Secretary.

The loss of the *Daily Express's* co-operation was a
severe blow to Edward's hopes, which he felt particularly
because of his close friendship with Mr. Gill. But he
found new encouragement unexpectedly in other directions. The first performances at the Ancient Concert
Rooms had been an unquestionable success, and the
uproar by angry interrupters had only focussed attention
upon an experiment which would otherwise have passed
almost without notice. And in so far as popular audiences
were concerned, Edward's *Heather Field* had made a
much deeper impression than Mr. Yeats's *Countess
Cathleen*. He was already feeling that he had made
history when a flattering invitation reached him from
Mr. Charles Henry Meltzer in New York, inviting him
to cable his immediate consent to the production of *The
Heather Field* by his Independent Theatre in the American
cities. Edward naturally agreed at once; and through
the winter he had all the excitement of knowing that his
play was going to be produced in America in the spring.
That it would succeed there, after having been rejected

by every experienced producer in London, was too much to hope; and Edward's sense of humour was equal to receiving any sort of news concerning it with equanimity. In May word reached him as to how the play had fared. 'It may not surprise you,' wrote Mr. Meltzer with engaging frankness, 'to hear that although a small minority was delighted with the play here, the production was generally received with resentful and stupefied amazement. Vile weather kept our usual supporters away to a large extent in Boston and New York. As for the Irish Americans, to whom we had appealed chiefly and directly, by circulars and advertisements in the Irish papers, they are evidently indifferent to literature.' A fuller report, a week later, said that the receipts had been 'almost nominal.' Mr. Meltzer 'did not think that twenty Irishmen came to see the play. None the less I am convinced that it is an exceptionally *good* play,' he wrote, 'which should appeal to thinking people anywhere. Even *The Master Builder* drew larger houses than *The Heather Field*.' Mr. Meltzer could scarcely have expressed failure more vividly than in that sentence. Nevertheless he declared himself to be by no means discouraged, and he asked Edward to let him make another attempt at some more auspicious time.

While Edward had thus succeeded already in having his first play produced in America, he was preparing vigorously for the second season of his Irish Theatre. Mr. Yeats's suggestion that he abandoned the attempt at once because of theological objections is grotesquely wide of the mark, and shows how little memory can be trusted in such matters. It was Mr. Yeats who disappeared from the second season of the Literary Theatre, in February, 1900. This time the plays produced were Edward Martyn's *Maeve*, Miss Alice Milligan's heroic drama *The Last Feast of the Fianna*, and *The Bending of the Bough*, which was a collaboration between Edward and George Moore, Mr. Moore having completely re-written Edward's political play *The Tale of a Town*, by Edward's permission. The success of the first experi-ment was thus repeated, and in the following year a third season was inaugurated, at which a play in Irish, by Douglas Hyde, was produced for the first time, while *Diarmid and Grania*, in which Mr. Moore, Mr. Yeats, Lady Gregory and Mr. Tadhg O'Donoghoe had all collaborated, was also produced. This third season, however, was the last with which Edward Martyn was associated, and the Abbey Theatre, which developed soon afterwards, passed entirely into the control of Mr. Yeats and Lady Gregory, who had by this time become completely preoccupied with peasant plays.

A profound divergence of views had arisen between them and Edward Martyn, which has been so fully discussed in other books about the modern Irish drama that it need not be detailed here. The main difference was that Edward consistently desired to use the stage for the presentation of modern plays by Irish authors con-cerned with the problems of ideas and of life. He had no interest whatever in peasant plays, which conveyed no subtle psychological problem and merely reflected social customs or conditions. He was still absorbed in the new conception of drama that had been introduced by Ibsen and Strindberg. Mr. Yeats, on the other hand, had been devoting himself to collecting folk-lore with Lady Gregory, and she had developed a real interest in the

life of the peasantry around her in County Galway.
The absence of peasant plays from the repertory of the
Irish Literary Theatre was an omission that Edward
Martyn would have willingly made good by including
a peasant play, if he could have got one. But Mr. Yeats
had formed a definite policy for the Irish Theatre which
was to involve concentration upon peasant plays almost
to the exclusion of everything else. In an article in the
review *Samhain* which he produced in 1902, Mr. Yeats
stated his own views very clearly, and it was quite obvious
that he and Edward Martyn could not continue to
co-operate along the lines he now indicated. 'Our movement is a return to the people,' wrote Mr. Yeats, 'and the
drama of Society would but magnify a condition of life
which the countryman and the artisan could but copy to
their hurt. The play that is to give them a quite natural
pleasure should either tell them of their own life, or of
that life of poetry where every man can see his own
image, because then alone does human nature escape
from arbitrary conditions.'

The parting of the ways had clearly arrived, and a
breach became inevitable when Mr. Yeats discovered the
group of amateur actors who had been got together by
the brothers Willie and Frank Fay. They had formed an
Irish National Dramatic Company which produced a
number of new Irish plays, including A. E.'s prose-poem
Deirdre, which the poet Mr. James Cousins had persuaded him to entrust to them. The Fays had, curiously
enough, given their first dramatic performances in the
hall of the Carmelite Church in Clarendon Street, where
Edward Martyn was about the same time making his
first experiments in encouraging a boys' choir to demon-

strate the possibilities of plain chant. Edward had watched the new theatrical venture with real sympathy, but it was not at all what he had in view; and even though he desired much to have Irish plays performed by Irish actors, he was convinced that such players as the Fays could never do what he required. They were, however, just what Mr. Yeats desired for his own sort of plays, and for their second season Mr. Yeats gave them his own *Cathleen ni Hoolihan* to produce. Their remarkable natural talents and their enthusiasm gave to Mr. Yeats exactly the material he wished to find. They collected the necessary number of actors, and trained them to a high perfection in the simplest form of character acting. And by 1903 Mr. Yeats had found it possible to provide them with a theatre of their own, when Edward Martyn, with his usual generosity, negotiated for the acquisition of the derelict Abbey Theatre, incorporating the adjacent disused morgue of Dublin in the older building. Through Mr. Yeats, Miss Horniman of Manchester became interested in the scheme soon afterwards, and provided an annual subsidy, besides giving them the theatre rent free for six years. The simultaneous discovery of J. M. Synge as an Irish dramatist gave a wholly unexpected impetus to this new phase of the dramatic movement, and, dominated by his genius, the Abbey Theatre became almost exclusively devoted to peasant plays very soon after it had begun.

By that time Edward Martyn had fully realised that his own ideas were to be discarded, and even ignored. But Mr. Yeats, with his restless energy and his surprising adroitness in manipulating men, was still doing all in his power to keep Edward Martyn in their original association. He tried to flatter him by professing his own lack of knowledge of Catholic Ireland, which Edward must instinctively understand. And among Edward's papers there survives a curious, though very characteristic, note from Mr. Yeats, scrawled in haste from a Dublin hotel: 'My dear Martyn. Please don't forget that I expect you to speak to-night at the Abbey according to promise. It is very important to have somebody there who does really know the Irish peasant.' With the rise of the Abbey Theatre, Edward Martyn, as well as George Moore, drops into the background. But his influence upon the origins of the modern Irish drama was so important that it is of interest to reproduce some of his own early articles on the subject, of which he had assembled a series for publication in a book of his collected essays.

His travels in Germany had convinced him of the possibilities of national support for a revival of theatrical art. In Ibsen he had discovered the modern genius whom he regarded as the author and inspirer of a new dramatic tradition in Europe. But in Germany, even more than in France, he had been impressed by the results of organised and official encouragement to serious drama. Among the papers which he collected for publication at the end of his life were several, written at the turn of the century, which described the impressions and the hopes he had thus gathered, and which show how he was dominated particularly by the influence of Ibsen.

'After the wonderful modern drama in Scandinavia,' he wrote in 1899, 'the modern drama of Germany, if we are to judge by its best work, is the finest and most intellectual in Europe. And this drama, strange to say,

is popular, and what is stranger, perhaps, is, that there is
a very inferior drama popular also. I do not mean to say
that the strangeness consists in an inferior drama being
popular, but in the good and the bad being popular at the
same time. If the Germans seek their pasture over fields
of such varied quality, it is because they are an omnivorous
people; and thus it is possible that sometimes they may
hunger for the husks, when they cannot have their fill of
the ambrosia of art. The theatre with them is, indeed,
held in high honour as the home of great thought and
great art. They understand its fascination when it
becomes truly elevated, and if at the same time they can
be interested in its degradation, through either silliness
or sensuality, I can only account for the contradiction in
the manner I have said, or perhaps, by the fact that there
must, after all, be two publics — one for the good and one
for the bad. And this would seem to apply, in a measure,
to other countries also, but not to England. There the
public is wholly for bad modern drama, and for bad art in
general, for the most part. That is why, I suppose, when
returning to England from the Continent, it always
seems to me like entering a comparatively half-civilised
country.

'The contrast has always struck me as peculiar between
the upholstered drawing-room-like shapelessness of an
English theatre, designed for an addled, overfed audience,
who loathe, above all things, any performance on the stage
that would appeal to a lofty and æsthetic sense in humanity, and the grand lines and noble austerity of some
foreign theatres like, let us say, the Théâtre Français,
where the first consideration is not materialism but art.
It is easily seen that English theatres are commercial

institutions by the manner alone in which they pander to the mere creature comfort of the audience. And, after all, what else can they do? If they will not pamper the multitude with just the food that the multitude desires, they are speedily neglected and fall into ruin. Since, therefore, in England, the multitude prefers its creature comforts to anything else in a theatre, the modern drama is like to be in a bad way for some time to come. Nothing short of a State subsidy or a subsidy from private individuals, whereby a theatre might be made independent of public favour, and so might become a public instructor, can rescue the drama from the slough in which it is wallowing. And I must say public or private subsidies seem to me eventualities extremely unlikely in so purely commercial and political a nation.

'Almost every town in Germany has its theatre subsidised by the State, where serious high-class plays are acted, and long runs are unknown. For, like the Théâtre Français, a different play is acted at every performance. This is the only way to have a vital drama. Long runs are the death of the drama; and it is hard to make theatres commercially successful without long runs. It is hard to keep the drama vital without experiment; and the multitude, if left to itself, nearly always dislikes experiment in such directions. That this State-aided freedom of experiment has had most satisfactory results in educating the multitude in Germany to an appreciation of good modern drama, scarcely can be doubted. We have only to look at the works that hold the stage, and the names of dramatists who, whatever their errors may be, have become almost European in the interest they have awakened among all the best students of the drama.'

In an essay on Ibsen's *Little Eyolf*, written about the same time, he insists, with his mind always centred upon his Irish hopes, upon the strongly national character of Ibsen's work, in opposition to the tendency to regard him as a cosmopolitan figure. 'I have heard Ibsen described as the international dramatist,' he wrote, 'in contradistinction to our national dramatists, by a critic of not much insight, who apparently cannot understand that this greatest and most original of dramatists is primarily intensely Norwegian, and is only international by reason of his immense genius, as any of our national dramatists, when he can show sufficient intellectual force, may also become international.

'After the performance of this play in the Little Theatre, I went away with its exquisite music still trembling in my heart; I wished to be alone so that the exaltation should not be interrupted. For the way with these wonderful plays, where subtle mental poetry finds expression in the most direct realism of speech, as here and in *Rosmersholm* and above all in *The Master Builder*, is to give the sensation of rare harmonies, to produce with their triumphant construction the effect of a symphony where idea grows naturally from idea, where dramatic effects are but the natural outcome of logical combinations of circumstances, where profound knowledge of the human heart and character is set down with such certainty of intellect as may be seen in the lines of a drawing by some great master.

'*Little Eyolf* may not be one of Ibsen's greatest plays. The master genius soared to its highest peak in *The Master Builder*. But, like Solness, it fell; and no one can say that the next work, *Little Eyolf*, is equal to the daring,

original, wonderful *Master Builder*. But if it is quite
inferior — indeed the beginning of a decadence that
increased in the following play, *John Gabriel Borkman*,
until it led Ibsen in the next and last, *When we Dead
Awaken*, almost to travesty his life work — *Little Eyolf* at
least has this in common with its predecessor: in those
scenes between the husband and wife, especially in the
third Act, there is the same symphonic beauty, with an
exaltation of beauty that lingers haunting our souls.
When, out of the psychological subtleties of the characters of Alfred and Rita Allwers, the respective mental
tragedies of husband and wife rise to a climax of conflict,
there is brought home to an audience with tremendous
impressiveness how greater far is the dramatic situation
of psychology than that of the mere exteriority expressed
only in bodily action. It is this very dramatic psychology
coming in logical sequence that is just the quality which
makes the work of Ibsen repellent to average playgoers
who, in the miserable decadence of serious drama
throughout England and America, and of course, worst
of all, throughout Ireland, abhor above all dramatic
requirements, the requirements of having to think con-
secutively in the theatre.

'On the other hand, if the drama is a mere jingle of
words combined with violent exterior dramatic actions,
however unconnected in sequence and improbable, and
thus offensive to good sense, they are delighted and cry
out: "What character! What originality! What genius!"
Nay, without even the jingle of words these very qualities
are what made the fortune of Pinero, as far as his serious
plays are concerned. However, when he wrote one
serious play, by an odd chance perfect in sequence and

K

drama, in fact the finest by far of all his works, namely, *The Thunderbolt*, I understand it had by no means the success of the inferior.'

In another essay, he insists that 'those peculiar qualities of poetry coming direct through realism have never been more splendidly displayed by Ibsen than in his beautiful prose poem drama *The Lady from the Sea*. Certainly Ibsen is the most original as well as the greatest of dramatists. And yet I imagine how some will start at this announcement. How they will raise their eyebrows and mention Shakespeare and Sophocles, and perhaps even Calderon. I hasten to add that I do not say he is by any means the greatest of poets, but just the greatest of dramatists. Yes, I think he is certainly. He has invented a whole new world for drama, even more interesting than any of the old. He has invented the drama of the mind, where outer action is all subordinate to the tremendous strife of wills and emotions, which work out to their inevitable conclusions with a mastery of art that intellectually delights a thinking audience. To be sure, much of this was in a way foreshadowed in the ancient Greek drama; nothing happens on the stage, only the action of emotion is advancing. This is how there is subtle affinity with the antique in the Ibsen drama.

'While, however, the emotion is large and simple in the antique, with the great Norwegian it is intellectually subtle. Moreover, it is unpopular as the antique would be with those British and American, or imitation British audiences such as there are here, whose only outlook upon the drama is as either mere amusement or bestiality, and who render inane or disgusting any theatre that depends upon them for support. That is why civilised countries have always felt themselves obliged to subvention theatres so that art may be possible in the drama thus freed from the influence of popular support. This subvention is as necessary for the theatre as for museums and galleries of painting and sculpture. What degraded and horrible places indeed would these become, if, like the theatres, they had to live on popular support?

'It is, therefore, nothing derogatory to Ibsen that he is not understood by such audiences. Even those who set themselves up for critics are often unable to see in him any transcendent merit. As an example of their obtuseness I may cite the case of a would-be critic in one of our papers, who complained of me as a dramatist who was trying still to "do Ibsen," as he, or mayhap she, elegantly expressed it, and was consequently nearly twenty years behind my time. This critic — save the mark — believed evidently that there had been several inventions by dramatists since, each a great improvement upon Ibsen, and that I was hopelessly stupid in not being influenced by such recent developments of art. This is the sort of fustian that does duty for criticism in our country, where there is as yet no real literary criticism to speak of.

'I should like to know the modern dramatists who have since made old-fashioned the art of Ibsen? Who are they who have caught its least excellence, to say nothing of improving on it? I thought that I had developed something from it in my *Maeve*, where I made a girl pine and die for a lover who had no existence, and gave it a semblance of truth. Ibsen was so great, so far before his time, that up to this the best dramatist since is but a pigmy compared with him.

'I am not one of those who prefer the study of the

inferior to that of the great masters. It would be well for many more to study this great national and, because so great, a world dramatist, whereby they might be led to understand his unapproached excellences, and be put out of conceit with their delusions about their own. They need not agree with Ibsen's opinions, some of which I am far from accepting myself. His opinions do not affect the quality of his technique, which is so original and beyond all rivalry, and rewards the severest study, as also does that of Tchekoff, though in a much less degree. The reason why so few have benefited by a study of Ibsen is because they have mistaken the craftsman for the teacher, and so instead of acquiring mastery in setting forth their subject, they are only led to exaggerate what may already be preposterous in their ideas. Such monstrosities as *Mrs. Warren's Profession* and *Damaged Goods* are some results of this error.

'*The Lady from the Sea* gives expression to that yearning and enchantment which the ocean has for certain natures. An enchanted sea! How can I tell the feelings that rise to the heart when we look afar to sea — from the barren coast in West Ireland, for instance? The illimitable Atlantic with all its mystery and beauty calls to us. We see its waves shake out their foamy manes like a champing host of cavalry, and we think of the old Irish saga —

'Sea horses glisten in summer
As far as Bran has stretched his glance.

'We are lost in reverie as the delicate indentations of the coast line, the ruined tower on the promontory, the outstretched calm of the ocean fill us with a sort of elegiac rapture. The poets of all time are drawn to the sea. . . .

'And Ibsen likewise is haunted by the same yearning beauty. Far away, exiled in inland Munich, he craves for the sea, and when in 1887 he returns to it, he gives vent to his enthusiasm and all his homesickness in this exquisite play, *The Lady from the Sea.*

'It is necessary that the audience should feel all this if it is to find profit and pleasure in such a work. One might have thought that the mere seeing the play properly performed would of itself be sufficient explanation, since the work so triumphantly explains itself. But the temper of audiences is so odd, and the vogue for dramatic inanity and bestiality so prevalent, that they seem to deprive otherwise intelligent people of their understanding as soon as they enter a theatre. In this way it may be doubted if even all the explanation in the world would be sufficient, seeing the way matters stand. Still, it may be of some service to the actors, and increase their interest in so spirited an undertaking by riveting their attention to the more poetical parts of the play. For, bad as it is to be misunderstood by the audience, it is far worse to be misinterpreted by the actors. One has to be oneself a writer of plays to know what mental torture this is.

'*Rosmersholm* is one of the master's finest and most absorbing studies in psychological action. As you follow the unbreakable, if delicate, thread of the idea, you are fascinated by that fertility of invention and triumphant craftsmanship which are the despair of all other dramatists who have sufficient intelligence to understand what is great in drama. Indeed, Ibsen resembles Beethoven in his marvellous fertility which, with the musician, mani-

fests itself in a thematic development seemingly inexhaustible and certainly unrivalled by any other
composer. It is wonderful to analyse those dialogues of
the dramatist, and to watch where each idea is exhibited,
and made recur and explained, and coloured with turns
which are like changes into varied keys. In this way those
great plays have been compared to symphonies, so
exuberant and so condensed withal are they, so poetic in
their realism, so evanescent in their charm.

'When writing about *The Lady from the Sea*, I showed
how the central idea of that fascinating play brought
straight to our hearts the homesickness which falls on
lovers of the sea who are exiled far away from its frag-
rance. The idea of *Rosmersholm* is more grim and tragic.
It is avenging conscience here that works itself out in an
extraordinarily vivid atmosphere. The old Norwegian
country house which gives its name to the tragedy fills
the background with its ghostly, still life. Johannes
Rosmer and Rebecca West, the survivors of the dead
wife Beata, are paralysed by their consciences, because
they believe they are the cause of her suicide in a mill-
race near the spectral old house. The whole progress to
the catastrophe is fearful and merciless as a Greek
tragedy, and like a Greek tragedy, too, it exalts us with
its great poetry, which gives by the very contemplation
of this mental suffering so depicted, a satisfaction to our
souls. This is called the joy of art.

'What a fascination there is about the theatre when
true art thus enters it! What a relief from the sterility
the ordinary theatre of England brings us, which has
practically fallen to the level of an unintellectual, and
often bestial, means of making money. As if the theatre

was ever intended to be a commercial speculation any
more than were Museums or Universities! All civilised
countries have recognised this. But, of course, only an
ignoramus contends that the government which we
enjoy is civilised when compared with those on the
Continent of Europe.'

Bitter words have been written by some of his more
intimate friends about the neglect of Edward Martyn's
part in creating the modern Irish drama. Mr. R. J.
Kelly, K.C., of the *Tuam Herald*, wrote feelingly on the
matter after Edward's death to claim that Edward 'paid
the initial expenses which no one else could be found to
do. The others, except Lady Gregory, came in later on
and reaped the profit and got the credit.' The complaint
is scarcely just, for Lady Gregory collected the small
financial guarantees from a number of public-spirited
Irishmen whom Edward alone could never have enlisted
in the enterprise. And although Edward's generosity
made it unnecessary to call upon the guarantors for any
expense, her activity had provoked a widespread curiosity
and interest before the first performances. But Mr.
Kelly is certainly right in claiming that 'it is no exaggeration to say that but for the money given and the enthusiasm thrown into the movement by Edward Martyn in
those early days of struggle, the Abbey Theatre could
never have lived nor continued its existence for one year.'
Certainly also it is true that Edward's indispensable and
untiring assistance in the early days has been most
unfairly ignored. A writer in *Irish Truth* is one of the
few who have paid any real tribute of gratitude to his
memory. His *Heather Field*, the writer points out, 'had
won the approval of Arthur Symons and some others of

that Beardsley and post-Beardsley band. He did not wish to have it produced in England. He wanted Ireland to have a national place in international art. If it was impossible for her to gain that through works in Gaelic, then he was determined that she should put her distinctive stamp on the works of her sons who wrote in English. He has often been accused of vacillation in that early period. But his strength was that he put wisdom and righteousness in art, as in all things, above a superficial appearance of consistency. It was he who did the hard work of gathering, in London, the first casts to play in *The Heather Field* and *The Countess Cathleen* in Ireland. He who bore the cold and bitter wind of public misunderstanding in the dawn of the Irish dramatic revival, felt little of the noonday warmth of approval that was vouchsafed to those who had shared his work and helped to bring his idea to fruition. Honour is due to all that band of early Abbey workers — to him and to Miss Horniman, to the brothers Fay, to James H. Cousins, Marie Quinn, Dudley Digges, Fred Ryan, to Seumas O'Sullivan, Maire ni Shiubhlaigh and Maire ni Gharbhaigh, to George Roberts and to Sara Allgood, as well as to Lady Gregory and W. B. Yeats. But Edward Martyn and J. M. Synge have a very special claim to Ireland's gratitude and admiration. Without Edward Martyn, the modern Irish drama might never have been born. Without Synge, it would have died in early childhood. In congratulating the Abbey on its coming of age, let Irishmen pay tribute to the memory of Edward Martyn — a man of ideas, a man of courage, and a man who loved his people and his country well.'

From time to time in the later years, his earlier plays

would be produced, for one or two performances only, by literary theatres in America, in Germany or Switzerland; but he had long ceased to look for any popular success. Seldom indeed would he even suggest that any of the plays he continued to write as a means of self-expression might be suitable for production. He was sensitive enough to dislike being rebuffed, and even Miss Horniman, who was well aware of his contribution to the founding of the Abbey Theatre, did not spare his feelings in declining a play which he submitted to her in 1910. 'Please forgive my candour,' she wrote with a condescension that was hard to bear; 'it really is a compliment, for I don't write more than a few lines in most cases when refusing plays.' Her letter had opened with a disconcerting abruptness: 'Dear Mr. Martyn. When I get plays sent in by office boys, all about titled people generally, I beg them to write about the kind of human beings they associate with. Now, have *you* ever associated with lady doctors, even unsuccessful ones? If you want to imply that the worry of an incapable husband has upset a weak mind, you should have made it clear. If your play were put on the stage, it would justify another *Playboy* row, for you have made your fellow-countrymen appear in a light which may be true, but it is not kind. To get one's self shot in order to annoy someone else is to carry out the saying "to bite off one's nose to spite one's face" to the uttermost limit.' And she added in a postscript, which can scarcely have offered much enticement to Edward Martyn: 'If ever you come to Manchester, I'll show you the Gaiety and some most attractive lady doctors.'

A few years later he gave his views concerning the

relations between actors and plays in a statement so characteristic that it deserves quotation: 'The greatest difficulty with which a reforming dramatist in Ireland has to contend is the kind of people whom he is forced to employ as actors. Here he is up against a class of people for the most part whose very last thought is reform. Who indeed expects to hear of a performer being a reformer? On the contrary, is it not he, or rather she, that has got the drama into that state of decadence as calls for the reforming dramatist, whose first work must be to depress the performer, since it was the latter's too assertive personality and importance that mostly brought about the decadence in question? Mind, I wish it to be understood that I am now speaking of the ordinary commercial actor and actress. If any of their unprofessional brothers or sisters take my remarks as alluding altogether to them-selves, it must be for the urgent reason that their con-sciences, upon examination, convict them, and they are naturally indignant at an exposure of their being found wanting in amiability and lofty concern for the advance-ment of art. I may say at once that for some of the unprofessional brotherhood I have much respect and appreciation.

'What is it then that makes the performers' influence so fatal in general to the drama of ideas? The answer is very simple. To promote such a drama, you must be interested in ideas. This is obvious. But at the same time it is obvious that the performer is as a rule only interested in the vanity of his or her own personality. It is im-possible for two such interests to be more dissimilar. You cannot reconcile them. One or other must prevail. One must extinguish the other, and in this world in-

feriority often prevails. It is not surprising that this
ignoble content has over and over again led to the shame-
ful decadence of the drama.

'And how silly it all is when you consider the average
performer's attitude towards an average audience and the
attitude of the audience to the performer. One vies with
the other in puerility of aim and abnegation of good sense.
Now these people in their ordinary vocations are often
sensible enough, often even intellectual, but there is
something about the atmosphere of the theatre which
induces a mood of silliness that precludes all sufferance of
intellectual pre-occupation. It is needless to say that in
such an atmosphere the work of a reformer with aspira-
tions towards the realisation of an Art Theatre is anything but likely to arrive at an approach to usefulness or
any hope of satisfactory results. And yet with a few
enthusiasts who are undoubtedly to be found, there is
still hope nevertheless that we may gather and keep
together a company that will be more interested in Arts
than in Philistinism and personal vanity. Then we may
be sure that none of these will scrap rehearsal for some
twopenny-halfpenny tea party, or swagger about to
victimise the unhappy playwright by boasting that the
first two or three performances must only be considered
as rehearsals, nor frighten the manager with vapours into
abdicating his authority in the settlement of the cast, nor
join in hostile combinations nor in fine practices, any of
these old bad insubordinations which somehow have
been the disconcerting weakness of the acting crowd.

'No, I feel in future I may hope from my actors a new
era of Art and peace.'

Many years passed during which he was obliged to look

on at the successful development of the Abbey Theatre
within limitations that precluded most of what he had
originally hoped to achieve. The Irish Literary Theatre
that he had hoped to found had become narrowed down
to a venture which scarcely ever attempted to produce
other than peasant plays; and instead of the school of
versatile Irish actors which he had hoped to train, the
directors of the Abbey Theatre had taught their group of
brilliant players to confine themselves almost exclusively
to peasant parts. At last, a few years before the war, he
found new allies in a younger generation of enthusiasts,
and he decided that the attempt to revive his first experiment should at last be made. In an unpublished
manuscript among his papers there is an essay, stating
the aims of his new venture, which sets out very frankly
the tale of his own disappointments, and contains, not
without touches of gentle malice, some criticisms of the
Abbey Theatre's directors that reveal his feelings towards
their abandonment of his own early ideals.

'That the Abbey Theatre has survived its numerous
contemporaries and rivals in theatrical experiment must
be a genuine satisfaction to those who have so ably
guided its fortunes; the whole of its success is due to two
persons, namely Mr. W. B. Yeats and Lady Gregory.
Without them it would never have been heard of. When
they disappear (and may they live long) it will most
likely go the way of all other dramatic enterprises. The
qualities by which Mr. Yeats has made the theatre are
Napoleonic and consummate. A fine poet and subtle
literary critic, he has above all a weird appearance which
is triumphant with middle-aged masculine women, and a
dictatorial manner which is irresistible with the con-

siderable bevy of female and male mediocrities interested
in intellectual things. In this way he practically dictates
to the critics who reproduce subserviently his opinions.
Lady Gregory, although not intellectually profound, is
intellectually acute in the most extreme degree. She has a
knowledge of mankind and a social mastery and tact that
can only be described as genius; thus equipped she
dictates to leaders of society and their hangers-on who
acquiesce to make the theatre fashionable. A combination
of two such efficient and unique personalities for the
special work they had to do, I suppose, the world has
never seen before. The result is that they defied opposition and have built up from nothing at all a remarkable
and lasting structure. The manner in which they com-
menced the work always seems to me, who have had some
experience in such concerns, as particularly wonderful.
We all know how useless it is to push a person without
talent. You may give him all advantages, but he cannot
avail himself of them and soon fails to justify expectations.

'These are the sort of persons, however, whom Mr.
Yeats and Lady Gregory triumphantly succeeded in
pushing. Mr. Yeats discovered some people trying to act
in a little hall among the by-streets of Dublin. Their
acting and performances were puerile, if acting is to be
considered more than feebly drawling out the words,
and stage managing more than occasionally wandering
about the stage at individual whim. Mr. Yeats at once
pounced upon these most unpromising players, and
proclaimed a wonderful discovery. He proclaimed their
merits in his most dictatorial vein until they actually got
to believe in themselves and even to show signs of some

improvement. Meanwhile the mediocrities taking their cue from the dictator went about fussing over the art of those players until they made them notorious enough to attract silly little people with silly little plays like *Cathleen ni Hoolihan* and *The Pot of Broth* to the amused surprise of those who were in the habit of thinking for themselves. Afterwards by degrees some of these players improved, some left, and others came along, and much good work was gradually done until the Abbey players are now recognised as the best actors of peasant plays probably in the world.

'This is a truly wonderful result from such beginnings, and one worth careful study by those who want to promote successful production of Irish drama. Going to work, therefore, like a student of strategy and tactics when he examines the campaigns of great generals, I will endeavour, from examination of the means whereby Mr. Yeats and Lady Gregory made the Abbey Theatre such a success, to point out to other Irish impresarios the causes of their several failures, myself to imbibe such salutary lessons as may help me to make a success of the dramatic project which I propose to unfold in this treatise. At the same time I am humbly conscious of my inferiority as an impresario to the two experts whose feats I have the temerity to imitate. Indeed beside them I am only as a *Duc de Bourgogne* compared with a Marlborough and a Prince Eugene. But while that unfortunate prince, owing to his inexperience and unfortunate advisers went to pieces before his great adversaries, I, by no means an adversary but a sincere admirer of my models, hope with patience and application to their methods, to arrive at a tolerable success, and so establish

what will be in no wise a rival but rather a complement
to their work.

'After a careful examination of the material of the
Abbey Theatre, the fact that chiefly appears to have aided
the impresarios all along is that, whether intentionally on
their part or not, the type of actor and actress evolved by
the undertaking, is such as would be practically useless
for making money on the English stage. By confining
themselves to acting peasants and the lower middle-class,
they are totally unfitted to portray the upper classes.
There may possibly be exceptions in a few of the men who,
having especial talent for acting, might with study arrive
at success in such parts; but the rest are hopeless. This
limitation has been the strongest bond for holding the
company together; and to hold a company together is the
chief difficulty for the impresario of an Irish theatre.
Another cause of cohesion is the ill success of the various
offshoots from the Abbey Theatre. They simply became
other peasant-acting companies, inferior to the parent
stock and lacking the most important arm of all, the
prestige of Mr. Yeats and Lady Gregory. Then the
individual players who seceded at various times and could
find no field on the English stage for their peculiar
talents, if they did not return to the fold, sank quickly
into obscurity. Thus all these causes contributed to the
conviction that it was better to be famous under directors
so able, than obscure on the great commonplace commercial stage.

'Now in the new theatrical company which we hope to
establish for the production of native works, dealing with
the lives and problems of people more complex and
refined, we have not such safeguards as I have described

for helping our players from deserting us to take lucrative parts in the fashionable drawing-room plays of England. In fact this has been a chief difficulty with me hitherto in the production of my own plays, which are of the nature I have just described, requiring performers who can create characters of complexity and intellectuality. When these are or believe themselves to be really capable, they have only one desire, which is to get on the English stage, and in pursuit of this object they are most difficult to interest in the literary and psychological drama; so that the dramatist who practises an art so fascinating to himself is at more disadvantage at present in Ireland than any other of his brethren.'

These reflections lead him to describe his own experiences and comparative failure as a dramatist with a great deal of shrewd and illuminating criticism. 'That is why,' he writes, 'although I have written more plays than anyone else, which are of course quite useless for commercial purposes, I so seldom get a chance of being produced. If I could have written capable peasant plays, which I could not because they do not interest me, in that the peasant's primitive mind is too crude for any sort of interesting complexity in treatment, I have no doubt I should have found my place naturally in the Abbey Theatre. But I could not, and as the Abbey Theatre could not produce work like mine, which was obviously not suited to their powers (they acted during one week-end *The Heather Field* on the whole so unsatisfactorily that they never attempted it again), I naturally became an isolated figure, who had to depend on my own efforts with amateur players of varied efficiency for seeing my dramas on the stage.

'My experiences were anything but encouraging; for although I met with considerable talent, it was not accompanied with any sort of taste. I suppose I have no right to be surprised that the only thought of these amateurs was to show themselves off. Any idea of discovering a native work of art and interpreting it with understanding was as far from their minds as from the mind of an average English actor or actress. Would it be believed that one day when I was discussing the possibilities of a society for producing native drama and continental masterpieces the leading lady proposed that I should produce *Madame Sans Gêne* at the Ancient Concert Rooms with an elaborate series of dresses for herself in the title part. That poor lady evidently thought that to show off silly players was the real motive of my interest in intellectual drama! It is little wonder that the Abbey Company is the only theatre that has come to anything.

'Thus with this material, which was alone capable of grappling with the work that interested me, I produced some plays of Ibsen and of my own with varying results. There were individual performers of extraordinary merit; but it was impossible, owing to irregularity of attendance at rehearsal, to get anything like finish or to avoid a tiresome accident. In the case of works previously produced with success, carelessness in performance at revivals is bad enough, notwithstanding the fact that the actors there must be blamed for any failure of representation which at the first production was absent. On the other hand, when it is a case of a piece being first produced, the delinquencies of the actors are generally visited by an indiscriminating audience on the head of the

L

unfortunate author, as was the case at the original production of my play, *An Enchanted Sea*, where the performers with few exceptions seemed to vie with each
other in an unconscious contest as to whether they should
make themselves or the work most ridiculous.

'After this misfortune, I was naturally not over anxious
to try my luck again with amateurs. However, some
years later Count Markievicz, the able director of the
Independent Theatre Company, whose absence since
from Ireland is an irreparable loss to the drama, produced
my *Grangecolman* with intelligence and success. This has
naturally revived my hopes somewhat, and emboldened
me to come forward with a project which, if carried out
with care, might lead to something like such fame for our
amateur actors as those of the Abbey Theatre have so
deservedly won.' The recent failure of the Repertory
Theatre, 'which exhibited some really clever acting,' had,
he held, proved that 'the Dublin playgoers will not
patronise amateurs in plays that they are accustomed to
see acted by the best English professionals. This is the
chief fact of the situation which had better be faced at
once.'

On that basis he proceeds to expound his own new
scheme and to consider its prospects of success. 'When
the Repertory Theatre, in the vain hope of making money,
chose to act plays of this sort they at once wrote down
their doom. They tried to pose as professionals, and I
wished to consider them so; but the public would not
look at them as other than amateurs who just wanted to
show themselves off before their friends like all other
amateurs, without a thought of helping by intelligent
interpretations the production of native drama, and in the

vain hope of somehow passing on to the English profession. How different was this folly from the intelligence
displayed in the management of the Abbey Theatre,
which created a flourishing school of native drama.

'What is my project then? It is not original. It is
simply to apply the methods of the Abbey Theatre to an
organisation of the most talented amateurs for the
encouragement by production of native Irish drama other
than the peasant species and thereby see if by study and
perseverance we may similarly create a bond of young
dramatists who will devote themselves to this department of dramatic writing. I feel that however depressed
and ruined we may have been by English government
and our own inept acquiescence by often playing into
the hands of the enemy, we have still some inhabitants
left in Ireland besides peasants, and that a theatre which
only treats of peasant life can never be considered, no
matter how good it may be, more than a folk theatre.
Consequently only partially representative of Ireland, it
cannot be compared with those other national theatres in
Europe which represent so thoroughly the minds of the
various countries where they exist, and it will be seen too
that this project is not strange nor original, any more than
others which have benefited us, such as the Agricultural
Organisation Society, which was known to be a success
on the Continent and had only to be properly applied in
Ireland to be the success it undoubtedly is. In the same
way we have only to apply the methods of that undoubted
success of the Abbey Theatre intelligently upon the
talented amateurs of the stage here in Dublin, and after
time and perseverance I feel sure to produce equally
good results.

'The great question is, of course, will the amateurs respond to my invitation. I know I am a very inferior showman compared with Mr. Yeats and Lady Gregory, and am further attempting what they never hoped for, since their choice of plays was at first from among the lowly and unsophisticated, while my appeal now is to the superior and refined. It would indeed have appeared presumptuous in the highest degree to have attempted this at any previous time, but now when they have met with such repeated failure, it behoves the more intelligent who have an ambition beyond showing themselves off in amateur theatricals before their silly friends (where surprise at the least accomplishment is so great that such accomplishment is considered wonderful, in the same way as are a few words from a parrot), to consider and see if this project of mine is not at least the one most conducive to performance and perhaps even fame.

'We can begin tentatively in the Abbey Theatre if they will let it to us, if not in some hall. Our plays, both native and translations of foreign masterpieces, shall be those not usually acted by professionals. We will also act plays, co-operating with the Gaelic League Players, in the Irish language, from which of course peasant subjects must not be excluded. Here they are fitting in every way. Above all, we will take the greatest pains, so that our performances may be intelligent and finished. We will not expect to make money; and in this respect we can be no worse off than we have been hitherto, nor than the Abbey Theatre was for many years when it had to bravely forge ahead before empty benches. But the Abbey plan was intellectually sound, and it triumphed by creating a thinking audience for itself, as I hope we

W. B. Yeats

From the drawing by William Strang. Reproduced by kind permission of the National Gallery, Dublin

may for ourselves in the end. To do this we must persevere.

'Well, we have now what the Abbey Theatre had not, namely a successful example before us; and I can hardly think that the more intelligent may now at last understand that this is the only possible way by which they may be taken seriously as artists. Ever since I helped to found the Irish Dramatic Movement in 1899, I have had this scheme in my mind, and made repeated efforts to carry it out. But owing to the blighting effect of the English stage on our thoughtless amateurs, I have met with disappointment and even disaster. However, now after their numerous failures to circulate the commercial theatre, I may hope for some sympathy perhaps with intellectual ideals, from the more intelligent among them at least, although I must confess that I never expect to be understood by types of players represented by the lady who wanted me to run her as Madame Sans Gêne. Those sort of people always will be hopeless in all artistic enterprises; but when I can point to actors like Mr. George Nesbitt, who in the ordinary commercial drama is merely mediocre, while in such psychological characters as Almers in *Little Eyolf* or as Carden Tyrrell in *The Heather Field* excels all professionals I have seen in those parts, it would seem nothing short of blind perversity to continue in their former methods. As the same criticism applies to others in a lesser degree perhaps, there is reason to expect that performances of merit and interest might with diligent work be given, that would end like those at the Abbey in compelling recognition and success. The artistic success of the Ibsen performances also at the Theatrical Club should strengthen this

expectation; so let us go forward with the title which I
invented for the foundation of the Irish Dramatic Movement in 1899 — *The Irish Literary Theatre.*'

The story of that later experiment has been fully told
by other writers, and only Edward Martyn's own personal impressions need be recorded here. When he
collected his essays for re-publication before his death,
the preface alluded to 'the foundation of the Irish Literary
Theatre in 1899, which was the source of the whole
modern Irish Dramatic Movement' as 'the most significant action of my life,' and described the progress of his
later venture as 'flourishing beyond all my expectations.'
'In these four past years,' he wrote, 'if we have not
discovered as many dramatists as we expected, we have
at least produced with remarkable effect several plays in
Irish and in English by natives, and many English
translations from masterpieces of the modern European
dramatists. Our chief discovery of a dramatist is Mr.
H. B. O'Hanlon, a writer of extraordinary imagination
and dramatic power. His three plays we have produced,
To-morrow, Speculations, and especially *The All Alone,* are
real additions to our dramatic literature and promise
much fine work in the future. He is only thirty years of
age, and has already made his mark. Mr. Eimar
O'Duffy's *The Walls of Athens* is remarkable for classic
style and finish, and his *The Phœnix on the Roof* is a
singular achievement for so youthful an author. I was
glad to produce them, and hope that advancing years will
enhance rather than dim the plays I expect from this
brilliant creature. In the late Mr. Thomas MacDonagh's
one act *Pagans* there was interesting psychology, while
his brother John, our manager, gave us two one-act

comedies, *Author, Author* and *Just Like Shawe*, touched with original humour and as felicitous as his own volatile personality. Among the artists, Mr. Paul Farrell has become famous in his incomparable delineation of Carden Tyrrell, surpassing any previous actor of that part. Messrs. Kerry, Norman, and Kenneth Reddin have also gained much experience and application, and given us good help, as also have Mr. Joseph MacDonagh, Miss MacCormack, Miss O'Carrol, Miss Coyne, Mr. Hayden, Mr. Purcell, Miss Nell Byrne, and others. Those who persevere with us will be heard of, for they are interpreters in a dramatic enterprise which is surely, if slowly, making a reputation, and if persevered in may make those connected with it famous.

'As for those other amateurs or semi-professionals who vie with the commercial actors, I cannot understand the reason of their existence. Who has ever heard of them beyond their Dublin acquaintances? What real achievement can be theirs? They can never hope to equal professionals in the sort of play acted by professionals. And still they are perverse. On the other hand they might attain considerable distinction by rendering faithfully and naturally uncommercial and therefore unacted modern dramas of ideas which are free from the mechanical sterility of conventional play actors. Thus they would derive reputation from the fame of the works they interpret, as is the case of the Abbey performers, and indeed a condition that has prevailed during the healthy periods of all drama. It is the feverish egotism of actors and actresses that bring about its downfall, for when the mummer becomes of more importance than the playwright, he will enslave him who should be his master,

and thus call into being miserable scribblers with no
literary distinction in ideas who, as in countries where
the mummer is triumphant, write plays with parts suited
to show off the particular tricks of their conceited
tyrants.

'For it must always be remembered that it is primarily
to witness the antics of the actor that the public go to the
theatre, and not to study the play. Therefore, great
drama would be in the way of disappearing altogether if
enlightened governments were not prepared to subsidise
theatres for artistic productions independent of the mob,
for all classes, high and low, rightly considering that a
theatre should chiefly be a centre of education and refinement like a museum or a picture gallery, and would as
soon think of consulting the mob in one as in the other.
Imagination is mocked at the thought of a picture gallery
filled with art of public choice, the intellect equally
revolts at the theatre being under the sway of a mummer-
ridden mob. It may be judged then how profound is the
sagacity of those owls and Handy Andys who say that the
test of a play is popular approbation, when there is not a
single theatre in Europe devoted to dramatic literature
that does not receive a government or some other sort of
subvention. These wise-acres want to make out an
impossible condition of affairs here which has never
existed anywhere, and they ridicule those who only seek
to reform our theatre by private subsidies, the only way
possible, when seeing (as in England which, compared to
such countries as France and Germany, is only half
civilised) all State aid is here denied. But indeed the
censure of Handy Andy, like the disapproval of master
works by that stable companion of his, our genial Bank

Holiday boy Jacques[1] is comforting in that it is a certificate of being in the right.'

In a section of his projected collection he included also a short appreciation in praise of the play which he found most satisfactory in the repertory of his new theatre — Mr. O'Hanlon's *The All Alone*.

'This fine play, *The All Alone*, is the first satisfactory work discovered by the Irish Theatre, which I founded in 1914 for the production of non-peasant drama by Irishmen, of plays in the Irish language and of English translations from European master works for the theatre. It is useless to deny that I am disappointed at the very meagre response from those non-peasant playwrights whom it was expected this hitherto untried medium of encouragement would stimulate. It only proves the falsity of those excuses the futile sometimes make for not producing good work, when they say that they are only prevented doing so from want of a stimulating demand. From such evidence clearly it is not the demand that makes the masterpiece; the founding of theatres for acting of such make those who have never tried, but rather are contented not to write above inferior drama, into great dramatists. On the contrary the great dramatist, eager before all to express himself, never waits upon the patronage of the theatre but rather sets about to revolutionise and reform it to his own uses. In this way it may be said that it is the dramatist makes the theatre and not the theatre the dramatist.

'And what is said of the theatre may be applied equally to the actors: for experience has always proved (to take no further instance than England and America) that

[1]The dramatic critic of a leading Dublin newspaper.

where the actor is predominant the drama is worthless. Who has ever heard of a great play written round the personality of an actor? And yet that is the beginning and end of the performer's idea of what all drama should be. On the contrary, in those continental countries where the dramatist predominates there is to be found an original and living drama. This is of course natural and as it should be, because actors and actresses, who resemble nothing so much as performing dogs with their antics and artificialities, are as ridiculously out of place in judging intellectual works, and cause as much confusion and mischief, as animals would if they were to be put at the conduct of affairs that required for their working the direction of intellectual men!

'But while the establishment of intellectual theatres will never turn the commercial playwright into an artist or enable him or any of his like to write good plays, still it is useful to the artist who may by witnessing and study of master works be stimulated to express himself in drama. In this way the Irish Theatre is responsible for the making of a few interesting works, the most complete and considerable of which is *The All Alone*, whose author Mr. H. B. O'Hanlon may be said to have first realised at our playhouse what a drama essentially should be. This naturally led to his study of continental masters. He understood from the great models what the miserable commercial hack, a slave of players and audiences sinking into barbarism, can never understand, namely that every great drama, every work worthy to be thought Art, must be founded on some philosophical idea. What is the idea of *The All Alone*? Let us examine it.

'*The All Alone* is a drama of the sea. The idea is the

vague charm and longing which the sight of the ocean awakens in the human heart, and the fatality which results from over-mastering obsession by this or any other mental passion. In this lies material for the most awful tragedy, all the more awful because it is psychological in the truest sense: for it is only when a particular passion gets into the head, so as to become a sort of cult, that the sufferer is to be pitied as the most unfortunate of men. The more highly strung or imaginative he is, the greater is the difficulty of his deliverance; because the poetry and idealism with which he looks out on life are lighted up with the flame of this fatal beauty, and without it his prospect of the world appears to him in uninteresting gloom. It is only those who conquer know, that there is no happiness in passion, that happiness was not made for this world, and that the nearest approach to it is the peace its conquest brings. So truly is the soul made for immortality! Very powerfully has the dramatist set forth the personality of his protagonist Esmond Everard, whose father, himself a sea-captain, has brought him up to live on the ocean, and dying, has solemnly left to him the injunction "to learn the secret of the sea." Very skilfully are the family set as a background, the mother with her unrelenting antipathy of her son's enthusiasm, which she sees will destroy him; Sheila to whom he is engaged to be married, and who now sees him fading away from her; the two trustees of his father's estate, who are so anxious to turn his splendid seamanship to their own advantage. They all arrange everything to capture him, when suddenly he rescues from the wreck of a nameless ship an apparently drowned woman whom he just manages to rob from death, and who proves to be the incarnation of all his sea-nostalgia. This Lyra of the sea, as she calls herself, takes such possession of him, that in the end, recognising her as the ghostly figure-head of a phantom ship he has seen in sea-visions, he goes away with her to the ocean, there to sail through the ages, as his mother, in her madness at the failure of all her hopes, now prophesies will be his destiny.'

III

CHURCH MUSIC AND DECORATION

III

CHURCH MUSIC AND DECORATION

EDWARD's passion for music had been evident from his childhood, and his special interest in religious music had always been remarkable. By the time when he left Oxford, and the modern Gothic mansion was being built at Tulira, it had been assumed as a necessity that an organ should be installed there for his personal use. He had made his first musical pilgrimages before he left the University, and they were soon to lead him to many other places besides the Wagner festival at Bayreuth. Long before he had aspired to write serious musical criticism for the reviews, he was already familiar with isolated instances of the revival of polyphonic music in continental churches; and by the time he made his first appearance as a serious musical critic in the 'nineties, he had formed vague ambitions of organising some similar reform of Church music in Ireland. In 1895 he published an appreciation of Palestrina which may be taken as the starting-point of his subsequent endeavours, by which he set himself to popularise Palestrina in England as well as Ireland. 'I have often wondered,' he wrote in 1895, 'whether the countless pilgrims to Bayreuth, who are wont to pass through Cologne, know that in its famous cathedral any Sunday morning at High Mass they may hear rendered on a scale of rare magnificence the masterpieces of another art reformer mighty in his day as Wagner is in our time.

'Giovanni Pierluigi da Palestrina, called the *princeps*

musicæ, whose sublime works are still unrivalled in the
domain of vocal composition, found indeed the ecclesiastical music of the sixteenth century in much the same
degenerate state as dramatic music was found by his great
successor forty years ago. Beauty and inspiration had died
out of it, withered by an arid mechanism that found its
highest triumphs in mere grotesque devices such as perversity of repetition, which destroyed the meaning of the
liturgy, sometimes causing the singers to utter simul-
taneously sentences mutually contradictory; or a use of
well-known airs from the troubadours as leading themes;
or even, in some instances, the composition of scores that
might equally well be sung upside down, or backwards or
forwards.

'It cannot well be argued that these absurdities and
abuses, which Palestrina was commissioned by Pope
Pius IV to reform, were due to mere incompetence, when
such musicians of genius as Orlando di Lasso and Claude
Goudimel flourished at that epoch. I am rather inclined
to suppose that they arose from an error, common enough
at all times to musicians, except perhaps to the very greatest, of supposing that vocal music may seek to become
absolute and to supersede the importance of the words to
which it is wedded. How this error has led generations of
composers astray, Wagner has shown with irresistible
argument in his *Oper und Drama,* where he defines music
as a purely emotional art, capable only of becoming absolute when in instrumental form, but when set to speech
taking necessarily a second place as the interpreter to our
feelings of the hidden sentiment in that speech, which
mere words must fail to express. His fidelity in practice
to this all-important law is the secret of the overwhelming

interest awakened by the hearing of his vast music-
dramas, which have now practically killed by their sincerity of purpose those operas of other composers who
sought to do the impossible, in their endeavour to make
great music at the expense of the verbal text. The fidelity
of Palestrina also to the same law is the chief secret of his
immortality. He, truly, and not Gluck, must be considered as the real predecessor of Wagner in reform.
Their common work was to define the limits of vocal
music. For in the same spirit as the Bayreuth master
treated the dramatic poem, the old Italian treated the
Liturgy of the Catholic Church.

'This spirit manifests itself in the single-mindedness
with which his music, regardless of all profane or ex-
traneous influences, reverently evokes and emphasises
the purely religious sentiment contained in the words of
his sacred subject. In order the more surely to accomplish
this effect, he resorted for inspiration to those profoundly
religious tones which had mysteriously grown up with the
Christian ritual, becoming inseparably associated with its
character. The influence of the plain chant on his works
is at once apparent to any person who may examine
separately their various parts, which will often be found
almost identical with it in style. This is the case in the
supremely beautiful *Kyrie* of the *Missa Papæ Marcelli*,
which might very well be described as contrapuntal
Gregorian. Often, indeed, the principal theme which he
chose for a composition consists of the Gregorian melody
itself, belonging to some antiphon, as in the Masses
Assumpta est Maria, *O admirabile commercium*, *Ecce
sacerdos magnus*, and others too numerous to mention.

'It is from this influence may be traced the breadth and

M

solemnity and ecclesiastical grandeur which characterise his music. But for the sweetness, the rapture, the strange beautiful harmonies that resolve themselves at intervals into silver voice chords, he is indebted alone to his transcendent genius. In those qualities, indeed, he reigns prince among musicians, as all lovers of song must confess who have listened to an adequate rendering of his finest works. Take, for instance, that arrangement for two choirs, each of four parts, of the *Improperia* sung on Good Friday morning. The old chant of the *Trisagion*, in the Greek Church, is the germ from which is evolved this truly inspired harmony, with its divine pathos, its exquisite antiphonal changes. It is unsurpassed for sheer beauty and fervour by any of Palestrina's masterpieces, not even excepting his *Missa Papæ Marcelli*, that glorious voice symphony and model for all time of ecclesiastical song, whereby the maestro saved contrapuntal music from being banished, for those very abuses before mentioned, from the Church by the Council of Trent.

'It is futile to attempt without a large company of singers to render the finest Masses of Palestrina which were written, it might be said, for an orchestra of voices. At Cöln, however, the Chapter may boast of a choir proportionate in vastness with their cathedral, and in training and tone certainly the most beautiful I have heard on this side of the Alps. The trebles are especially exquisite for their quality of sound—those wonderful child notes one hears only on the Continent. Their intensely masculine and ecclesiastical character—so opposite to the womanish round-toned singing of English boys—suits in a peculiar manner the music of this celestial master, who knew as no other how to call forth the rarest qualities of vocal sound. Here the various parts rise or fall with incomparable art, the one above the other — the alti above the trebles, who sink for the moment to their low entrancing notes, and then the tenors above the alti, to fall in turn below a high point in their bass. And all meanwhile, though changing their register, maintain their proper quality of sound, thus producing effects of which no conception can be formed by any arrangement on even so rich an instrument as the organ.

'For no music suffers so much as this by such experiments. Nay, it loses much of its charm if sung by mere concert choirs, who can never be in touch with the spirit of Roman ecclesiasticism. But in this great cathedral it is heard with the perfection of tradition, and amid a surrounding of unique mediævalism that would seem a survival of the scenes that inspired the old painters of Cöln. Here are the tall, lance-shaped arches, the ancient delicate glass of the chancel windows — this old part of the cathedral which the new emulates in vain — the attendant canons in their seats, the congregation crowded confusedly beyond iron gates, and the little altar-boys flitting hither and thither like the child-angels of Meister Stephan, who encircle his "Madonna in an arbour of roses."

'It is indeed a picture of wondrous devotion and beauty, whose sentiment is quickened by a music the most appropriate. And listening to the sublime unaccompanied song, so free from those verbal repetitions and other abuses that ill accord with the solemn grandeur of the Liturgy, one cannot but recall the exclamation of Pius IV, when the most famous of these master works was sung in the Sistine Chapel, and think that such must have been the harmonies heard by the Apostle St. John

in his vision of the New Jerusalem. It is a bold word;
but I feel, if I were constrained to choose for myself, I
would relinquish all — even Bach, Beethoven, Wagner —
for the incomparable Pierluigi.'

That eulogy of Palestrina, collected long afterwards
for republication from his innumerable articles, was an
indication of the plan that gradually took shape in his
own mind, of attempting to persuade some one of the
Irish bishops to undertake a reform of ecclesiastical
music in his own diocese and to restore the traditional
plain chant of the Church's liturgy. To anyone who knew
the conservatism and indifference of the Irish clergy as
well as he knew them, the idea must have seemed almost
fantastically impossible. But his experience abroad, and
his own increasing influence with the Irish hierarchy,
as one of the very few Catholics in Ireland who had
sufficient public spirit and religious sense to provide
handsome subscriptions for the furtherance of religious
art, encouraged him, as time passed, to pursue the
possibilities further. In the year after his article in
praise of Palestrina had appeared in the *Speaker*, he was
in Paris, and there had opportunities of studying the
remarkable work that had been done by a choir-master of
genius, M. Charles Bordes, who had actually obtained
permission to revive the ecclesiastical music of Palestrina
and especially of his disciple Vittoria. When he was in
London afterwards, Edward returned to the charge in
the same paper with a eulogy of M. Bordes and his work,
which expressed his feelings vigorously in regard to the
neglect of church music by the clergy.

'The assertion sounds strange,' he wrote, 'but nevertheless it may be maintained with sufficient truth that the

chief enemies of the great old composers, whether by active traducement or contemptuous neglect, have been themselves musicians. We need not go out of our way to search for proofs of this assertion. A few of the most obvious will suffice. Has not everyone heard of Gounod's vandalism in making the most refined and happy inspiration the first Prelude of Bach do service as an accompaniment to a vulgar sickly air of his own? Has not the Purcell festival of last year left a record, for the most part, of unparalleled misrepresentation? If Handel were to hear *The Messiah* as it is now executed, could he possibly recognise his own work? Instances such as these might be multiplied. Yet there are some musicians who are honourable exceptions among their brethren. At those concerts in Bloomsbury directed by Mr. Arnold Dolmetsch, the chamber music of old masters is performed with an exquisite taste and feeling upon the various ancient instruments for which it is written. His are consequently the most interesting and delightful of Chamber Concerts.

'Then upon the score of contemptuous neglect, of course the chief delinquents are the choir-masters of the Catholic churches. With an inexhaustible treasury of the grandest ecclesiastical song at their disposal, these profane and somewhat grotesque arbiters of religious music yet prefer to produce, whenever they are able, work so frivolous, mean, and unecclesiastical, as render attendance at a musical service almost maddening. The clergy are often accused of being the cause of this abuse, but I think very unjustly. They are a hard-worked body of men, who, in the midst of so much to which they must personally attend, are glad to leave, as of secondary

importance, the conduct of the choir to the organist, and
would be just as satisfied if he gave them good music
instead of bad. That this is generally a fact, I see no
reason to doubt.[1]

'Not only, indeed, would the better change be a case of
indifference with the priests; but I am sure they would
welcome it if they could once understand that their
organists might promise them, with every prospect of
fulfilment, such an increase of funds, through adequate
productions of the old polyphonic masters, as under the
auspices of M. Charles Bordes has found its way into the
coffers of the old Parisian church of Saint-Gervais.
However, I fear such a choir-master as M. Bordes is not
to be found often. This admirable artist has laboured long
in the service of true ecclesiastical music. With the
enthusiasm of a Proske or a Baini and an instinct for the
traditional methods of execution directed by untiring
study and observation, he has edited in modern clefs,
containing directions for time and gradations of sonority,
a vast selection from the school of which Palestrina is the
chief. Besides several works by that unapproachable
master, Masses or Motets may be found bearing such
signatures as "Gregor Aichinger," the old German of the
glorious Regina Cæli, "Felice Anerio," "G. F. Brissio,"
"Clemens non Papa," the Franco-Flemish master so
great that he was thus called to distinguish him from the
Pope of that name, "G. Corsi," "A. Gabrieli," the
Venetian, "Claude Goudimel," "Josquin de Près," of the
Franco-Flemish school, also "Morales," the great Spanish
pre-Palestrinian priest, "G. M. Nanino," of the exquisite
Hodie, "Pitoni," "Orlando di Lasso," whose works

[1] 'I was much less experienced then than now.'—E. M.

have defied time, and last, but of all the most largely
represented, "Tommaso Ludovico da Vittoria."

'The compositions of Vittoria seem, on the whole,
those most in favour with the choir of Saint-Gervais. A
pupil of Palestrina, this wonderful Spanish priest pre-
serves still so strong an individuality that his music is
always recognisable from other works of the school. It
is simpler than that of the master, and lacks his marvellous adjustment of parts and beauty of texture, that
seem to come of themselves, like the growth of a flower.
On the other hand, it is more passionate and in some
respects intense, with strange chords suggestive of a
suffering spirit, which sound like anticipations of the
Passion music by J. S. Bach. The religious sentiment is
not of that serene celestial beauty, transcending earth
and its sorrows and deformities, which the Prince of
Music breathed into his harmonies, but rather of an
exquisite sadness, arising like sighs for mercy from our
vale of tears. The sad Spanish prayer of Vittoria is what
causes the Requiem Mass for six voices to live as his
greatest work, and the greatest of all requiems. Prayer
and wailing suited his genius and compassion with agony,
so divinely inspiring his "Responses" for Tenebræ.
They are indeed the strange rare flowers of his sombre
genius — strangely beautiful in the harmony of their
tones, and modern in the sense of a character intimately
revealed. They also at times, as in the *Judas mercator
pessimus,* exhale a half-Oriental pathos, curiously re-
sembling the melancholy as from chords made by
cymbals of Chinese porcelain that Chopin has written to
commemorate the sorrows of his Polish countrymen. . . .

'Volume, tone and training are the requisites for

rendering this class of music — not a small band of singers accustomed most of the year to yell debased music accompanied by a powerful organ. No, a couple of screeching tenors or a few boys, each of whom may perhaps be able to simper out a solo like a fifth-rate *prima donna*, are not the material for grappling with the larger works of the polyphonic school. Many voices are necessary to produce the grand orchestral effects of this unaccompanied song. Last Lent I had an opportunity of hearing the *Missa Papæ Marcelli* at a London church celebrated on most other occasions for the extreme bad taste of its music. The choir, partly from weakness, and partly from a pernicious profane mode of singing, left the masterpiece of Palestrina, for me, almost unrecognisable. It sounded like some little piping quartette — very much the same as the C minor Symphony would sound if played hesitatingly with only one instrument for each part.

'This instance of incapacity discloses the real value of a choir which has the reputation of being one of the best in London, and which, I believe, is most costly to maintain. It tends also to prove that if organists were minded to reform their music, they would first have to reform the composition of their singers. Instead of a few showy, expensive voices, accustomed to bleat an operatic solo with a self-conscious method of vocalisation, it would be necessary to collect many voices, and to train them for singing in the traditional ecclesiastical style. The change would be a saving of expense, most likely, although it might impose upon the choir-master considerable additional labour. But nothing of any value is done without much labour — and for him who has courage and ability, the reward is great. See the crowds and the money that have come to a small poor parish in Paris through the genius of its choir-master. Surely it cannot be but that among Irish organists there is left an artist who may yet come forward to emulate M. Bordes in his revival of Vittoria at Saint-Gervais.'

The years passed, and his connection with Mr. Yeats and George Moore in the foundation of the Irish Literary Theatre gave him a certain celebrity, and a consequent increase of self-confidence. He opened the question boldly in the Catholic weekly, *The Leader*, in an article on 'Catholic Church Music in Dublin' in 1900. He had already been publishing articles deploring the lack of taste among the Catholic clergy in matters of church decoration, and he was probably the only Catholic layman in Ireland who had the courage to attack the clergy openly for their indifference, or whose criticisms could be expected to be taken seriously. But *The Leader*, under Mr. D. P. Moran's vigorous editorship, had provided a platform for free speech which he eagerly accepted. 'The chief causes of why our church music is so bad,' he proclaimed boldly in the organ of the young Catholic Nationalists, 'are (1) the laziness of our Catholic musicians; (2) the want of knowledge and taste on the part of the clergy; and (3) the unpardonable laxity which, among a large Catholic population, permits such an unecclesiastical and unæsthetic custom to prevail as the singing of women in liturgical choirs. The general public appear to like great, true liturgical music, as, whenever I have given them an opportunity, they have come in crowds to hear the Palestrina Choir. At the same time, they tolerate bad. But, then, we are a somewhat careless people, very hard to rouse.

'I unhesitatingly lay the chief blame for the state of our church choirs on the musicians. They ought to know better; but it looks as if they have no taste, or, having it, they are too lazy to let it appear. They have not the taste, or are too lazy to take sufficient trouble to produce the proper liturgical music of the Catholic Church, or to collect a boys' choir, which, in a large Catholic city like Dublin, with so many schools, ought to be easy, considering the work is done in London with a comparatively insignificant population of Catholics. The Dublin musicians prefer to do what gives themselves the least trouble, and if by any chance the clergyman in authority demands that a proper choir and proper music should be started, the organist immediately overwhelms him with such a swarm of imaginary difficulties and objections that he, most probably inexperienced in such matters, retires in despair. So much for our Catholic musicians.

'Those who are next, although very much less, to blame, are the clergy. I have the greatest veneration for the clergy of Ireland. Among them are men of shining talents; but their greatest admirer could not with any sincerity say that they were gifted with æsthetic taste; and in this respect the English priests are even more deficient — for anything lower than the low standard of musical taste at such churches as, for instance, the Brompton Oratory, is hard to imagine. Among those of our clergy who are reputed to be scientific musicians, I have only met one who gave me the impression of having a classical musical taste, and that one is the present and eminent, versatile Archbishop of Dublin. The others seemed only full of the grammar of music. But a knowledge of the grammar of music will no more give a taste for good music, than the knowledge of the grammar of a language will give a taste for good literature. Æsthetic taste is a born faculty, which, moreover, needs much cultivation, if it is to be of any practical use. It is by no means a necessary complement of great intellectual faculties for matters other than those of art. But in all matters of art it is indispensable, and in none more than in the selection and production of liturgical music. This lack of æsthetic taste, then, causes our clergy to see nothing anomalous or censurable in the present state of our church music, otherwise they could not allow its continuance. They are a hard-worked body of men, and have so much to attend to besides the choir, that they doubtless consider the music safely left in the hands of a professional musician. They consequently permit, without heeding, these many abuses of it.'

His own vehement prejudice against women, which he made no attempt to hide, contributed very largely to his enthusiasm for Palestrina choirs; and his outspoken denunciations of women in church music must have added enormously to the difficulties of the few ecclesiastics whom he persuaded to support his plans. 'For instance,' he asserted now, 'if they only knew how incongruous it was, they would not permit the musicians to shirk their proper work and consult their own convenience by such an abuse as employing women to sing in liturgical choirs. Apart altogether from the violation of the rubric, the practice, from a merely æsthetic point of view, is most offensive and reprehensible; because that peculiar aloofness and evenness necessary for giving an artistic sensation of true liturgical phrasing cannot be conveyed by a woman's voice. The only proper place for a woman's voice, with its volume, passion, and essential earthliness, is the stage. Women have always been unrivalled at depicting the violent passions of life. Acting is essentially the female art; and the voice of the female realises, more than any other form of voice, the idea of opera or drama. But the liturgical idea is not *dramatic*. It is *epic*, which is something very different. It therefore requires a singing which shall be passionless, and shall give a sensation of cerebral fervour exalted above earth. These are essentially masculine qualities; and the sense of them can only be conveyed by a male choir. They are what give the naïve voices of boys such advantage over women's self-conscious voices in liturgical singing.

'All judges of singing are agreed on this. It is only the æsthetically ignorant, with no appreciation for the most exquisite effects of *timbre* or quality of sound, who consider fulness and volume of a female voice more beautiful than the marble seraphic tone of a boy. It may easily be excelled in power, training and flexibility, by that of the *prima donna*; but in quality of sound, never. I suppose because it is so beautiful, it is so short-lived, even as those other two most exquisite revelations of nature, that for their evanescent beauty would seem to be its brethren — the sunrise, the rainbow?

'There is no hope of any improvement until women are prevented from singing in our church choirs. This is the first and most necessary reform, without which all other attempts at reform are useless. It is necessary to impress the clergy with this fact. And for the reasons I have stated, they will, I fear, require much impressing. Strange to say, the Religious Orders, whom one would think, from their discipline and asceticism, would be the easiest to convince, appear after all the most determined to retain female singers in their choirs. This so scandalised the General of one of these Orders, an Italian, when over in Dublin on his visitation, that he refused to enter the church while women were singing in the choir. He did his best to stop the abuse; but the community was evidently too much for him. Another Order, I am told, are much in awe of their female sodality, who, according to my informant, flock into the choir on Sunday evenings as a change of amusement from the music-halls which they are wont to frequent during the week. I have heard of a female singer when reproved for her bad singing by an organist, going into hysterics, and a friar coming to expostulate with and reassure her.

'These in themselves are harmless and ridiculous stories, which have been told to me, but they scarcely redound to the credit of the singing of our divine liturgy. The proper singing, of course, for female sodalities is congregational singing. The women should sing in the body of the church, and the organist should accompany them from above. The fact is, all these abuses in our church choirs and church music are remnants of penal times, when we had to do with whatever material we could get. But now, in a free Catholic country — free at least in this — such arrangements are indefensible; and the more civilised of us have a right to demand that the incomparable and imperishable art of the Church be given to us at least in the ecclesiastical centres. Indeed, we might well be living in the gloomiest of Protestant countries for all we know of the grand æsthetic distinction of Catholicism. And to those who do know it, how difficult and

weary it is to live in a Protestant country — how the heart
is drawn to Paris, or Ratisbon, or the Rhine, to St.
Gervais, or Notre Dame, or Cöln, where the choristers
at the Little Hours, sing that enchanting melody of the
Responsorium breve. Of all music, the Gregorian from
the voices of boys is the most divine!

'But we are deprived of this. We are told that the
banishment of women from our liturgical choirs is
premature, etc., etc.; that it would cause an outcry now.
Of course, it would cause an outcry now, as it will cause
an outcry a hundred years hence, if the reform is deferred
till then. It will always cause an outcry. But what of
that? Is there not always an outcry from the Philistines
at enlightened reforms? So the sooner the outcry is
manfully met and got over, the better.'

Having delivered himself of these provocative exhor-
tations, Edward Martyn could scarcely fail to discover
that he had committed himself to a programme which
must fall into irrevocable discredit if he did not himself
take steps to translate words into actions. Yet nothing
could be done without the active co-operation of at least
some one of the Irish bishops. Edward knew the limitations of his own county well enough to realise that he
could hope for no revolutionary developments there.
But if he could not exert influence in County Galway,
where he was incomparably the most important Catholic
layman from the Bishop's point of view, where could he
hope to obtain sympathy and practical co-operation?
Except for County Galway, he was well known only in
Dublin; but there his influence as a rich and public-
spirited Catholic layman was no greater than that of
many others. His resources as the proprietor of ancient

landed estates could not even compare with the more recently acquired wealth of Catholic stockbrokers or merchants in Dublin, and the difficulty of banishing women from the choirs of a cathedral — which was what Edward's plan must probably mean — was certain to provoke more opposition in Dublin, where so many Catholic ladies had enjoyed exceptional advantages in musical training, than in any other part of Ireland.

It was a most exceptional chance that the see of Dublin was occupied at the time by an Archbishop who was not only a scholar of wide culture, to whom Edward Martyn's tastes and enthusiasm made a special appeal, but also an enthusiast for liturgical music. Almost any other bishop in Ireland would either have been quite indifferent to any suggestion that the prevailing musical standards were not as they should be, or else would have considered that the idea of banishing women from the church choirs would arouse more opposition than could possibly be worth while.

But Archbishop Walsh was a remarkable figure in the Irish hierarchy. As President of Maynooth he had made his reputation as a solid and versatile scholar, and he had made extraordinary progress in modernising the educational system of Maynooth. He had become involved in litigation over the lease of certain lands that the College had farmed for a number of years, and the arbitrary increase of rent which the Duke of Leinster's agent had demanded because of the improvements effected by the College in the land they cultivated, had opened the eyes of the young President to the realities of the Irish land question, converting him from a conservative disapproval of agitators generally, to a definite sympathy with the

Land League in its efforts to establish the tenant's rights to security of tenure and compensation for improvements. He had been elected with an almost unprecedented majority of votes as the choice of the Dublin diocese in recommending to Rome their list of preferred candidates for the vacant archbishopric. And after his appointment as Archbishop of Dublin, Dr. Walsh had soon become by far the most prominent and ablest figure among the Irish bishops. Only the active intervention of Cardinal Vaughan and the Duke of Norfolk at Rome had prevented his becoming a Cardinal and had raised Dr. Logue to that exalted dignity in his stead. An uncompromising Nationalist and Land Reformer, he ruled his diocese with the austere discipline of an ecclesiastical autocrat, fully conscious of his own intellectual superiority, and regarding it as a duty to keep in touch with the wider culture of his time.

In such a man Edward Martyn found a degree of sympathy that he could scarcely have looked for elsewhere. He approached the Archbishop to ascertain his views on the question generally, and as an incentive to further interest in the matter he made a definite offer to give substantial financial assistance if Dr. Walsh would take the necessary steps to establish a Palestrina choir in his own pro-Cathedral. The result of his tentative approaches was an almost incredible success. Not only had he discovered an Irish bishop who shared his views, and was willing to substitute plain chant for operatic music. The Archbishop was willing to make the innovation in his own cathedral; and the church where the experiment thus promised to make so auspicious a beginning was actually the pro-Cathedral in Dublin itself.

By the beginning of August 1901 the idea had borne such fruit that although Edward had set out on one of his musical pilgrimages to Ratisbon, Archbishop Walsh wrote to him after his departure to announce that: 'I have made my first move in the direction we had in view when you were last here. I am appointing one of the priests of the pro-Cathedral to be "Choir Director." There was something like this in Cardinal MacCabe's time, but it never came to anything practical. I had great difficulty in getting the documents that establish the precedent — in such matters I like to act, as the lawyers do, on precedent; when there is a precedent, no one can seriously object to the turning of a sham into a reality. Fr. Williams, C.C., is now my "Choir Director." I have explained to him that we must move prudently, but always in the right direction, indicating that "quartette" parties will have to go, sooner or later, and the sooner the better — and that we must no longer allow the Protestant cathedrals in Dublin to be ahead of us in fidelity to the remnant they have of the old Church musical tradition. I am getting away as soon as I can for six weeks on the Continent. I want a vacation badly, as I have had a lot of worry (which I knew when I faced it could lead nowhere — for the present) at the National Education Board. I hope to be able to see you in October. Meanwhile I am telling Fr. Williams to let our organist know that, through your kindness, we are to have a worthy celebration of the Feast of St. Cecilia in Marlborough Street this year.'

On his return to Ireland in the autumn, Edward pursued the matter further, and committed himself more definitely to promises of large financial support. The

N

Archbishop made careful inquiries and shortly before Christmas reported that: 'Since our last conversation, I have been endeavouring to ascertain how far it will be feasible to make a real reform of our church music in Marlborough Street. The cost, of course, will be heavy. But from the detailed information I have got from a friendly source, of the cost of the music at St. Patrick's Protestant Cathedral, I have no doubt that, allowing for the difference in the requirements of the services there and with us, the munificent provision which you have so generously offered to me, will enable the thing to be done. I find that what we can contribute from church funds to the choir expenses in the pro-Cathedral is £225 a year. Of this, Mr. Rogers gets £100 a year. So, *for the present*, we have £125 available.

'The *singing* part of the choir in St. Patrick's costs £1,220 a year. It seems that Lords Ardilaun and Iveagh contribute £250 a year each, i.e., £500 a year. The rest comes from the fund which the so-called "Disendowed" Church was able to carry off under the "Irish Church" Act. I have mentioned above, "the difference in the requirements" as between St. Patrick's and ourselves. *They* have, in addition to two *full choral* services every Sunday, two services every day of the week, one of these (morning) with boys only, but the other (4 p.m.) full choral, with boys and a certain number of men. I propose now, as soon as possible, to break finally with the existing "quartette" system, and start a male choir of boys and men, Mr. V. O'Brien, of course, to be in charge.

'We need not, I think, embarrass ourselves by having a *very* large choir for the ordinary Sunday work. But it would seem to me *essential*, if we are to make an impression (or rather to keep up the impression that has undoubtedly been already made) upon the public mind as regards what constitutes *real* church music, we should have, from time to time, a really effective rendering of one of the great masses. I have had a talk with Mr. V. O'Brien, letting him know that my thoughts are running in this direction; but, of course, I made no special reference to Marlborough Street, though I daresay (after the success of November 24th) he may have inferred that this was what I meant. I have also had a talk with Dr. Donnelly [the auxiliary Bishop in Dublin], to whom I mentioned in confidence your generous intentions. I am happy to say that I find him in the fullest sympathy with us.

'I ought to mention to you a point that he put before me in reference to what I told him of your proposal to make a foundation. He at once remarked that the only way of securing the stability of the work would be to have a duly constituted *trust* set up, which would make it impossible for anyone, to the end of time, to divert the fund from the purpose intended by you as the founder of it. This is a wise suggestion. I happen to know enough of law to be able to state with absolute confidence that the purpose is one for which a trust can be established *in perpetuity*. The details of this can easily be arranged. I only mention it now as a very gratifying evidence of Dr. Donnelly's real earnestness in the matter. I always knew of this; but you, of course, had not the same opportunities of judging of his views that I had. Altogether, the prospect now seems, thanks to your great generosity, a very bright one.'

This evidence of enthusiasm and practical decision on the part of the Archbishop filled Edward with joy. The letter reached him on his return to the Kildare Street Club late one night, and in his reply on the following day, he was in the happy position of being able to tell the Archbishop that his readiness to consider a permanent endowment was as yet premature. 'You have lost no time in entering upon the good work,' he wrote to Dr. Walsh. 'As regards the question of the foundation, I am quite prepared to consider it under certain conditions, and clearly see its necessity for making the work permanent. At the same time I think it is at present premature, as we really do not know how much it will cost us to do this work to your satisfaction. Would it not be better for you and Mr. O'Brien to begin the work at once while I would supply money over and above what you could give? Or would you leave the work to Mr. O'Brien and myself, giving whatever money or other help you could? At the end then of a couple of years or so, we could form some idea of what the amount of a foundation should be. I expect to be here until next Sunday evening when I go direct to Paris for Christmas. So I am at your service. I think it would be well if you could start Mr. O'Brien in the Cathedral as soon after Christmas as possible, as he should be preparing for Holy Week immediately.'

The Archbishop, however, was not given to making excited decisions, and in his reply by return of post, he impressed upon Edward the necessity of looking ahead, and planning on a permanent basis, if any really big change were inaugurated. 'With every desire to get our music into working order on the new lines with as little delay as possible,' he wrote, 'I don't see how I can break up the existing arrangement until we have something of a permanent character to put in its place. I would suggest that we make all our calculations as soon as possible with the view of beginning definitely in Holy Week. I think Mr. O'Brien would be well able to give us all the requisite information between this and then. As for my wishes in the matter, I should of course wish to have the *really great* music on as many occasions as possible, but even as a matter of cultivating a sound musical taste amongst our Dublin public in the matter of church music, I think we ought not, especially at first, to be too lavish of what is really of the first rank.

'By, of course, *never* having anything that would be out of joint with it — I mean never having *any* music but of the *polyphonic* style — and having the masses of Palestrina and his immediate school on the greater festivals, Christmas, Easter, and so forth, we could put the music of that school in its proper place, and show all concerned what music it is that should be looked up to.

'Our first-class days, according to the usage of the pro-Cathedral, are the 1st Sunday of Advent (Quarant Ore opens), the Feast of the Immaculate Conception, Christmas Day, St. Patrick's Day, Holy Week and Easter, the 29th of June, and St. Laurence's Day (14th of November) — that gives nine or ten days for the *full* choir, and I think it would be well to add one or two other days so as to bring the average up to about one day for each month. Holidays falling on week-days in Dublin are not really suitable for anything elaborate in our churches; but the 8th of December, which is the Feast of the pro-Cathedral, and the 14th November, which is the Feast of our diocesan patron saint, cannot be passed over. Would it be well for us to monopolise the annual Cecilian celebration? I am inclined to think not. Something has been gained by having it in different churches from year to year.'

Edward on his side had his own stipulations to make if the question of a permanent endowment had to be faced at once. He was willing to make the necessary final arrangements, but he was anxious that his friend Vincent O'Brien should be placed in charge of the choir, and he replied accordingly that if any permanent endowment was being considered, Mr. O'Brien should be given a permanent appointment as conductor of the choir. 'I quite agree with what you say in your letter,' he wrote, 'and think that by doing a fine and complete Holy Week music in the pro-Cathedral we should best make a beginning of the work. It will be necessary for Mr. O'Brien to make preparations for this soon after Christmas. I suppose you would permanently appoint him to the pro-Cathedral some time before he produces the music. Unless he were to get a permanent post there, you could hardly expect him to give up his present place. And it will be impossible for him to conduct the Holy Week music in the pro-Cathedral while remaining organist of St. Saviour's, as the Dominicans in that event would naturally require his services in their church during Holy Week. If you would allow me to make a suggestion I would say that after Christmas when I return here, I would ask you to give Mr. O'Brien and myself an interview. We could then much better discuss the details of the work than by letter. My wish will always be to do everything that will satisfy you in all respects. I think your idea for carrying out the musical services of the year eminently calculated to have the best results. As I told you, I propose to go to Paris to-morrow night for Christmas; but if you wish me to remain here in order to begin preparations at once, I will willingly do so.'

By return of post, and even with apologies for not having been able to write until the evening, the Archbishop replied that he agreed entirely with the suggested appointment, and that, while he would regard it as 'cruel' to keep Edward from going to Paris for the musical festivities of the new year, he would be delighted to meet him and Mr. O'Brien together for a conversation in January.

With the new year, however, the Archbishop felt it necessary to place the whole matter on a more stable basis. He wrote a friendly letter towards the end of January which was plainly intended to test how far Edward Martyn was really in earnest. 'I regret to say that we have encountered a hitch,' he wrote. 'I cannot speak of it as an altogether unforeseen one. I have for my part been quite prepared to take the responsibility of the change in the pro-Cathedral music in an experimental way. For at the worst there would be no difficulty at any time in falling back upon some working system or other if the continuance of the reformed system was found to be on any ground impracticable. I foresaw, however, that unless I was able to guarantee to Mr. O'Brien that the system for which he was to be brought in would be permanent — so that he could have the ordinary security of an organist's position — he might not see his way to giving up the position that he has.'

It was a dexterous thrust, to inform Edward that the

whole plan was now put in jeopardy, through the reluctance of Edward's own nominee to assume charge of
the new régime unless he were guaranteed a permanent
position. 'Now this is exactly what has occurred,' the
Archbishop explained. 'He is not in a position to give up
his present secure position, since I can only say to him
that I wish to have him as a trainer and director of a choir
of boys and men in the pro-Cathedral, without being able
to add that I can give any guarantee of the stability of the
new system. I should regret exceedingly if the great
reform on which I had begun to count as all but effected
were to end in a disappointment. But I trust it will not
come to this.'

The success of the whole enterprise, in other words,
now depended upon Edward himself. He had succeeded
beyond anything he had reason to hope for, in winning
the support of the Archbishop of Dublin, to such an
extent that His Grace was now writing of his own
feelings that 'the great reform was all but effected.'
But it now remained for him to give definite concrete
proof of his intentions by handing over to the Archbishop a large sum of money to provide a permanent
endowment for the choir which he had proposed to train.
He had already made up his mind to do this, and his
reply to the Archbishop's letter hastened matters at once.
By the beginning of March, Edward had already got his
friend, Serjeant Charles O'Connor to draw up a scheme
for a legal endowment; and before the middle of the
month the Archbishop was employing his expert canonist
to scrutinise the proposed scheme with a view to avoiding
any possible flaw. 'It would, of course, be useless,' he
wrote to Edward on March 16th, 'to get a scheme that

you and I would personally approve of, and that would also be approved of by the lawyers, if in the end it turned out to be unworkable on account of its being in some way at variance with ecclesiastical law.'

Edward was to find, in fact, that the presentation of even so large a sum as he had set aside, to an Archbishop for the fulfilment of a purpose which inspired them both, was a much more difficult business than he had ever anticipated. The difficulty, he soon found, lay chiefly in the Archbishop's generous desire that the aims of the pious donor should be completely safeguarded. Their joint proposal had been that the fund should be vested in trustees, who would require certain conditions to be fulfilled by a committee of responsible experts on musical matters. But the canonist immediately discovered obstacles to the constitution of any such authority. The rights even of the Archbishop to interfere with the administration of a cathedral were limited. But what would the Cathedral Administrator say to interference by a committee? 'Subject to certain essential conditions,' there was no canonical objection to having the arrangements for the music of the cathedral vested in a committee. But the committee could not possibly include the Archbishop, as both Dr. Walsh and Edward had suggested in their own proposals. The Bishop, being the supreme authority in the diocese, must always remain the court of appeal; and as such he could not possibly be a member of the proposed committee. Nor could the committee include Canons of the Cathedral Chapter nominated for the purpose; since they must either be nominated directly by the Archbishop or else they must be elected by the Chapter itself. Above all, it was out of the question that a lay authority should in the ultimate resort exercise supreme control over the music of a cathedral church. 'Possibly,' added the canonist in conclusion, 'a way out of the difficulty might be found if the Founder were willing to consent to arrangements conformable with the Canon Law. As a canonist, I have only to say that the arrangement set forth in the Draft Scheme is one to which the Archbishop is not free canonically to assent.'

To Dr. Walsh this discouraging opinion was undoubtedly, as he told Edward in writing, 'a great disappointment.' The surprising feature of the subsequent negotiations is that he appears to have borne no resentment towards the suggestion — which had so scandalised his canonist — of a layman controlling the music of a cathedral church. On the contrary, he devoted an astonishing amount of time and ingenuity to trying to devise some means by which Edward's personal wishes might be secured, not only during his own and Edward's lifetime, but for all time. Another difficulty was to determine what music should be included or excluded under the scheme. To meet this the Archbishop suggested that a list of music should be drawn up by three experts — who might be, he suggested, one a nominee of Edward's; Mr. O'Brien as conductor of the choir; and a third nominee of his own, who he suggested would be Fr. Bewerunge, the professor of music at the Dublin diocesan seminary. Edward's reply met this engagingly frank offer in an admirably diplomatic spirit: 'You know now what my wishes are as founder in the matter,' he replied at once. 'They are simply to secure that a particular kind of music should be sung by a whole choir in an efficient manner, and that a competent conductor in the person of Mr. Vincent O'Brien, who I believe is alone capable at the present time of doing the work properly, should be appointed and maintained. If these conditions can be secured by means of Canon Law, I am perfectly satisfied. If not, I am not prepared to part with money which on a subsequent occasion I might wish to spend on the same object under more favourable circumstances. I would therefore welcome any scheme in accordance with Canon Law drafted by you, which my legal advisers might consider safe for the furtherance of my ideas regarding this foundation. As far as I can gather, these ideas are identical with your own.'

The arrival of this letter must have brought considerable relief to the Archbishop. He replied by return of post: 'Of course we shall be able to get things into shape.' Meanwhile he suggested that Vincent O'Brien and he should go through the scheme together, and then submit the result of their consultation to the assistant bishop, Dr. Donnelly, who was enthusiastic about the whole plan. The eventual result could then be submitted to Edward himself for his approval. A postscript to the letter reveals the real eagerness of the Archbishop to fall in with Edward's revolutionary scheme. 'I don't know whether you have come across an Italian (Roman) monthly, the Gregorian Review *Rassegna Gregoriana*,' he wrote. 'It is altogether on Solesmes lines, and this seems to me to open up a very hopeful prospect. Of course as a Bishop *emphatically exhorted* (though not commanded) by the Holy See to use the Roman Medicean text, I am not free to use any other. But I think the case will be a strong one for an application for permission to use the Solesmes text. It is *practically* the one that I was accustomed to and was brought up upon in Maynooth from 1858 to 1885!'

A few weeks later, what Dr. Walsh now called 'the great musical scheme' had advanced a stage further. He was writing again to Edward to suggest that, as by a fortunate coincidence he was already employing Mr. Charles O'Connor, who always acted for the Archbishop in legal affairs, a meeting should take place between Mr. O'Connor and another of the Archbishop's legal friends, Mr. D. F. Browne. They would, he believed, 'get the thing into shape for us by meeting and talking it over together far more expeditiously than if they were working at arm's length, each with a solicitor at his back.' Meanwhile, Dr. Donnelly had got a copy of the endowment scheme of the choir at the Protestant Christ Church Cathedral, and they were studying that to discover practical hints for their own scheme.

A fortnight later, the result of the lawyers' consultations was available, but the Archbishop was by no means satisfied that they had provided against possible difficulties in the future. A long experience in Irish public affairs had made him quick to perceive possible causes of future controversy, and he now exercised his ingenuity in warning Edward against the pitfalls of a scheme which the lawyers had already sanctioned. First about the committee of experts. Fr. Bewerunge, the professor of music at Clonliffe, was a German, but so highly respected as a musical expert that if the Archbishop appointed him (as he intended), as his own nominee for Edward's scheme, there would be no serious cause for objection. 'Fr. Bewerunge is all right,' he told Edward, 'but there is really no security if we depend upon his successors in office. I dare say that when the next vacancy occurs there will be a cry raised that the bishops are betraying the interests of the country if they don't appoint an Irishman. Lots of candidates, able to sing well, will be forthcoming, and any one of them may be elected. It occurred to me to-day to suggest—and before writing to Mr. O'Connor I should like to know what you think of it—that we should make it a *sine qua non* of future appointments that the "expert" musician should have gone through a recognised course of training either in the Music School at Ratisbon *or in some other regularly organised School of Ecclesiastical Music*, having at least— Professors (or otherwise fulfilling specified conditions which I could get Fr. Bewerunge to give me as really defining what such a school of music ought to be). It would not do to specify Ratisbon *in individuo*. I am not without hope that, as a result for what you are doing for us, a real school of real ecclesiastical music may grow up in Dublin. We should keep this possibility in view, but at the same time we should so specify things that until there is a real *bona fide* school in existence, we should insist on the qualification of the one school that we know of as a reality. I should have fair confidence that any priest who went through a course in such a school would be all right. Without some such requirement, I should regard the whole thing as left unprotected for the future. Moreover, I don't see how the future can be provided for at all except in the way I suggest.' Another letter, reporting progress some weeks later, added the further suggestion that not only Fr. Bewerunge's successor but also Mr. Vincent O'Brien's should, under the terms of the trust, be required to have completed a course at some such musical college, at any rate within twelve months of being appointed as conductor.

The search for securities to bind the future evidently gave real enjoyment to the Archbishop, though the delays became exasperating to Edward. Having already pointed out to the lawyers their failure to provide for the appointment of dependable trustees, he now sought about for means of controlling their actions in case the conditions of the trust were not fulfilled. On this point Mr. Charles O'Connor had confessed inability to produce any safeguard. The Archbishop, however, had made the drastic suggestion 'to give some one such as the Bishop of Galway the right of capturing the fund for a charitable purpose. The person so entitled to £10,000,' he argued, 'is not likely to let the chance slip. Still there is no real security.' Even so he had devised yet a further expedient, of providing 'some one whose duty it would be to decide the question.' What suitable person could be stipulated for? Or what office was there, the holder of which could be named to exercise this invidious censorship, over the actions of trustees who were themselves interlopers in the administration of a cathedral church? The Archbishop's ingenuity was not to be baffled. Possibly, he now thought, 'something might be done on the line of the certificate mentioned in Section 2. Suppose we required that the commissioners, before paying the interest, should have a certificate from the Treasurer of the Committee that the conditions had all been complied with? We can imagine people getting careless about the observance of the conditions. But it is another thing to suppose them acting fraudulently by certifying—for the purpose too of getting money from a public body—that conditions had been observed which in point of fact had not been observed.'

More than six months had passed and Edward might well hope that the scheme had by this time been made water-tight. But in June a new series of objections were forthcoming—this time from Bishop Donnelly, who had been considering the whole project more from a musical point of view. 'He prefaces his criticism,' Dr. Walsh reported, 'with the remark that no one could be more opposed than he is to "eclectic programmes." ' But the auxiliary bishop had reflected that 'there are several liturgical things for which we have no music of the Palestrina time. He instances the *Te Deum* and the Sequences of the Missal (*Lauda Sion, Veni Sancte Spiritus*, etc.)' These were certainly serious gaps in Edward's scheme, and above all for a cathedral church! The matter had indeed cropped up already. 'You may have observed,' wrote the Archbishop, 'that at the pro-Cathedral we had a bad hitch on the Christian Brothers' day—the *Lauda Sion* was not sung at all, though the Mass was of a day within the Octave of Corpus Christi!' Nevertheless, the Archbishop's resourcefulness was by no means exhausted. He had already thought of a possible solution of the difficulty—'to add a section immediately after our prohibition of mixture of the two categories of musical composition. This section would provide that the prohibition would not apply in any case in which the experts would certify to the committee *in writing* (to make it a formal deliberate proceeding) that for the purpose required there is no music of the 17th century extant, and that in that case the committee would

be empowered to sanction the performance of music of a
later date, as to which the *experts* would similarly certify
(1) that it complied with the general requirement of
Clause 8, i.e., in accordance with the laws of the church
and the spirit of the liturgy, and (2) that it was composed
in a style similar to that of the earlier works so that it
could be performed at the same liturgical function
without contravening any canon of art.' Even so there
were legal difficulties, in Mr. O'Connor's view. But
once again the Archbishop came to the rescue, by
suggesting that this could be obviated 'by the inclusion
of a "short preamble" declaring your object in the
foundation of the choir to be the cultivation of that style
of music which the supreme authority in liturgical
matters has declared to be best worthy of a place in
Divine worship.'

Edward, in marvelling at the apparently tireless
patience of the Archbishop, must have wondered at
times whether the whole affair could not have been
settled long ago if there had been a less meticulous and
analytical brain to deal with. 'I am glad to know that you
are satisfied with the draft scheme, as it now stands,' Dr.
Walsh wrote in his next letter a few days later. 'But even
now,' he adds, 'it occurs to me that one or two slight
changes will have to be made.' This time the difficulty
concerned the contingent powers to be given to the
Bishop of Galway, in the event of his being able to claim
the trust fund, on account of neglect on the part of the
Dublin Cathedral to fulfil the necessary conditions of the
endowment! The difficulty, he held, was a serious one.
'It will, of course, be altogether for you to consider what
particular kind of charities (to be selected by the Bishop

of Galway) in the dioceses named the money should go to, You could say, for instance, "the poor" or "the encouragement of technical education" or "the building of churches, or of schools, and so on." '

It was not mere casuistry, however, but a long experience of the ways and habits of the Board of Charitable Bequests, that induced the Archbishop to spend so much ingenuity in circumventing every possible objection or difficulty in advance. By the end of June he was able to report that he had actually seen Judge Carton, who was one of the Commissioners; and that the Judge had been so fully satisfied that he believed the Bequests Board would now pass it as a matter of course at their next meeting. Dr. Walsh would make it his business to attend the Board in person 'so as to ensure its not being postponed.' Meanwhile, there were still three slight amendments necessary. The principal one still concerned the prospective reversionary powers of the fortunate Bishop who might possibly benefit by a failure to comply with the conditions of the trust in Dublin. The Commissioners would, he found, 'not take a trust that might involve them in the responsibility for things impossible to foresee. Their approval would of course be given to *rational* charitable application of the fund.' Edward's hands would, therefore, be left entirely free in the matter, in the event of his having to recall his endowment and divert it to some other purpose. 'It may put a useful check,' was Archbishop Walsh's comment, 'upon the possibly fantastic projects of some Bishop of Galway in the 30th or 40th century!'

At long last the negotiations thus reached their conclusion. The scheme dated November 26th, 1902,

o

bearing the names of Edward Martyn and Archbishop
Walsh as principals, was duly approved by the Board of
Bequests. Securities to the value of £10,000 were paid
over by Edward to the Commissioners of Charitable
Donations and Bequests, for them to pay the income to
the committee appointed for the administration of the
choir. The first detailed clause in the agreement was a
stipulation that 'the said Choir shall consist of men and
boys only, who shall all be Roman Catholics, and there
shall be at least eight men and twenty boys regular
members of the said Choir, and they may be supple-
mented by others. On no occasions shall females be
employed.' The income of the fund was to be supple-
mented by the annual sum of at least £276 from the
funds of the Cathedral. 'The music to be sung shall be
Gregorian and that of Palestrina or in the Palestrina
style (being that which has been declared by the Supreme
Liturgical Authority of the Roman Catholic Church to be
most worthy of a place in Divine Worship) and no music
composed later than the end of the 17th century shall be
sung unless registered on a list to be drawn up and added
to from time to time by the Committee.' The Committee
was to have Edward himself as its chairman, and was to
include the Administrator of the Cathedral and two other
priests nominated by the Archbishop, as well as the
Professor of Sacred Liturgy for the time being in the
seminary of the Dublin diocese at Clonliffe.

On that basis the choir was constituted and began its
work. There were signs of widespread interest in the
experiment, though the austerity of the Gregorian chant
was a bitter disappointment to many. One of the first and
greatest encouragements was that when the new Bishop

in Edward's own County Galway, Dr. O'Dea, was about
to be consecrated, a request was received that the choir
should be lent for the occasion. Archbishop Walsh
viewed the invitation with some suspicion, fearing that
such a precedent would make it difficult to refuse other
applications of a similar kind. But he decided to meet the
request generously. 'Is it an Irishism,' he wrote to
Edward, 'to say that it is a good "sign" of the new
Bishop that he is anxious to have the right kind of music
on the occasion of his consecration? Of course we should
do what we can to meet his wishes. The danger is that if
we let the pro-Cathedral Choir go, there will be no end to
the applications that may be made for the extension of the
permission. Let us guard against this danger and then
do what we can to meet the wishes of the new Bishop.'
And he concluded with a strongly worded recommenda-
tion to the Committee that they should regard the
occasion as being so exceptional as to justify even the
abandonment of High Mass in the pro-Cathedral in
Dublin.

The first year's record, however, was by no means
encouraging on the whole. Edward, in his enthusiasm
as a regular attendant at the High Mass each Sunday
when he was in Dublin, put forward towards the end of
the year a suggestion that the choir should be installed
in a new tribune specially built for them, instead of having
to sing in the Organ Loft. Dr. Walsh, who had had to
endure much persistent hostile criticism since the experiment started, and who had become painfully aware of the
increasing decline in attendance at High Mass on
Sundays, met Edward's suggestion in the first week of
1904 with a douche of cold water that was enough to

damp any man's enthusiasm. 'As to building a tribune,' he wrote, 'I fear the pro-Cathedral funds would not stand the strain. I hear there is a VERY NOTABLE falling off in the collections at the doors, which means in the attendance. This was foretold by "croakers." I dissented from that view of the case, because I had faith in the attractiveness of real ecclesiastical music. But when the music of the church is sung Sunday after Sunday dismally out of tune, it is impossible to make a stand. Candidly I don't see how we are to go on.'

But such occasional outbursts of petulance in a harassed and very human Archbishop were scarcely surprising. The way of the reformer in Ireland is never a gay one, and Dr. Walsh was never blessed with a sense of humour that might have mitigated the irritations of having to combat ridicule and passive resistance. What mattered much more was his unfailing, if dour, perseverance; and under the protection of his austere encouragement, the experiment gradually gained strength as its execution improved. In time even the hopes that he had expressed in one of those early letters to Edward was fulfilled, and the choir became an official Schola Cantorum, or school of ecclesiastical music, where the future administrators of the choir could obtain their training, so that the clamour for appointing a native Irish musician — which had so exercised Dr. Walsh in prospect at the outset — might be gratified without lowering the standard of qualifications required. In time, too, as happened with all of Edward's ventures, real genius was discovered once he had provided the means for it to find expression. It was no small achievement to have been the means of 'discovering' the future Count John MacCormack. The memories of famous men concerning their own beginnings are often uncertain, and Mr. MacCormack's own version of his early connection with the Dublin choir provoked a correction from Edward before his death. 'The following are the facts,' Edward wrote in a letter to the *Irish Independent*. 'When forming the cathedral choir at the end of 1902, I wrote in answer to an application from Athlone, that Mr. MacCormack would come up to Dublin to let us hear him. He came early in 1903, and when we heard his astonishing voice I immediately secured him for the choir. It is not a big voice, although its quality of tone is unapproached. So far from my ever having thought it too big, I was disappointed that it did not seem to dominate and improve the tone of our men, with which in those early years I was dissatisfied. I am thankful to say that in these later years it has vastly improved — notwithstanding the loss of Mr. Mac-Cormack.' It was impossible in any case to expect that Mr. MacCormack should have remained in Dublin, once his voice had become famous all over the world. And few Irish musicians have shown an equal interest in their own country in these later years.

Looking back some fifteen years later, when he was writing the introduction to his *Paragraphs for the Perverse*, Edward alluded to liturgical music as 'the chief interest of my life.' Although he had not found in it any scope for the accomplishment of original work as a means of self-expression, yet it had 'always filled him with a sort of rapturous interest' arising from 'an instinctive and indeed mediæval love for the liturgy of the Catholic Church. The red letters of the Rubric,' he declared, 'are to me what the stars are to the astronomer, or (to put it so that all may understand) what a pack of cards, a racecourse, a music-hall or a golf links are to Handy Andy. I find in the liturgy an artistic compilation probably unsurpassable, with a music unapproached certainly.' In retrospect he recalled the origin of his own hopes of achieving some improvement of ecclesiastical music in Ireland. 'After many years wandering on the Continent to Rome, Paris, Regensbourg, Cöln, Mainz, Munster, where liturgical services were magnificent and the music varying in excellence — except at Regensbourg where it was always splendid and the best — I often wondered why in my own land, the most Catholic of all Europe, where much money had been expended on new churches, where the Church was most flourishing, there was so little to be seen of her wonderful art. In fact one would never suspect that she had any, if judged by her aspect here in Ireland.

'I set about thinking,' he went on, 'how such anomalies might be changed. I did not believe we could be so savage as to go on contented with them. Then in the autumn of 1898 I first met Mr. Vincent O'Brien, just after his production of the *Missa Papæ Marcelli* at St. Teresa's Church in Dublin, an enterprise which filled me with interest. With his aid and that of Rev. Mr. O'Mahony, one of the most influential of the Christian Brothers, I started a choir of men and boys called the Palestrina Choir, the object of which was to give renderings of that master's works, and of others of the same school, from time to time at Church functions, as a model of what the true liturgical music should be. During the four years of its activities the Palestrina Choir, under the extremely able conductorship of Mr. Vincent O'Brien, was a very popular institution. Vast crowds attended whenever it was to be heard.

'When, however, His Grace the Archbishop, who all along showed intelligent sympathy, made it the Cathedral Choir, or the Schola Cantorum, to give it its canonical designation, of the Dublin arch-diocese, there came about a curious change. The Handy Andys at once took alarm. We might trifle with the question as much as we liked. It was all very well so long as there was no reform. But now here was an official organisation in obedience to the commands of His Holiness actually set up, and all admonished to take it as a model. This was too much for the Handy Andy musicians and others who admired their methods. The thing must be disparaged, spoiled by all the farcical and ineffective tactics of Handy Andyism. It must not be given a chance. At the requiem for the late Pope, when the whole hierarchy of Ireland was present, the otherwise splendid function was spoiled by the choir being crowded out into a hole, so that the sublime Mass Vittoria composed for the obsequies of the Empress Maria, although well rehearsed and very well sung, sounded weak and muffled as if it were away somewhere outside the church.

'But although mortifications had to be borne, we forged along in spite of terrible difficulties. We gathered some powerful friends. Bishop Donnelly, Dean of the diocese, one of the most accomplished men of his time, in whose well-appointed church a fine choir is worked on the same lines as that of the Schola, and Monsignor Dunne, an expert in Liturgy and Gregorian Chant, both on the Cathedral Choir Committee, have given un-wavering assistance. But above all, His Grace Dr. Walsh, who could extinguish the whole work any time he thought proper, has thrown over us his all-protecting mantle of authority. Some time ago I heard there was a round robin sent to him from the pro-Cathedral requesting him to change the music of the choir. As was to be expected from a learned canonist and musician of taste, he took no notice of such a document. In fact no one, except perhaps my humble self, has been opposed and annoyed by Handy Andyism so persistently as this distinguished man, whose ideas for the betterment of Ireland have, as far as I can judge, been so very far-seeing. If we landlords had listened to him thirty years ago, we would have come much better out of our troubles. He was absolutely right in his advocacy of the Catholic College in the one Dublin University. This would naturally lead to a separate University in Cork, and as we could have the management of our affairs, an Irish University in Galway, where everything would be taught in the Irish language. He is particularly suited to our time of educational reform. Indeed there is no one to take his place.

'And so the choir has fought along for sixteen years, always gaining strength and efficiency from the splendid training of Mr. Vincent O'Brien, who to his other achievements as composer, shown in the Easter Cantata and fine symphonic poem *Samhain*, voice producer and conductor, is by far the best, if not the only, liturgical musician in Ireland. He has imbibed a unique knowledge of Gregorian from the teaching of the Solesmes monks, which he shows in the fine taste of his accompaniments and in the splendour and true Church feeling of his improvisations on the plain chant of the day, whether as voluntaries or leadings into the Cappella music, of which he gives most effective renderings despite the wretched acoustics of the crowded pro-Cathedral. How gorgeous it would all sound in a fine church like St. Patrick's for instance! He has also produced with great effect, amid much concert work, the Graal Scene of *Parsifal* and the *Dream of Gerontius*, which no other musician here ever dared attempt. Moreover he has discovered and taught all the chief singers of his time. He is a very rare product of our country.'

The foundation of the Palestrina Choir was probably the most durable achievement of Edward's public life in Ireland, and he followed its development with affectionate interest and enthusiasm till his death. From time to time he would contribute articles to the Irish Press about Church music; and in an essay which he contributed to the *Irish Review* he makes the interesting confession that: 'It must have been, as with me, through Wagner back to Beethoven, through Beethoven to Bach, through Bach to the super-human perfection of Palestrina, that the few who were gifted to perceive so celestial a beauty, have revived the cult of liturgical æstheticism.'

In the preface to his collected essays, Edward Martyn wrote before his death that the section of his *Paragraphs*, devoted to modern Church Ornament, 'will probably show the perversity of my countrymen more clearly than any of the previous sections. It is not surprising, because in modern times almost everywhere this subject more than any other seems to draw the nations along the easy way where misapplication of things to purposes is the rule of action. Here, however, in the original home of Handy Andy, it hurries at a rate to make us "whip Creation," in the elegant idiom used by transatlantic paladins of small nationalities. For instance, could any practice better illustrate the symbol of using the bootjack for a hammer than the perversity everywhere, but nowhere so much as in Ireland, of preferring the tradesmen to the artist for the production of ecclesiastical ornament? And yet so it is. To produce art a tradesman is used instead of an artist.

'To remedy this I hit upon an expedient so simple that the wonder it excited at the time has always puzzled me since. It was nothing more than to proclaim that the artists in Ireland should decorate churches and that tradesmen should be obedient to them. I showed how the only demand for art in Ireland was from the churches, how the artists who were starving for want of work were the proper persons to supply it, and how the tradesmen would not suffer, as they would always be required to do the mechanical part of the work. In fact the whole arrangement seemed eminently conducive to the dignity and prosperity of Ireland. But although this obvious discovery was rather popular, as it resulted in chasing from the country foreign purveyors of stained glass that looked like crudely painted window blinds, and lifted from poverty to affluence the native makers (one of whom, Mr. Earley, wrote to thank me for being thus the cause of his return to prosperity), still it aroused such an amount of blank astonishment and mulish opposition from Handy Andyism as prevented anything like its general acceptance then or since. It was triumphantly asked: Who was going to be so foolish as to hand over his church for a *corpus vile* to be experimented on by artists, as if the experiments of artists could be worse than the mechanical formulæ of the tradesmen!

'Evidently they failed to understand that the difference

T. P. Gill
From the painting by Miss Sara Purser, R.H.A.

between an artist and a tradesman was not in degree but
in kind, as the difference between a hammer and a boot-
jack. Neither can be compared with nor put to the uses
of the other. At last, when Handy Andyism was brought
to bay, it was boldly asserted that art had nothing to do
with decoration, an opinion not surprising when we see
instances of so-called decoration in our churches. I
remember a mosaic scheme in a dominant tone of dirty
yellow that made me feel as if a plate of stirabout was
thrown in my face. The most notable example of this is
imported work by modern Italians, than whom none,
who were once so great, have sunk so low in the practice
of modern arts.

'Nevertheless in this reform also my interference bore
some fruit. I succeeded in persuading Mr. T. P. Gill to
settle in the School of Art, Mr. Childe, a pupil of the
celebrated Christopher Whall, and a most efficient teacher
who since 1903 has trained many an Irish artist in his
stained glass school. I also at the same time suggested
to Miss Purser the advisability of opening a studio where
he should be the chief artist. At first she was inclined to
jib; but being a woman of great business capacity as well
as an artist, who, of course, would understand the
situation, she took the hint, and now she and his pupils
at *An Túr Gloinne* have been painting for several years
many beautiful storied windows. That great man, the
late Archbishop Healy, when Bishop of Clonfert, was the
first to allow the artists to "experimentalise" in his
cathedral at Loughrea. The work was carried on by his
successor, Bishop O'Dea, with the result that few modern
churches can compare with it in the fine taste of its
interior ornament and furniture. Among its many fine

works, the Virgin and Child, by Mr. John Hughes and
the altar rails with their bold and varied carvings by Mr.
Sportal, are especially noticeable. There may be more
beautiful altar rails in existence, but all I know is I have
never seen more beautiful.

'The side altars and iron woodwork were designed by
Mr. W. A. Scott, Professor of Architecture in the
National University. Some years before I heard from
artists vague talk of there being a young architect somewhere in Ireland who was also an artist. This seemed to
me so wonderful a thing that when some friends in
Spiddal told me they wanted to build a new parish church,
and that I must advise them as to the best way of making
it really beautiful, I was determined to find out at once
this prodigy, whom after some difficulty I found. He
was none other than the now fine designer, Professor
Scott. He entered into the project with enthusiasm,
which resulted in a little masterwork of design and
charming appropriateness to the situation. It is admired
by every artist and man of taste. Scott now began to
be talked of everywhere. He had invented something
like a modern Irish architecture inspired by our old
buildings. In any other country he would be overwhelmed with clients, but of course Handy Andyism is
arrayed against him. Still he has built a fine diocesan
college in Galway, and for the isle of St. Patrick's Purga-
tory a marvellously proportioned hostel, a blending of
simplicity and austere grandeur of design.

'These reforms, however, are only exceptions to the
general resistance to reform. In Dublin only two churches,
St. Teresa's and St. Andrew's, both noted for artistic
possessions, have been decorated under the supervision

of Professor Scott. The results are really fine. It is in
Dublin that we should most like to see the work of our
artists in churches, because of its convenience as a centre
where clients might study examples of our aims. But
evidently our educational methods have forced to a more
acute viciousness here the passion for batin' the cock
with a bootjack, none the less barbarous from its veneer
of self-satisfied respectability, that we find the passive
resistance of Dublin the most difficult of all to break
down. Thus I may say that Dublin, if the capital of
Ireland in some matters, is surely not so in matters of
taste. The results of course are deplorable. The new
churches built are as unshapely as sacks of potatoes.
They disfigure the old churches. In MacCarthy's master-
work, one of the most noble of modern churches with a
nave worthy of the thirteenth century, they have done
little (with the exception of the new aisles which are not
bad) that has not tended to disfigure what was left by the
master. The side altars and statuary are very bad and fit
clumsily into the architecture. The stained glass is
worse, with the possible exception of Clayton and Bell's
window. But worse than all, they have scraped the fifty
years' mellowness off MacCarthy's high altar, which
gave it such an ethereal look, and added ugly extensions
on either side, ruining the design so that the general
effect is now that of some fantastic fabric of sugar in
some confectioner's window.

'It is almost as bad as the machine-made classicalism
with which some atrocity from London has covered the
noble Lombard wall spaces of Kildare Street Club,
another architectural master-work. It is a shame that
people who are unfit to have the care of such fine build-

ings are not restrained from doing such things. Passing over such trifles of misuse as the lighting of domestic fires with the music-stands of the pro-Cathedral, I proceed to the misuse of an architectural device which is nowhere so prevalent as in our midst. I mean the modern mania for so-called reredoses at all cost. Now a reredos is properly a sculptural decoration on a wall at the back of an altar, which on no account should be attached to the reredos. One should be able to pass all round the altar. It follows, therefore, that when the altar is backed by windows or colonnades a reredos must be out of place, and an absurdity. In this case an open altar under a pillared baldacchino is correct. However, such an arrangement prescribed by authority is characteristically repugnant to us, for the same spirit that impels us to misuse nearly everything, here impels us to fix mock reredoses to the backs of altars, even if they block the light from windows or break in upon the beauty of apsidal arches or chapels. It is hard to account for such misuse of means to ends, unless by my usual method, for the spaces at the back of such altars are always very ugly and useless for any purpose, except as places where that most famous of all adepts at batin' the cock, the clerk, may throw his old rubbish.'

In his efforts to improve the ecclesiastical art of Catholic Ireland, Edward Martyn had indeed undertaken a herculean labour. From the first years after he had left Oxford he had been most generous in his contributions to the improvement of Catholic churches, and by his will he eventually provided much larger sums for the adornment of several Irish cathedrals that were still waiting to be built. But his own efforts could never be more than a very small contribution to all the church building and church decoration that were constantly in progress, and it was necessary to undertake a vigorous propaganda to make people, and the clergy especially, familiar with his own ideas. He had started on the simple assumption that to employ artists would always produce better results than to employ commercial decorators; but in Ireland all artists were so suspect of eccentricity or irreverence that the idea was by no means as convincing as it sounded.

It did much to promote confidence when Mr. T. P. Gill was able to organise official classes for various handicrafts and arts under the safe auspices of the new Department of Agriculture and Technical Instruction; and it then fell very largely upon Edward's shoulders to provide work for the few young artists who received training in the schools. There was no one else who commanded the confidence of the clergy in artistic matters as he did, and he was in the supremely strong position of being a generous donor to many ecclesiastical undertakings. 'I am exceedingly grateful to you for your munificent contribution to our new church in Loughrea,' wrote Bishop Healy of Clonfert, shortly before the Boer War. 'You are the first "outsider" from whom we have received anything, and the example will have an excellent effect. May God bless you and yours.' Before long Edward and his friends succeeded, by a judicious offering of important subscriptions, in obtaining almost a free hand to supervise the interior decorations of the new church at Loughrea, and they made an admirable use of this opportunity.

Edward's faith in the native talent of such artists as he

hoped to discover had been amply justified. He was willing to wait, and at first he had to employ Christopher Whall and Mr. Virtue to make the stained glass windows he erected to members of his own family in the parish church at Ardrahan — the only glass by them in Ireland. But it was not long before Miss Purser's stained glass works produced a very remarkable succession of young artists under the experienced direction of Whall's pupil, Mr. Childe. In sculpture, Edward was able to recommend the work of two Irish artists of real genius, Oliver Shepherd and John Hughes, and he gave them several useful commissions from his own resources. And in architecture his discovery of the work of Professor Scott was to produce opportunities, that would not have occurred otherwise, for demonstrating, at Spidall and in Cork and elsewhere, the great possibilities of a return to the early traditions of Celtic-Norman designs. But his chief work consisted in a vigorous sustained propaganda in favour of employing Irish artists to design and decorate Irish buildings and, when necessary, in trenchant attacks upon some of the new buildings that were being erected at great expense with the approval of an ignorant Press. In Ireland the scope for artists of every kind was inevitably very limited, and the work for the Catholic churches was by far the most important field in which they could hope to find employment. Edward, as a munificent donor to many churches, had seen the possibilities of his own personal influence, and he used it with really powerful effect.

It happened that while Edward and his friends were actively concerning themselves to establish new standards of culture in Ireland, one of the most ambitious churches built in any part of Ireland for many years reached its completion and was consecrated with most exceptional ceremonial. For many years before the completion of St. Adamnan's Cathedral in Letterkenny the whole Catholic peasantry of Donegal and of the surrounding counties of Western Ulster had been aroused to enthusiasm by the efforts of the young Bishop of Raphoe, Dr. O'Donnell, who, some twenty years later, was to succeed Cardinal Logue as Archbishop of Armagh, Primate of all Ireland, and the only Cardinal in the Irish hierarchy. In no part of Ireland was the traditional piety and devotion of the peasantry more intense; and probably no bishop in Ireland had the same hold upon the affections of his people as the brilliant young ecclesiastic who had been one of the most cultured scholars, and the most independent character, among the younger members of the professorial staff at Maynooth.

Dr. O'Donnell had become a national figure already before his appointment as Bishop of Raphoe, and he was particularly in sympathy with the new manifestations of the Nationalist Movement. Born of tenant farmer stock in Donegal, he was a native speaker of Irish, and could preach as fluently, and with the same scholarly grace, in Irish as in English. Moreover he was a power in Irish politics, the intimate friend of many members of the Irish Parliamentary Party, and in later years was to be one of the trustees of the Party funds, as well as one of the most influential of its political counsellors. It was not surprising that he should undertake the building of a cathedral in Letterkenny soon after he was appointed at an early age as Bishop of Raphoe; and he had succeeded in arousing extraordinary enthusiasm among the poor

P

people, in appealing to them to offer gifts either in kind
or in money to build a great church that would confer
dignity upon the diocese and would be the principal
feature of their market town. The money was in due
course collected and the big new church was dedicated to
their local saint, St. Adamnan, whose ancient biography
of the great Saint Columba is one of the most vivid
memorials of the primitive age of the Irish Church. It is
a big Gothic building with a spire which towers above the
squalid little streets of the poor market town; and the
contrast between its ambitious proportions, which represented so faithfully the idealism of the peasantry who had
built it out of their little savings and their generous gifts,
and the squalid backwardness of their own homes was to
provide the theme for Mr. Michael MacCarthy's elaborate onslaught on the Catholic Church in Ireland which he
published under the title *Priests and People in Ireland.*
On the wrapper of that egregious compilation Mr.
MacCarthy published a composite photograph, showing
a great modern church towering above the streets of little
hovels surrounding it, which was in fact based upon the
photographs of the new cathedral at Letterkenny.

On the question of whether an impoverished peasantry
should spend their slender resources, at the cost of great
and prolonged self-sacrifice, in building a church so much
out of keeping with their own standard of living, the
views of Edward Martyn were not likely to coincide with
those of his intellectual friends in the new literary movement. For him, as for any other devout Catholic, it was
no more scandalous or inappropriate to find a magnificent
cathedral built as a citadel of devotion amid poor surroundings, than it would be to come upon similar

contrasts in Chartres or other cathedral towns all over the Continent. But the question of what sort of cathedral had been erected at such cost and by such sacrifices, as a symbol of the philosophy of Catholic Ireland, was a very different matter. The Nationalist Press had been filled with verbose accounts of the magnificent ritual with which the new cathedral had been opened and consecrated, and with the customary ignorant effusions in praise of its architectural and decorative beauties. It required courage in Ireland at that time for a prominent Catholic layman to publish a deliberate onslaught on the artistic standards of the new cathedral, and no one but Edward Martyn was likely to express such criticisms. But the opportunity was too important to be missed, and he came forward without hesitation to denounce the whole proceedings in the *Leader* over his own signature.

'If a reader should turn to the daily papers in 1900,' he wrote, 'for an idea of the new church just finished and opened with such advertisement, he might be led to think from their eulogy that it is a perfect gem of art. Now it is no such thing; and what is more, many of us know it is no such thing. At the same time nobody will dare to say so. It is with very great reluctance that I say so; I feel it a most disagreeable duty, but a duty all the same, if our labours for the improvement of ecclesiastical art and the development of native talent are to bear fruit. I hope, therefore, that everything in this article will be taken in the spirit in which it is meant — namely, as criticism, in all sincerity at least, with a view of bringing about betterment, thereby showing the superiority of native work over foreign importations of an inferior kind, which have led to a decadence in ecclesiastical art more debased than at any previous epoch in our country's history.'

'It is no exaggeration,' he went on to say, 'that among the unsatisfactory works in any new church the foreign works are by far the most unsatisfactory, and that whatever is good is Irish. I will begin with the decoration. This, I understand, is the work of an Italian. I can well believe it; for it has all the decadent senility of a worn-out tradition which was once great and made Italy mistress of the arts, but which now makes her their meanest drudge. It has always seemed to me astonishing that there should still be a belief, even with the un-initiated, in the power of that country to produce tolerable works in painting or sculpture. All persons of taste know that she cannot. If there is one subject upon which every artist is agreed, it is this. Still there are many among our clergy who seem not to know that this is so. How easy it would be for them to become enlightened and saved from wasting good money on such worthless work, if only they would take the trouble to seek advice. They would not act in other matters as they are acting in matters of art. If they were going to law they would take the advice of a lawyer, if they were sick they would call in a physician for advice; but in matters of taste, which is quite as technical a subject as either of these, every man thinks he knows what is best himself. The result is what we see in our churches.

'This mania for Italian art has become, in Ireland, a perfect scandal. I was informed that a marble group came from Italy to go under the high altar of a church, and had to be rejected on account of its very badness of workman-ship. I was informed by the head of an Irish firm that in the case of another church they were actually employed to make models for the wretched Italian sculptors to work from. This is certainly degrading our craftsmen. But it is all on a par with the general stifling of the Church's great art traditions, such as the degradation of church music, the perversity of permitting women to sing in church choirs, etc., etc. And what I have said about the badness of decoration here may equally be said about the badness of the stained glass. This, too, is chiefly of foreign importation. Here for instance is a large West window, which I was told was by Hardman of Birmingham. In order to show to what inferiority a firm may sink when freed from the influence of a great genius like Pugin, it is only necessary to compare this work with the little window (mentioned in the "Paragraph" on stained glass[1]) from Celbridge Catholic Church, which the same firm executed in the year 1858. Of the Munich windows it is, of course, unnecessary to speak. At least I was told some were done in Munich, and I can well believe it from the peculiar vulgarity some displayed.

'Of the two works, however, belonging to this church, executed in Ireland, it is my pleasant duty to speak in the highest praise. One is the beautiful peal of bells, which, for its size, could scarcely be surpassed in quality by any country. The other is some figure-carving inside the arch of the nave where it joins the transepts. This carving, despite a certain rudeness, appears to me to be a work of genius. It represents scenes from the life of St. Columbcille, divided by a bold if somewhat rough, rope framing. The composition of the various sections is full of simple charm. The figure of Our Lord at the top is

[1]See page 233.

conceived in that true spirit of power and dignity which is inspired by the finest periods of ecclesiastical art; while the whole work pulsates with a feeling and life such as I have not seen nor thought possible in modern church sculpture. The artist, I heard, was from Belfast. I hope that this may be his beginning of manifold work for the Church.

'I have said it is not a pleasant task to find fault; but it is necessary to prevent the miserable foreign work in our churches from being held as models for future church decorations. Until lately the clergy do not seem to have realised that they have made grave mistakes, that the majesty of Maynooth College Chapel, for instance, where the architect, Mr. MacCarthy, did his work so well, has been nearly ruined by its stained glass and most of its decorations. Even now some clergymen look with suspicion on the movement for abolishing the foreign art commercial traveller and for employing the best Irish artists at adorning our hitherto disfigured churches. They see in it a dangerous experiment, and hesitate to allow their churches to be, as they term it, "experimented on." I wonder they cannot understand that even the wildest experiments of artists must produce superior results to work of which I complain, and which differs from art work not so much in quality indeed as in kind. Is it possible that our artists should produce a worse effect than common tradesmen who degrade the practice of art to mere commerce? Are apothecaries superior to doctors or law clerks to barristers? Was the statesmanship of the Parliamentary Party superior to that of Parnell? Does the boasted intelligence of a quick-witted people show itself conspicuously by holding an analogous

opinion? Oh, we are too quick-witted. We have become
so suspicious of the good that we have become the dupes
of the bad.'

Only a few weeks earlier he had contributed to the
Leader an article in denunciation of the general standard
of stained glass in the Irish churches, which certainly
could not have been published in any other paper that
appealed to a Nationalist public at the time. 'Among all
the bad forms of decoration in modern churches, that of
stained glass is undoubtedly the worst,' he wrote. 'Never
since over a thousand years ago when, I take it, the art
was invented, has that art fallen so low as just at the
present time. I think this may be safely asserted without
fear of contradiction by anyone possessed of æsthetic
taste. The reason of its decay and the general decay of the
decorative arts can be traced to the democratic educational movements of the early part of last century, which
sought to give to everyone, irrespective of wealth, equal
facilities of learning. To the doctrinaire, no doubt, such
systems appeared to be ideally philanthropic. Perhaps
they were. But doctrinaires have never been noted for
their knowledge of humanity; and the last thing, I
suppose, they then could have been expected to understand was the serious blow they dealt to human intelligence as a ruling force, by their well-meaning designs.

'What was the result of this work of theirs, for instance,
to those highest of intellectual ruling forces, literature and
the fine arts? Let us see for a moment. It is generally
admitted that the greatest literature and art were produced in times when there was none of this fever about
promiscuous education. People then were educated who
could afford to pay for education, both intelligent and

stupid alike. The intelligent, as yet unhampered by the
uneducated masses, were able to control the taste of the
stupid rich people, and to keep literature and the fine arts
up to a high standard. From among the masses the only
persons influencing the intellectual world, were individuals of genius who are always sure somehow to educate
themselves, as is the custom with real genius which can
never be suppressed but must sooner or later shine forth
before men. These individuals of genius were, of course,
on the side of true intellect and taste. The rich, clever
and stupid alike, could afford to pay a proper price for
things of rare and costly art, and they paid it. Even the
stupid rich were not numerous enough to vulgarise the
world's literature. The uneducated masses looked upon
costly art as beyond their resources, and were satisfied
with plain furniture and decoration, which, although
simple and unpretending, were in excellent taste; for as
yet the world had not made that wonderful democratic
discovery of how to produce an object which was not in
its way a work of art.

'Then came the indiscriminate education of the
masses; and when I say education, I mean a so-called
higher education, not the mere teaching of reading,
writing and arithmetic, which should be compulsorily
taught to everyone. This so-called higher education may
have helped individuals of genius. It may also have
impeded them; for, as I have said, genius educates itself;
and, somehow, men of genius seem to have risen from
the masses more in the old days than now. But with
mediocre persons of small pecuniary means, the higher
education appears to me to have been an unmixed evil.
The only result it has had with such persons is to develop

in their mediocre heads an inordinate idea of *respectability*, that mean English word which came into vogue over here with the decay of our language and national individuality. All over the world mediocre persons of small means, having their heads turned by this education, at once passionately desired to appear something above what in reality they were. They despised the occupations of their fathers and the beautiful simple art of their fathers' dwellings, and having no genius to become famous, they found nothing left for them but to become *genteel*.

'Hence, in response to their demand to appear like their betters, at small pecuniary cost, there quickly arose, for the first time in the history of the world, a supply of the cheap sham. Sham furniture, sham decorations, sham jewellery, sham wine, sham literature of the lowest type, were poured out upon the mediocre masses, who eagerly swallowed all the rubbish because it was cheap, and to them undistinguishable from the real and good. By degrees they were joined by the stupid rich, to whom good and bad were, naturally, undistinguishable. Thus there grew to be an immense public in the world who soon so got to prefer the cheap and sham, that with the distortion which familiarity with inferior things produces on the intellect, they actually ended by viewing with detestation anything truly great in literature or art. It will, therefore, readily be seen by the impartial observer, that a revolution, more or less, recently has been effected, the greatest ever heard of in the history of the world. For the first time in history, genius and intellect, now reduced to an unprecedented minority, have ceased to guide the world in matters of literature and art. The intellect of the world stands aghast at this monster that has been let loose.

To rail at it is useless. It seems impervious to ridicule or contempt. On it marches, growing and throwing out fresh feelers of destruction until, I suppose, it will eventually reduce the world of the arts to a primeval barbarism, whence a new artistic era may be brought to birth.

'In this wholesale effacement of the beautiful, there is little wonder that so delicate and refined an art as that of stained glass should have been the first to suffer and die under the clumsy hand of the Philistine. Here the cheap sham has worked greater havoc than in other departments of decoration, so much so indeed, that now it is impossible to have an artistic window made by any firm, home or foreign, if the firm is left to itself for the execution of the order. It is futile to think that, if the order is sent to firms abroad or in England, good work can be assured. The work is really no better than what is produced in this country; and if we are determined to have bad work, it is better to have it bad Irish than bad foreign: for I think few of us will deny that we ought to keep the money in the country under such circumstances. But whether those who have the sole authority for ordering stained glass, will admit the state of the circumstances, is doubtful. For the most part they have never seen good stained glass in their lives, yet with a light heart they lay out thousands of poor folks' money in such a way, that it would be preferable for them in the interests of art to cast it into the sea than thus to waste it on the daubs with which the whole of Catholic Ireland is now wellnigh plastered.

'Since a study of the world's finest glass at Chartres, or Tours, or Bourges may not be practicable, I would ask those about to order stained glass, to look at a little window in this country, at a place easily accessible. In the Catholic Parish Church of Celbridge, over Our Lady's altar, this little two-light window, with medallion scenes from her life, surrounded by a prevailing brilliancy of blue, is the finest stained glass I remember to have seen in modern times. You have to go back to the thirteenth century which has inspired it, to see excelled its ecclesiastical design, its jewel transparency, and its severe subordination of pictorial to decorative effect. I could not discover who was the maker. I was told it was there for over forty years. I concluded it must be a work done under the masterful influence of the elder Pugin who, among his many inventions, revived the mediæval art of stained glass, which has been gradually deteriorating as we get farther away from the time and genius of that great artist. Whether those whom I now advise to see this beautiful window, will admire it when they see it, I think problematical. For this is real stained glass, and totally different from the pictorial window daubs they seem to love. It is to be feared that there they may rather admire the new German stations of the Cross, than which it is impossible to conceive anything in worse taste.

'If we take pains to search about, we may still have fine windows made for us, not by firms, but by stray individual artists who practise the craft as a fine art, and not as a mere commercial industry with endless repetition of commonplace pattern, and at a price as cheap as the goods are nasty. For, let it be known at once that good stained glass cannot be produced unless a proper price is paid for it. The first necessity is proper design, which should have greater regard to transparency, colour, and general decorative effect, than to the production of a mere picture. In the execution of such a design it is imperative that *pot metal*, which is the technical name for glass stained through and through, alone should be used. Thus, if a red colour is required, there should be red transparent glass, if blue, blue transparent glass, and so on, with all the different colours leaded together, while for the face and hands, there should be white glass, with the features and fingers drawn in severe lines of brown pigment, which also must be used for the shading of all colours, because it is alone lasting and indelible. What is known as silver stain for putting gold on another colour is also lasting; but it was not discovered until the fourteenth century.

'No attempt should be made at realism, or heavy shading, or colouring by enamel, which in times of decadence was plastered over the window in order to deaden its transparency and make it appear what it should not be, namely a bad picture. This enamelled glass (always a sham because painted and *not* stained glass) was, of course, destined to find high favour in this our time of shams. It is not lasting. Indeed, I hear of the enamel already peeling off several recently set up windows with the expansion and contraction of the glass in hot and cold weather, so that these once dreadful windows are now merely patches of white glass. I also hear many complaints about this matter, but I think, on the contrary, it ought to be a subject of general satisfaction to know that there is a chance of our country being thus soon rid of such disfigurements to her ecclesiastical buildings.

'Since we have seen that only the individual artist, therefore, can give us artistic stained glass, our aim, if we wish to improve matters, must be to find such an artist, who would design windows, and superintend their execution by a firm in this country. In the first instance I regret it will be necessary to import the artist, since, after careful inquiry, it is not believed that the country possesses one of sufficient merit at present. However, such a state of affairs would be only temporary, as this artist would train several Irishmen to his methods, so that soon a native school, according to the best traditions, would be formed. Already the proprietor of a well-known studio for stained glass has expressed his willingness to execute the designs of such an artist under the artist's immediate supervision. Thus good art of the kind will be executed in Dublin by Irishmen; and we would only ask the clergy to abstain from giving foreign orders until they first see what may be done by their countrymen under such new and favourable circumstances. The work is high in aim, and national in the best sense; and while an appeal to their æsthetic taste may seem to a few of the clergy somewhat visionary, an appeal to their patriotism has never been made without satisfactory results.'

While Edward Martyn was contributing these occasional criticisms of church decoration to the Irish newspapers, another critic, who had not the prestige of Martyn's family connections, and still less the power that Martyn exercised as a potential patron of new churches, had been working on similar lines in the same newspapers. Mr. Robert Elliott decided to publish a book of his own collected criticisms in 1906, and he persuaded Edward Martyn to write a preface to the volume. The preface was one of the most trenchant things that Martyn wrote on any subject. 'If there are doubts,' he wrote, 'and differences of opinion, and justifiable repudiations of those reproaches made by the enemies of Catholicity in Ireland, who say that the means of the people are squandered on the building of churches in a quantity altogether beyond its needs, there can, among those who are best qualified to know, be no doubt or difference of opinion, or repudiation whatever of the fact, that, as far as artistic excellence is concerned, the money laid out on those churches has, in the great majority of cases, been lamentably squandered. It is not pleasant to think of this; and the feeling of dissatisfaction is scarcely lessened by the further fact that our so-called church art is not in a very much worse state than the modern church art of any other country.'

IV

THE GAELIC LEAGUE AND IRISH MUSIC

IV

THE GAELIC LEAGUE AND IRISH MUSIC

As a landlord who owned properties in County Roscommon as well as County Galway, Edward was in some sense a neighbour of Douglas Hyde, who had learned his first enthusiasm for the Irish language revival by listening to the Irish-speaking peasantry around him. Hyde was not in fact the real originator of the language revival, for the first steps had already been taken by Professor Eoin MacNeill, who organised a small class for teaching Irish to a few enthusiasts in Dublin. But Hyde and MacNeill very soon joined forces, and the captivating personality and magnificent oratorical gifts of Douglas Hyde made him an ideal President for the Gaelic League. Edward Martyn had been interested in the movement from its earliest days, and he had formed vague ideas of learning Irish well enough to write plays in it, as a language with an astonishingly varied vocabulary and a great undeveloped tradition. But it was not until the Irish Theatre had come into existence that he became a really active member of the Gaelic League, accepting a seat on its executive committee. Committees were never suited to his own peculiar gifts, and he was usually a somnolent member, even though he attended conscientiously; and his co-operation was to cause the new movement considerable embarrassment when it resulted in bringing Mr. George Moore as an ardent recruit.

It is difficult nowadays to realise that even in Mr.

Moore's own boyhood the peasantry of the western counties had still spoken Irish habitually as their native language — so much so that their landlords generally had to speak it well enough to conduct business with them in Irish, while the children of the gentry used to listen to it in wonder, when they went out rowing with the local fishermen or entered into the peasants' cabins. A few decades had wrought a rapid change in the rising generation which had been compelled to attend primary schools where everything was taught in English; and by the early 'nineties, when Douglas Hyde launched his great effort to revive a dying language, the struggle seemed to be a very forlorn hope indeed. But Mr. Moore had returned to Dublin to assist Edward and Yeats in founding their Literary Theatre, with his mind full of sentimental recollections of his own childhood, and the idea of creating a new literature in an undeveloped language with so rich a literary tradition induced astonishing outbursts of enthusiasm on his part.

Those who find it hard now to recapture that old enthusiasm, which then filled so many men who were quite incapable of learning to speak Irish as a living language, would do well to read a speech delivered by Mr. Moore at a meeting of supporters of the Irish Literary Theatre in February, 1900. 'My fellow countrymen,' said Mr. Moore, 'the language is slipping into the grave, and what you have to remember is that when the language is dead the soul of Cuchullin, which we all share still a little, will have vanished. The restoration of the language is the nation's need; even if we had a national Government, it would not be a real National Government if the language had perished, for the Celt would have been robbed of his original home. We want our language,' Mr. Moore continued in an impassioned appeal; 'we desire it with our whole heart and soul. Our desire may be foolish, unpractical, unwise, according to the lights of the English nation at the present moment; but our desire is our desire, our folly is our own, and if we wish to start ill-equipped in the business race of the world, knowing no language which is understood outside of Ireland, shall we be gainsaid like children? But this is not our desire; our desire is to make Ireland a bilingual country — to use English as a universal language, and to save our own as a medium for some future literature.'

But Mr. Moore was far from thinking that to write masterpieces in Irish would be to hide his light permanently under a bushel. On the contrary, to compel the attention of the whole civilised world to a masterpiece written in a language which was an obstacle to its being discovered, would add to the glory of the writer's fame. 'You will be told,' he impressed upon his audience, 'that if a genius such as Burns should arise to-morrow among the Irish peasantry and write his great work in Irish it would remain unread.' Let them be consoled by the reflection that 'Ibsen writes a language which is spoken by very few millions, yet his plays are read all over Europe, and the old Irish poems, written in a form no longer spoken, are known to European scholars. There is no such thing as a beautiful unknown page of literature, there is no such thing as a beautiful unknown poem, there is no such thing as a beautiful unknown line of poetry. Were a great work written in Irish to-morrow, in a few years it would have travelled all over Europe.'

As for writing in English, Mr. Moore had at this time
fully made up his mind that 'a language wears out like a
coat'; 'as it was with the Latin in the fourth, so it is with
English in the nineteenth century. From universal use
and journalism the English language in fifty years will
be as corrupt as the Latin of the eighth century, as unfit
for literary usage, and will become in my opinion, a sort
of Volapuk, strictly limited to commercial letters and
journalism.' This was a new note in the propaganda for
the language revival, and Mr. Moore's hearers must have
been tickled as they listened to him explaining how
'Walter Pater, England's last great writer, said that he
used to write in English as in a learned language. The
language, he thought, had reached the same stage of
decay as the Latin language had reached in the second
century. He knew he was writing in a decaying language,
and he treated it as such. Since his death, we have seen
the English language pass through the patty-pans of
Stevenson into the pint pot of Mr. Kipling. If we would
write with distinction we must do as Pater did, compile a
special vocabulary, and strip ourselves of all ideas and
words except those which seem to us to reflect the
intimate colour of our minds. It would seem that it is
only by narrowing our hearts and limiting our words
that we can write at all now.' Not only was the
English language imposing this insufferable restriction upon artistic expression. The ideals of modern
England had imposed themselves so far upon the
souls of every English-speaker that 'to begirdle the
world with Brixton seems to be her ultimate destiny.
And we, sitting on the last verge, see into the universal
suburb, in which a lean man with glasses on his nose

and a black bag in his hand is always running after his bus.'

It was 'dear Edward' who had shown the path of emancipation from that appalling nightmare to the novelist who — with his Irish background and his French education — had, in his own belief, written in *Esther Waters* 'the most English novel' that had ever been published. And with all the fervour of a neophyte, George Moore was appealing now to Edward's Dublin friends with a sublime apostrophe. 'My fellow country-men, the moment has come to save or let perish our language. It is the one sod of Irish earth on which we can all stand united. In this cause everyone may help, landlord and peasant alike, Nationalist and Unionist, and a cause cannot be a lost cause to which everyone can contribute; some by learning the language, some with sums of money, some by having their children taught their language. In my youth, Irish was still spoken everywhere; but the gentry took pride in not understanding their own language. It was our misfortune that such false fashion should have prevailed and kept us in ignorance of our language, but it will be our fault if our children do not learn their own language. I have no children, and I am too old to learn the language, but I shall at once arrange that my brother's children shall learn Irish. I have written to my sister-in-law telling her that I will at once undertake this essential part of her children's education. They shall have a nurse straight from Aran; for it profits a man nothing if he knows all the languages of the world and knows not his own.'

That peroration was a landmark in the Irish literary

movement. Mr. Moore had braved the inevitable
ridicule of Dublin by his promise to see that his brother's
children should follow in the paths of virtue that were
closed to him. Miss Susan Mitchell immortalised it
soon afterwards with her lines:

> 'I've puffed the Irish language, and puffed the
>   Irish soap;
> I've used them — on my nephew — with the
>   best results, I hope;
> For with this older, dirtier George I have no
>   heart to cope.'

For Edward Martyn, living much of his life in County
Galway, the question of learning Irish seriously could not
be so easily shelved. Nor was he the man to evade the
implications of his own propaganda. He bought and
studied the textbooks issued by Father O'Growney, and
before long he had been elected to the Executive Committee, or Coisde Gnótha, of the Gaelic League. It was
he who, at Mr. T. P. Gill's dinner to assemble all the
talents which were congregated around the *Daily Express*,
vociferated to Douglas Hyde that he should address the
assembly in Irish when he was called upon to speak.
Mr. Moore's personal dislike of Douglas Hyde had been
instantaneous at their first meeting; and he was humiliated
by Hyde's lack of responsiveness in not including him
also on the Coisde Gnótha. His description in *Ave* of the
'Irish streaming like porter through Hyde's long black
moustache,' when he responded to Edward's call for a
speech, showed a lamentable lack of enthusiasm when
precept had to be put in practice. And in *Salve* there is a

Douglas Hyde

From the painting by Miss Sara Purser, R.H.A.

melancholy account of the failure of his own speech at a
public meeting organised by the Gaelic League in
Dublin.

Edward's personal contribution to the language revival
consisted chiefly in a persistent propaganda in the newspapers. He had learned enough to be able to read it in its
modern form, and with the prevailing enthusiasm he
adopted the habit of signing himself in Irish, and having
his book-plate printed with his name and the word
Tulira in Gaelic. Most of his acquaintance with Gaelic
literature was, of course, derived from the translations
published by Douglas Hyde and Dr. Sigerson and others,
and from the intensely dramatic versions of the old Irish
sagas that were presented by Standish O'Grady in his
Cuchulain and his stories of Finn and his Companions.
O'Grady's own knowledge was even more derivative
than Edward Martyn's, and he was even unaware of how
the name Cuchulain should be pronounced. Patrick
Pearse, who had at this time been appointed as a very
young man to the editorship of the official Gaelic League
organ, the *Claidheamh Soluis*, corrected O'Grady when he
pronounced the name in its straightforward English
acceptation as Cutch-ul-ane, and told him that the right
pronunciation was Coo-hu-lin. O'Grady was overwhelmed by the discovery, and after a long pause informed Pearse that he would have written an entirely
different book if he had known the correct sound of the
name. But his sense of the vigour and chivalry of the
Irish sagas was superb, and he did more than anyone to
popularise them and make them known.

Edward Martyn, indeed, explained boldly in one of
his articles in the *Claidheamh Soluis* that 'my studies of

Irish have convinced me that it is finer and more beautiful
than any language I know, except Greek, which will
always be to me the most beautiful, the tongue of the
highest civilisation the world has ever seen. It was
indeed my Hellenism that first led me to the Irish
language through the subtle Greek refinements I found
in Irish ornamental art.' He was on surer ground,
however, in explaining his own attitude towards those
who decried the language revival as being of no practical
value. 'When that question is put to me,' he wrote,
'often by persons with a brogue as strong as pickle that
will float potatoes, I am sorely tempted to answer this-
wise: "In order, my friend, that you who would be able to
pronounce the Irish so splendidly, might for ever be
prevented from murdering the English."' No two
languages in the world, he argued, blend less well than
Irish and English. 'The English accent is horrible in
Irish, and the Irish accent horrible in English.' What
he resented most was 'our present mongrel state
of being neither one thing nor the other, where
we meanly ape with hopeless failure the gross opulence
of England, so that even a complete and thorough
anglicisation, which as I say I believe impossible, would
be preferable.

'It is to this mongrel condition, in which we are, that
may be attributed such loss of character and enterprise as
causes the general inefficiency pervading all effort in
Ireland, and the fatalistic doctrine that nothing Irish can
succeed. Nothing Irish will ever succeed until Ireland
shakes off her self-imposed slavery and becomes really
Irish again. Until then she always will be wanting in
initiative, and nothing that is attempted for her improve-

ment can permanently succeed. This is how her native language is necessary for her material welfare. She had, therefore, better set about de-anglicising herself and making herself Irish without delay if there is to be any hope, morally, intellectually, and commercially, for her in the future. Now the foundation of de-anglicisation and of Irish nationalism is the Irish language. The first and most necessary work is to make it again the spoken language of the country, because all other works undertaken in the interests of nationalism without this first foundation work are as efforts to construct houses after the manner of the Doctrinaires in Swift's quack university, whose project was to begin at the roof and work down to the foundation.

'Thus the national language, by awakening our dormant distinctive genius will render us virile and independent, and consequently fitted to obtain full benefit from the labours of reformers and economists who now find us so unmanageable because of our timid apathy. It will also be a check to the appalling emigration that threatens to totally depopulate Ireland; for the enemies of the language always say that Irish prevents people from leaving the country to earn their bread. Precisely. And if it does nothing else this will be an advanatge gained. But it will do more. It will educate and fit the people to deal intelligently and successfully with the wiles of brigand government in English interests against our prosperous development. It will enable Irishmen to make a living in their own country by changing Ireland from a desolate province with no distinctive existence, except the distinction of faded inferiority, into a small flourishing nation.'

He even contributed a penny pamphlet to the series published by the Gaelic League, with the challenging title of *Ireland's Battle for Her Language*, which took the form of a violent attack upon the National Education Board. 'At the present moment,' he wrote, 'the fate of the Irish language is in the hands of the Irish people. It is useless to try to shift the responsibility upon the shoulders of England or the British Government or any other of those scapegoats whom the lazy, the unpractical, the lovers of declamation rather than action, find it convenient to blame for their own shortcomings. Even that arch-enemy of our nationality and regeneration, the National Board of Education, upon whom the Chief Secretary now has shifted his own responsibility, cannot altogether be blamed if at this juncture the cause of bilingual education in the National schools is lost. The real responsibility is with the Irish people who have the power, if they care sufficiently for their language and distinctive existence to use it, of just forcing the National Board to agree with all their wishes anent the teaching and furtherance of our native tongue.'

The method which he proposed to achieve that object was simply to exercise the control over legislation which was in the hands of the political electorate. 'The people of Ireland have only to exercise that right and they can obtain all they want. They have just to see that this question of the language is made a test question for their representatives at the approaching General Election. Against a representation of nearly eighty members pledged to fight and vote in Parliament for the language, I should like to know how long half a dozen contumacious commissioners would continue their impudent opposition?

They would soon find themselves flung out of their seats of authority, and moreover they would drag with them in their fall many who, because of their growing insecurity and the rising tide of democracy, are now making one last despairing effort, aided by Freemasonry and kindred underhand helps, to maintain their bigoted anti-Irish ascendancy.'

The pamphlet continued in a hysterical diatribe against English vulgarity and hypocrisy, which showed how intensely anti-English he had become since the Boer War. This hostility became an obsession with him as he grew older, and it found expression in all his criticisms of social customs and culture in Ireland. A remarkable instance, which shows how his original power of vigorous writing and outspoken criticism was gradually being spoilt by his extravagant prejudices, was an article which he selected for the conclusion of his projected collection of essays, attacking the institution of public-house bars—which he regarded as a particularly degrading importation from England.

'One of our greatest misfortunes,' he wrote, 'in our subjugation by England and in our adoption of her language and customs is that, with the shedding of our national characteristics and culture, we appear to have sunk into such a sort of barbarism as forces us to assimilate from our conqueror almost nothing but his meanest and coarsest traits and institutions. The realisation of this melancholy fact has passed into a commonplace now; and we see even the upper classes in Ireland emulating England in her coarsest materialism, where they might be expected to set a good example to the rest of our countrymen. But then our upper classes, with less culture than their order elsewhere in Europe possesses, and with less patriotism than was even felt by negro slaves, are, for over a century passed, a disgrace to the country. Being what we are, therefore, it is not surprising that when we had cast off our customs, we should have given the go-by to whatever good thing England had to offer us — her great literature, her incomparable poetry, her culture, which, if much inferior to that of the Continent, is still considerable — and that we should have sought to emulate her in voracity for her gutter literature, her horse-racing, her gambling, her prize fighting, for the inanity of her theatres, the crudity of her music-halls, and lastly, for the demoralisation of her own unique invention — namely her public-house, with its standing bar.

'The standing bar is the thing! This is what has made drunkards of so many Irish people. Before the coming of this bestial English institution (to which I must admit our classes and masses took with amazing naturalness, in conformity with the ease with which they shook off national customs and language) drunkenness was never in any way remarkable in Ireland. But now this country, like England, has the reputation of being one of the most drunken in the world. There never was an institution like the public-house and standing bar so well calculated to make drunkards. The ease and convenience with which men and women can drink, the privacy, if required, of the snuggery, the physical fascinations of the barmaid who has to listen to the customers' coarse inanities — all combined to make that English invention, the standing bar, an irresistible inducement to drunkenness. So much is this the case that if we were to establish standing bars in those cities of Northern Europe which *A Rambler* says a highly-respected merchant tailor of this city found so sober, I am certain we would soon make them as drunken as Ireland was made by the same process.

'What then, is the remedy for our state of drunkenness? Nothing short, I say, than the abolition by law of the standing bar and the public-house and the substitution of the continental *café* system, where there are no standing bars, where everyone must sit at a table and be served by a waiter, where food can be obtained as in a restaurant, where there are no snuggeries, and where the passers-by outside may see in through the windows. This is the system of sober countries whose system we must adopt, if we can hope to become, like them, sober. There is not the least use in closing public-houses arbitrarily at inconvenient hours. The cause of the disease is in the institution itself. Here in Ireland our remedy seems to be as savage as is the cause of the disease. In order that people may not soak at standing bars, decent folk are prevented from having their meals in hotels or restaurants. I suppose there is not another country in the world, except Ireland, where you cannot have supper in a hotel after the theatre, or where on Sundays you may starve, except between 2 and 3 p.m., if you do not happen to be able to get your meals at your residence. Let us have restaurants, then, for the poor as well as for the rich, like on the Continent, and open at convenient hours, and let no intoxicating drink be sold except in such restaurants, and, of course, in shops where there is no drinking.

'Alas! I know these projects will, as usual, be considered exaggerated and absurd in a country, like this, inhabited by a slack-baked population whose so-called

education engenders general revolt against what is
considered reasonable or fine in any normal country.
But whether my project is absurd or unpractical, or whatever else my slack-baked countrymen of all classes may
elect to call it, I assert, and I think I have proved, that it
is the only means of sobering Ireland permanently. You
may have, as *A Rambler* suggests, a Father Mathew in
every street, you may improve people's dwellings, but all
your labour will be lost, and drunkenness will return, as
long as the bestial system of the standing bar remains.
The public-house and standing bar will make all our
temperance reforms in the present and in the future as
they made them in the past — ephemeral.'

For years he had been a loyal supporter of the various
manifestations of native traditions which were encouraged
by the Gaelic League. He was naturally in complete
sympathy with its remarkably successful and interesting
work for the revival of Irish music. Even the programme
of Irish dancing, which provided the lighter side of its
social activities, but could not arouse him to any real
enthusiasm, received his public support. He had always
detested dancing as a peculiarly idiotic form of recreation,
and all his queer hostility towards women rose up in him
when he was obliged to watch the competitions in traditional dances at a Gaelic League festival. At last his
impatience broke out in an article in the *Claidheamh
Soluis* in which he modestly proposed 'to hint merely at
such reforms as would make the spectacle of Irish dancing
more grateful to the æsthetic beholder.'

To write about dancing at all was, he admitted, rash
'for a man who cannot dance and who never could be
taught dancing.' 'I have painful recollections,' he con-

fessed, 'of having been when a small boy, forcibly dragged against my will, while protesting and kicking, to Monsieur Garbois' Dancing Academy in Stephen's Green, where that great man, whose real name was Garvey, dazzled my imagination with his talk about hunting and shooting, and his rooms in Vienna and Paris, and where I made scarce any progress beyond being taught to walk like a hen around the room.' Nevertheless, he now felt it to be his duty 'to call attention to the look of gravity which petrifies the features of every dancer. A more unsuitable accompaniment to what is supposed to be such a joyous performance as the dance it is impossible to imagine. And yet a naturally gay people like us Irish think it incumbent upon us to act in a manner so inconsistent. It would greatly enhance the pleasure of the spectator to see a gayer expression on the features of our dancers, who, I hope, will take the suggestion in good part.

'Then again, there is another fault in our dancers which has given rise to serious criticism, and that is the habit of hanging their arms down rigidly by their sides during the evolution of their steps. Surely this must be altogether wrong. No amount of appealing to usage on the part of our experts would convince me that this was the habit in ancient times, when such a thing as a common thought or an ugly action was unknown. Surely the object of the dance is to throw into grace of motion the frame of the dancer; and how can this object be achieved with such important limbs as the arms in rigid protest against the activity of the others?

'Lastly, I come to an objection against Irish dancing which, unlike the two previous criticisms, can be used against the dancing of all other nations in Western civilisation. I mean the gross unfitness of its practice by any except those of the female sex. I must say that it has always shocked my æsthetic sense to see a man, nay, even a boy, dance. There is something degrading in the male being thus engaged in this essentially female pastime, and it fills the heart with sorrow and commiseration, as when we see humanity lowered to some undignified use.

'On the other hand, there is nothing that shows the female to so great an advantage as the dance. For the time her unideal and somewhat absurd figure assumes a beauty of outline never to be imagined in any other circumstance. Truly the Palæstra of the female is the Dancing Academy! Therein is her fitting exercise, not in the athletic exercise which misguided people are now forcing on women, and for which females are most unsuitable, in that it only emphasises their limitations and ridiculous want of beauty in its highest manifestations. Such exercises should be left to the male portion of humanity — the pride of the Palæstra. How well the glorious ancients understood all this! Fellow countrymen, if you would be heroes, content yourselves with being spectators, but shun the practice of the dance!'

Looking back on his own activities as a Gaelic Leaguer, Edward wrote some candid criticism in his last years. His sympathy with its aims had never abated, and he had given an unhesitating lead to other Catholics in defying the disapproval of the bishops when they issued their manifesto against making the Irish language a compulsory subject for the National University. In his will he left a large legacy to endow the training of Irish teachers

in the Irish-speaking districts. But for years, until
Douglas Hyde resigned from the Presidency of the
Gaelic League, when he could no longer prevent it
from becoming a political body, Edward had been
discouraged by its refusal to adopt a strongly Nationalist
attitude.

'In the Gaelic League,' he wrote in the preface to his
collected papers, 'I make no special claim to be a reformer, for here we are all reformers, and I must say that
the Gaelic League has done great work in so far prevailing
with our country that did not want the Irish language — a
fact proved by the apathy of National School managers
who had the power, if they wished, of making Ireland
Irish-speaking ten years ago. For many years I was one
of the Coisde Gnótha, or governing body; but somehow
I have always felt out of my element at public meetings
and deliberative assemblies. It is only in moments of
great crisis that I seemingly awaken to the situation and
succeed in making order out of confusion. Thus at the
Gaelic League, when the question of compulsory Irish
at the National University appeared to raise a babel of
diverse opinions, I plunged amidst the babel and told
them straight that if they failed to procure this they would
fail in the chief object of their existence, and survive their
failure a very short time; and that unless the Gaelic
League put their whole strength into the fight, I would
publicly resign as a protest. This, I think, had its effect
on the talkers and the time servers. Shortly afterwards,
I addressed a vigorous public meeting at Castlebar,
which seems to have given the lead to all Ireland. The
District Council and other public bodies one after
another came effectually into line. The County Councils

R

threatened stoppage of scholarships, with the result on the party-coloured Senate that everyone knows.

'I had for a long time another conviction anent the policy of the Gaelic League which I carefully refrained from ventilating during the presidency of our distinguished friend, Dr. Hyde, who I may say created the revival, carrying enthusiasm for our native language around the world, and for whose opinion on this subject — upon which we differed — I always had the most deferential respect. However, now that he has seen good to resign on this very question, and that the Gaelic League is fresh and vigorous again owing to Government opposition, I do not think there is any need for my further reticence, especially as I think his resignation, being mistaken, has strengthened my conviction.

'My conviction is that the fundamental rule of the Gaelic League prohibiting politics was a fundamental mistake. Of course, I understand the large view of interesting all Ireland in the native speech which a non-political propaganda ideally sought, but I believe that view to have never been anything but a dream. It might as well be expected to unite her on any other reform. The Unionists as a body dislike the Irish language probably as much as Home Rule, equality of the Nationalists with themselves, or land reform. For them the language that European scholars revere is only the gibberish of natives whom they look upon just as the natives of this first of England's colonies in point of time, and whom it is preposterous to put on a level with themselves, the colonists. I do not think the Nationalists quite realise this, but I who have been in both camps know what is in the hearts of either side.

'That is why I hold, and I think recent events bear me out, that it is futile to placate the ascendancy. They simply must be made to accept the Irish language as they were made to accept other reforms hitherto. This being so, it is easy to see what a mistake it was for the Gaelic League to deprive itself of the chief driving force of all other language revivals in Europe for the sake of placating an unreasoning stubborn body whom they should have known they never could placate. All language revivals have been intensely political except ours, whose strength has been sapped for the miserable result of gaining certainly not more than twenty from the Unionists; while a Government, ignorant as usual of Irish ideals, has recently failed to differentiate the Gaelic League, in spite of all its efforts to be non-political, from the Gaelic Athletic Association.

'Of course it should have been violently political first. Instead of antagonising the Parliamentary Party and thereby making unnecessary difficulties for itself in the country it should have hung on to the coat-tails of the Emm. Pees, dogged them everywhere, supported them at all their meetings with Irish speeches, and always insisted upon their learning Irish. Thus it could have inserted itself into the powerful national life of Ireland, and gained great strength with the people, whom it could have educated effectually to avoid the pitfalls into which they were eventually led.'

Although his best-known and most effective achievement in raising the standard of Irish music was the foundation of the Palestrina Choir in Dublin, Edward was still prouder that he had been the first person among his contemporaries to rediscover the existence of a traditional Irish music, still surviving among the peasantry. 'My chief work,' he writes in the introduction to his *Paragraphs for the Perverse*, 'was the discovery towards the end of 1898 of a traditional singing among the peasantry, as a more or less rustic survival of the art of the Bards, and the evident corruption of its exquisite melody and tonality by subsequent musicians, as for instance, the editors of Moore's *Melodies*, etc. Of course I was ridiculed by our miserable musicians,' he reflects, 'the fitting brood of those who disgraced themselves by allowing our old harp tradition to die out at the end of the eighteenth century. My ideas thereon are now universally admitted, and with the foundation at University College, Cork, of a chair for traditional singing and music, we are in a good way of preserving Irish music from Irish musicians.

'However, in our efforts to improve music generally, success, although hopeful at first, has been dwindling. At one time the Dublin Orchestral Society and the Sunday Orchestral Concerts so ably conducted by Dr. Esposito promised great things. He is a pianist of the first rank and a composer of note, especially for his particular instrument. In his unselfish labours for the education of the people to an appreciation of orchestral music of the highest quality, he has shown himself a true artist, and among our many importations the only one practically useful to our country. He carried on his brave and civilising reforms from 1899 until they were suddenly stopped by the war of the Philistines for the alleged interests of civilisation.'

Dr. Esposito's concerts, like almost every other significant enterprise in Ireland during that period, owed much

to Edward's unfailing generosity. In this case he shared
the burden with a public-spirited gentleman who was
also the donor of notable pictures to Sir Hugh Lane's
Gallery of Modern Art, Mr. W. P. Geoghegan. Writing
to Edward after the conclusion of the first series of
recitals in the spring of 1906, Mr. Geoghegan reported
that the receipts had totalled £413 against an expenditure
of £442. 'I don't know how you feel about it,' he said,
'but in my opinion the result for a beginning is very good,
and I think Esposito deserves the greatest credit. As I
have embarked on the enterprise with the expectation of
a loss, I would not like to see Esposito quite unpaid, and
I therefore propose to you that we pay £25 each, which
would leave Esposito £21 for his own services and pay off
the loss.' It was not often that the public responded so
helpfully, and that Edward's share as a guarantor of
expenses was so light.

In music, no less than in art and in the drama, he was
more concerned with the cultivation of a national tradition than with the creation of popular enthusiasm for his
own interests. The mere idea of gathering together large
numbers of people who would not otherwise have thought
of coming to hear good music had little attraction for
him. His abiding preoccupation was to discover native
talent, being convinced that it would win wide recognition inevitably, if only it was encouraged to express
itself.

'If you speak of national composers at the present
time,' he wrote in an essay on Schools of National Music,
'you are frequently met with the remark that so and so is
only a hunter after local colour, and that the really great
masters neglected local colour, and were universal.

Then certain votaries of local colour are brought forward as examples of those musicians who had a fashion for a time, but whose fashions soon passed away. Among these notably was David, who went to the East, and returned and wrote *Le Désert*, a symphony built upon the airs and tonality of Arab music; so that the Paris of the 'forties hailed him as the chief prodigy since Beethoven. Only old Aubert seemed to doubt when he said: "Ah, yes, this is all very well, but I should like to see what our friend Félicien César could do, if only he were to come down off the back of his camel." And when he did come down off his camel, he no longer pleased people some-how — at least not by any means to the same extent as before. At the present day he is little more than a name. And so the world has grown suspicious of local colour, and rightly so, when local colour is seized upon by the composer for effect in order to give an air of originality to his work.

'There is, however, another kind of local colour, which is natural, and, indeed, indispensable to all genuine composers of genius. I mean the peculiar quality of melody and tonality which marks the mass of that mysterious, untraceable music, growing somehow out of the folk of his country. This is the material out of which all the great music in the world has evolved. This folk music of each country, with its characteristics of that country, stamps the national character of that country's school of cultured composers. This is a self-evident fact when we turn to such a composer as Grieg. There is no need to emphasise the influence of Norwegian tonality and melody in his compositions. In fact, their very colour has been made a plea that he cannot be very great, because he is so influenced by local colour. The answer to this is, of course, that Grieg is the creator and founder of the cultured music of Norway, which he was the first, or among the first, to develop from the folk melodies of his native country, himself first being thoroughly imbued with its native music.

'But it may still be objected that Mozart and Beethoven have never done this. That is true; and the reason is because they evolved their art out of some two centuries of cultured German music. But that music had originally been evolved from the German folk. And if the local colour of that folk music is, to many, unrecognisable in Beethoven now, it is because the evolution from it is so long ago, and the great German music has since flown all over the world, and established for itself an universality. But its local colour still clings to it all the same; only we cannot recognise it, because of the universality, the proof being that it is its local colour that distinguishes it from Italian music and from French music, which have their local colour each in the same way, and which differentiates them from each other and from the German. There can be no other way to account for their various differences. And manifest differences there are between them in style and character and colour, as any understander of music must see. What was the particular local colour that left its stamp on each? I will trace it briefly.

'The most ancient school, that of Italy, took its origin from the Gregorian Chant, the origins of which were partly Greek and Jewish chants, and partly also the pagan folk songs of the Etruscans. This Italian music arising from the Gregorian was vocal polyphony, as it was called, and was chiefly used for liturgical purposes. Thus the origin of the Italian school was religious, and, moreover, whether the Italians may like it or not, the finest music they ever produced was religious. Palestrina, whatever position he may hold among the world's composers (I think him the greatest of all, if I may be permitted an opinion) is certainly the greatest of the Italians.

'The purely instrumental music doubtless was better than opera. There were many great men like the Scarlattis, Marcello, and in a lesser way Galuppi and Boccherini. But that did not prevent the fact remaining that Italian music had been going down since Palestrina, until it reached its dotage in Bellini. Then came a mock revival in the egregious Verdi — that old opera banditti chief, with his hat on the side of his head, who pounced upon wandering Wagnerisms, and cast them into a big *olla podrida* pot always simmering in the grotto of his imagination, where the winds made grotesque sounds. He was the father of that later brood of Mascagnis, Puccinis, etc., who have helped with her other artists, in their different domains, to pull down the wondrous Italy of the Renaissance from her throne over the arts.

'The two other most important schools of music, Germany and France, started about the same time. Germany, by far the greater of the two, arose from the local colour of the *meistersingers* and *folk hymns*, acting on the splendid church polyphony of Aichinger, Jakob Handel (not George Friedrich of the vulgarised oratorios), Heinrich Schutz, and others. To an Italian or a French musician of that time, German music, so different in fibre from either of theirs, as it even appears to us to-day, must have seemed exceedingly coloured by German folk music. It is needless to trace its course. It produced three out of the four greatest musicians of the world — Palestrina, Bach, Beethoven, and Wagner. It is now suffering an eclipse. In Richard Strauss it has in some respects perhaps found its Verdi. What are to be the future German Mascagnis and Puccinis imagination shrinks with horror from contemplating.

'The French school is not nearly so important. It never produced a man to be compared with the giants of the Italian and German schools. At the same time it has had several fine composers, and a colour and style quite its own, due of course, as with the two previous schools, to its own peculiar folk music, which at the beginning, together with the troubadours, influenced the writers of madrigals and old church polyphony. At first this school was called Franco-Flemish, from its association with the great contrapuntalists of the Netherlands. Its chief exponents were the great Josquin des Prés, Pierre de la Rue, and later Claude Gondimel. There was a certain influence afterwards in Lulli, which again became very French in Rameau, a delightful contemporary of Bach. The French invented a native comic opera, of a bright, clean-cut quality, a very appropriate development from its lovely folk origin, and if they have not risen to the immortal heights of the Italian or German, they appear still to flourish, possessing the greatest of living composers in the exquisite Claude Debussy.

'It will be seen now that what people call world music is one of either three kinds, Italian, or German, or French, the differences between which are easily recognisable; and the only way to account for such differences must be the differences of origin, or local colour. The casual observer, I repeat, does not perceive this, because he is accustomed to the hearing of this world music in all countries. But already Grieg, who had but lately come out of the folk, is heard everywhere. So are the Russians and Smetana, the Bohemian. He therefore puts them down for local colourists only while they are really proceeding quite naturally. How could they do otherwise, and have a chance of being great? Do we ever hear of any one attaining greatness by writing in any other style than that of his native country?

'What moral, then, does all this point to for musicians who would be composers in Ireland? I say nothing of the foreigners amongst us. They will, doubtless, go along the lines of their own various nationalities. But what is the course for Irishmen? Why, it is obviously to do what all other nations have done when they founded their native school of music — to go to the folk and become thoroughly imbued with native tonality and rhythm and melody, and then to exercise their invention and learning in evolving a developed art under this influence. It is useless to study a number of so-called Irish airs out of collections, and think that you are filling yourself with the spirit of Irish music. These airs are nearly all altered and corrupted to fit the characteristics of world-music, which is either Italian or German or French, as we have seen. If peasant music is sophisticated, it dies, and can, consequently, be of no use to the Irish composer. In fact, such music as Moore's *Melodies*, where the real character of Irish folk music has, through some unfortunate process of sophistication got to be eliminated, are a barrier against the formation of an Irish native school.

As with everything in Ireland, everything has been gone about in the wrong way; so that any right thing, perchance now advocated, is looked upon as some monstrous eccentricity. If there had been a collection of Norwegian airs mutilated like some of our collections, Grieg might not have appeared. He might have been merely an obscure fumbler among native rubbish. But whether there were such collections or not, it is certain they had no influence on Grieg, who went straight to the folk, and became diluted with the finest qualities of folk music.

'The one musician in Ireland who followed — perhaps unconsciously — Grieg's example, was the late O'Brien Butler, who perished, with the half score of his opera too, I fear — to the irreparable detriment of Irish music — on the *Lusitania* in 1915. He was brought up among the folk singers and pipers of Kerry, so that he may be said to have the folk or real Irish music in his blood. His *songs*, his *violin and piano sonata*, and, above all, his opera *Muirgheis*, are as strongly marked with the folk character of Ireland as that of Grieg is with the Norwegian; and without wishing to make a comparison in any other way between the two, I may say at least that the work of O'Brien Butler is quite an interesting foundation for a native school of music. Let those who are better, or consider themselves better than him, go along the path he has shown, and overtake him if they can with superior works.

'Outside this path (for, as we have shown it is not only the path of Grieg, but of the founders of all other schools of native music) they may compose music, but it will not be Irish music; and it is seldom a man has attained real greatness as a composer in the school of a nationality foreign to him. In fact, I think the only one who ever did was the Irishman, John Field, who went to live in Russia, invented the nocturn, and became one of the influencers of Chopin. He appears to have been a person in himself. We see how David fared when he went abroad for local colour — no doubt momentarily successful — but then when he got down off his camel. . . . Dvorak, the Bohemian, was also not very successful when he left his natural local colour to take on that of the blacks of the United States. There is all the difference in the world in writing in one's mother tonality and in adopting a foreign one. It is like trying to write literature in a foreign language. How many have succeeded? One is genuine, the other is false.

'Therefore, until a number of Irish musicians become imbued with the genuine folk music of Ireland, and reflect it in their works, we shall never have a native school of music. But meantime we must also take care that the folk-singing, piping and fiddling are preserved among the people as jealously as the Irish language, because if they now were to go, all chance of this Irish school of composers would go with them. Then besides, Ireland is always late about everything. It appears from what I have written that the future of music mostly lies with the small nationalities. Now therefore is Ireland's time. Let her take advantage of it. For this reason I am anxious that she should have the necessarily right ideas before making the attempt.'

It was Edward's boast that he had himself discovered one of the most interesting forms of Irish folk music. In the autumn of 1898, he had written for Sir Horace

Plunkett's *Daily Express* an article on *The Use of a Provincial Féis*, describing his own impressions of one such event in his own county. Long afterwards, in including the article in his *Paragraphs for the Perverse*, he altered the title to 'How I was the First to Discover Traditional Singing.' 'On the 1st of September, 1898,' the article ran, 'was held at Galway, under the auspices of the local Gaelic League, one of those provincial music festivals which it has been a chief aim of the Féis Ceóil to inspire and encourage throughout Ireland. The excellence and success of this experiment will, no doubt, cause other provincial centres to follow so spirited a lead, and in time we may hope to see the whole country alive to that store of ancient art which is hidden away in her remote places.

'One of the chief characteristics of this competition and concert, where the performers were all peasants, was what might have been a surprise to most people, but was none to me, namely, *a complete absence of vulgarity* — that hideous art defiler which stalks like a skeleton at most art feasts of the present day. Here, on the contrary, it was a refreshing surprise to hear certain Irish airs, which in modern versions have grown so corrupted, now rendered in their ancient form, with those turns and closes of an unmistakable mediævalism preserved. A most conspicuous example of this preservation of antiquity was in the singing of what I had hitherto considered cloying and obvious as melody, until on this occasion, I heard it redolent with charms of mediævalism and sung to Celtic words, as it was, no doubt, handed down in the musical traditions of the old people. The effect was marvellously refined and redolent of ancient beauty, and sounded after

previous experiences much the same as the Benedictine
singing of the Gregorian chant of Solesmes sounds to the
one who has been accustomed to the mutilated and
vulgarised version in the Ratisbon Gradual.

'Such a discovery would naturally lead the lover of
music to inquire into the cause of the deterioration. Is it
because Irish melodies are set to English words that they
lose their genuine flavour? It is a well-known fact in
literature that the *anglicisation of Irish names results almost
always in sounds of a peculiar meanness and ugliness*. On
the other hand, these names, as they are pronounced and
spelt in Irish, are invariably beautiful. Indeed a fatal
deterioration of the Celt would seem to follow from his
contact with the Saxon. His incomparable sense of
refinement and elegance, which made him the most
exquisite of artists — witness the ornamental Romanesque
of Ireland and the Gothic of Northern France — fades
and vanishes before the comparative grossness and materialism of the Saxon touch. What remains after this
defilement of his nature is a certain emasculated
materialism, which gives him a character that appears so
colourless and mean. That is why in those parts of
Ireland which are much affected with English influences
we generally remark a certain air of second-hand, shabby
England defacing all objects and customs. Where,
however, there are no such influences, the face of the land
is not thus dismally defaced. The result is that while the
inhabitants of the shabby England are often vulgar, the
Celtic peasants of the uncontaminated West are naturally
refined; and that is the explanation of the fact that
vulgarity was absent from this little music festival of
peasants. For these considerations then, if for no others,

the Celtic language and art of Ireland should be preserved, and further efforts at anglicisation should be
strenuously resisted. After all, in Ireland, there is no work
of man of equal value or interest to that of her ancient
language and art. If they are allowed to die, the country
will become one of the most doleful wildernesses in
Europe. They are kept alive by those humble gatherings
and festivals.'

Some years later he contributed to the Gaelic League's
organ, the *Claidheamh Soluis*, an account of a particular
singer whom he had lately heard again at Tuam. 'I have
heard Bartly Walsh sing many songs on different occasions, and I find it difficult to convey all my appreciation
of what I believe to be the unique excellence of his
performance. I have really never heard anything of its
kind so good. It reminds me of beautiful Gregorian
singing, or of Orientals chanting in old mysterious tonality. The flexibility of his voice is very remarkable.
There is never an effort. Always well within himself, he
goes through passages of extreme intricacy of note and
delicacy of interval with an accuracy of ear and feeling
for expression that are equally admirable.

'It is obvious to any cultured person that the loss of
such a native art as this would be a national calamity,
second only to the loss of the Irish language itself. Here
we have evidently a remnant of the style of our ancient
bards. And what a noble masculine style it is! How
different from the drawing-room insincerities and puling
sentimentalities of latter-day melody singing, with its
mawkish modernisation of our melodies to suit the
sugary or, as the case may be, bombastic commonplace
of the words! This Irish singing is redolent of the beauti-

ful ingenuousness and sincerity of mediæval art; and the old music like the old sagas has a rich colour and a strong native flavour. Neither it nor the saga are perhaps finished works of art, but they are the materials from which the composer or the poet makes master-works. From such sagas floating about Greece, Homer fashioned his epics as Grieg and Smetana their music from the richly coloured peasant tunes of their respective countries. Traditional singing's chief appeal, like that of the great liturgical song, is to those of the highest culture, and to those who are simple and unspoiled. At the same time, traditional singers, however good, are curiously out of place on the platform of a large hall with their rustic art sandwiched between the varied layers of sublimer provincial respectability. Their home is by the cottage fire, among the mountains, or by the wild wet sea. But I can well imagine they are horrible and barbarous to superior-minded mediocrities, who are more victims of a false and perverse education, and who in their self-complacency have reduced this country almost to a wilderness of inanity.

'It remains, therefore, for us, Gaelic Leaguers, to consider how we may preserve this old music and dying tradition of Irish singing. An interest in it has been aroused in Tuam; and I think that Tuam should be made the centre in Ireland for its preservation and cultivation. The children must be taught it. A Summer School for Irish Singing might be established in Tuam. We hope at the next Féis there to give many prizes to the children for proficiency in this respect. It would also be well at the Dublin Oireachtas to give prizes both to them and the grown-up singers. By this means the old would be induced to teach the young and the young to learn of the old, when they see their ancient art once more restored to honour in Ireland.'

His friend, the composer O'Brien Butler actually wrote an Irish opera called *Muirgheis*, of which Edward published his considered criticism in the *Leader*, which shows his capacity for enthusiasm over a genuine attempt to provide what he so much hoped to discover. 'After my first hearing a complete performance of O'Brien Butler's opera *Muirgheis* in the Theatre Royal in December, 1913, where it ran for a week with great success, I became aware that its chief defect was in the libretto. The story as outlined in three acts is well constructed, but in its detailed working out it is overloaded with songs and dialogue through all the acts, which, as far as I can judge, not having read the libretto, seem unnecessary, and to delay and obstruct the dramatic movement. Then, in the second act, where Muirgheis is being enticed away to Tir na nOg, the fairy vision which breaks in on the marriage feast is, without adequate reason, cut in two by a sudden return to an interval of the real life, and thus has much of its elusive beauty destroyed. These faults have their effect upon the singers in some instances by producing unnecessary fatigue, and upon the music written for the orchestra also; because even in such scenes as the entrance of Donn of the Sandhills in the first act, and the duet between Diarmuid and Máire in the first scene of the third act, the orchestral illustration is clearly inadequate for the dramatic exigencies of the situations.

'With these reservations, however, I have nothing but praise for the work. The music is most beautiful, refined

s

and original. There is not a trace of vulgarity in it from beginning to end. The orchestra is always well balanced and often disclosed exquisite devices of instrumentation. Those other qualities of beauty in the music which I originally recognised, even in the meagre performances of the concerts, now came out in manifold intensity. Beauty is indeed the quality by which this music is most affected. It is hard to imagine a more refined beauty than that in the fairie music at the end of the second act, with its strange wistful chorus for soprano and alti calling Muirgheis away to Tir na nOg, where the moving melody of the alti touches the whole with colour like to saffron sunlight of the Sidhe.

'Except in the *Rheingold* or *Götterdämmerung* or *Parsifal* I have heard no choral writing in modern times more beautiful than this. The songs, too, have reminiscences of the old traditional singers' melodies, and are accompanied often by most charming and characteristic themes with great skill on certain instruments in the band. In the ballet music there is a reel full of movement and classic gracefulness where the passing from the first to the second part has so enchanting an effect. When the libretto of this opera is tightened and translated into Irish, and when the music is intensified in the more dramatic duets, it will be a real delight to see it performed again, for it contains some of the most beautiful modern music I know.'

To the Gaelic League he looked, and directly appealed, to assist in preserving the tradition of Irish folk music. 'The Gaelic League,' he wrote in another article, 'if it succeeds in preserving the folk airs in their purity, will be doing a work of the highest art value for posterity. The only satisfactory way it can preserve them it seems to me, is by having numerous records, now while so many are available, taken on the gramophone or some other improved instrument for recording sounds, because no matter what pains we may be at to induce teaching of the young by the old, many songs must thus be lost, and in all cases their preservation be precarious. This is sure to give an exact reproduction of the intervals and rendering. It is my opinion for reasons (as in the case of the Moorish melody) I have already stated that, except in dance music, none of our collections (not even the great one of Petrie) has successfully noted our music. The delicate intervals and rich colour of the song, as it is sung by a really good singer, is almost always absent. And that the singer must be good is, of course, indispensable. There are so many bad country singers, that for most people the folk song is a thing of disrepute. But there are fortunately, some excellent singers too, male and female; moreover, even in Dublin there are some who have learned the style amazingly well. One of the chief requisites for such a singer is to have a very perfect ear, without which it will be impossible to render correctly the exquisite refinements of phrase and oriental tonality in the best traditional singing.

'As an objection against the value of our folk music it is sometimes said that it never can be accurately preserved because we do not know in what scale or scales it is written. At all events, the experts are not agreed as to scale. I do not think this much matters. What we require is to preserve in their purity the songs as traditionally sung, by having them mechanically reproduced. This will ensure a body of folk art whose peculiar national

character will affect our future composers, who will
doubtless write their music in the modern major and
minor scales all the same. Some may consider this an
impossibility; but I do not think it is, because we do not
want to imitate the folk music. We only want to take our
colour and rhythm from it. No doubt it would be satisfactory if the true Irish folk scale was scientifically
demonstrated, because it would put the whole study on
surer foundations. But we must remember that the
preservation of Irish folk music is chiefly important not
for its own sake, but for the vital influence it may have
on the future as a means whereby immortal works may
yet arise out of Ireland. We may or may not have great
composers in the future. But there is one thing certain,
and that is we shall never have them at all, if we are only
to depend upon what passes for Irish music in the various
printed collections.'

Slowly, indeed, but with an undeniable success, more
evident even than in any other enterprise of the Irish
renaissance, the revival of Irish music has gathered
strength in recent years through the organisation of the
Féis Ceóil, or musical festival. Its first meeting was held
in Dublin in May 1897, and was so successful that other
meetings were held each year, nearly always in Dublin.
Looking back after fifteen years since that first experiment, Edward Martyn was able to write with his usual
straightforwardness in the *Leader* that: 'It is surprising
when we consider the state Ireland was musically
fifteen years ago, to see her progress, for although the
public taste is as low, if not lower than ever, still the
practice of music has multiplied out of expectation. This
is all due to the Féis Ceóil, and especially is this the case

in instrumental music which, according to reports of the
judges, seems to have reached quite a phenomenal degree
of excellence, far surpassing the choirs or other vocal
sections, notwithstanding the fact that the Féis Ceóil has
introduced some distinguished singers who have since
become celebrated all over the world. The Féis Ceóil is
an excellent institution; and those who are managing it
deserve credit for the success with which they have accomplished, under difficulties, so much good work. I would
not say a word to injure them for the world. On the
contrary, I here bear testimony to their ability and
achievement. The Executive Committee is a model
according to its limitations and its lights.'

Its lights, however, were not all that Edward Martyn
desired them to be, and he held that their dimness was
due to the limitations of the Executive. 'The result is
that, with all the best intentions of its management, the
Féis Ceóil is not what it really ought to be — the great
national festival of music like the Eisteddfod in Wales,
influencing and interesting the national spirit of our
countrymen. The reason, of course, is, it is not sufficiently Irish and depending on Ireland. That is the
great distinction between it and the Gaelic League,
which has had such overpowering influence on Irish
life, in preparing men's minds for all other movements,
such as literary, industrial, agricultural, co-operative,
etc., which would all have died away but for its vitalising
force.

'At first, perhaps, there was some excuse for this
failing on the part of the Féis Ceóil to probe funda-
mentals, because it was largely an organisation of musicians; and musicians, it is well known, have never been

remarkable for correct ideas of general culture. To have at such a period made any Irish musician understand that art, however it may benefit by foreign influences, must spring from native sources, would have been about as easy as to have made men then believe that a person in a few years could fly in a machine from Wales to Ireland. Indeed to judge by the very general contempt among our musicians for the folk music of Ireland, I doubt whether this fundamental idea is even to-day understood by them to any extent. Moreover, there were then as now among us several capable musicians of such complete English traditions and habits that they would have looked with horror at any departure which was not strictly according to the tastes of our *seonini* or imitation English.

'To these, as usual, the mildly national section of the promoters deferred. English and other foreign musicians were called over to adjudicate; and although there was a certain patronage of pipers and fiddlers, like the toleration of superior persons for a tumbler of whisky punch after a fashionable cosmopolitan dinner of many and elaborate courses, still the importance of the maintenance and study of our native folk music in its traditional purity as the original matter which was to colour and distinguish compositions of Irishmen from those of other nations, was contemptuously ignored with results of sterilising much of the good work the Féis Ceóil was accomplishing in the general cultivation of music.

'The Féis Ceóil will have to be reformed, or else it will die out before the national advance of the country. That it is only kept alive by the artificial support of the *seonini* is seen in the sparce attendance at all general meetings, which will grow ever sparser unless the Féis Ceóil is made in reality what it now pretends to be — the national music festival. Who ever saw such scanty meetings in organisations like the Gaelic League which is a vital movement? The music movement to be a success should be allied to the language movement.

'The Féis Ceóil should by right be the musical section of the Gaelic League, doing for Irish music what the other does for the Irish language. Of course this need not mean that it should adopt the methods of the Gaelic League towards music. These methods are not altogether satisfactory. As far as they aim towards the preservation and encouragement of our folk music they are well. And it must be remembered to its high credit that the Gaelic League was the first to produce an original opera by an Irishman in the Irish language. Still there is no attempt by the Gaelic League to promote the complete study and practice of music, as the Féis Ceóil has promoted them, notwithstanding its limitations and mistakes. It is to perfect the Féis Ceóil by example of Gaelic League methods in the cultivation of Irish music and the adoption of every other thing Irish, while maintaining and developing its already excellent work for the promotion of music in general, that I advocate those reforms which I think will result in a new and more vigorous life to the movement.

'Above all, the importation of English or other foreign musicians as adjudicators should be done away with. Their presence was always a mistake, even from the first, notwithstanding the plea that we should thereby have more detached, and fairer judgments, and that the Irish people would have more confidence in foreigners' decisions than in those of her own musicians. The contrary has been the fact. The Irish people, naturally irreverent, and rendered more so by recent reading and teaching, only laugh at those lisping epicenes and garrulous Cockneys, who come over here laying down the law, and showing off to us Irish. Besides there is too much Church of England music influence. The game of bringing in the foreigner seems nearly played out.

'If we get rid of the English adjudicators it will be a relief. Fancy, I heard one of those atrocities making facetious remarks about the Irish language before an audience of Irish people! Any other but Irish people would have sent him running before them. Why should we employ any English? We do not want them. Have we not several of our own musicians to do the work, and at probably a quarter of the expense? In this way we could afford to employ at least three judges in each competition who would be a check upon each other, and would at least avoid such a deplorable arithmetical mistake in marks as recently caused so much dissatisfaction both to competitors and the Féis executive.

'I should like to know, indeed, whether at English competitions they send to Ireland, or any other country than England, for adjudicators. I am sure they don't. Why, therefore, should we send to England? Already our countrymen have given us satisfaction in the persons of Mr. Joseph O'Mara, Mr. Plunket Greene, and the late much-lamented Denis O'Sullivan. We do not mind how severely we are criticised by our own people, but we object to be patronised by the English. Let this reform then be carried out, and let the acid element and brindled cat element of the committee strive to get over their anti-national prejudices, and to get more in touch with Irish movements and life. I have always advocated that the Féis Ceóil should be the musical branch of the Gaelic League. It is a pity the promoters of the Féis Ceóil will not see this. But they won't.'

V

POLITICS AND LATER YEARS

V

POLITICS AND LATER YEARS

NATIONALIST feeling had run high in Ireland towards the end of the Boer War; and while the Parliamentary Party was still split into the two factions of Parnellites and anti-Parnellites, it was to be expected that new men with the outlook of a younger generation should be eagerly sought. Never was there a more cordial welcome for converts from Unionism among the landowning class; and Edward's sudden leap to fame through his resignation of his magistrate's commissions had made him a popular hero in the West. As the elections approached, his name was constantly being mentioned as a very eligible candidate for his own county; and he soon began to receive personal letters exhorting him to enter Parliament. Some of them, as was usual in the atmosphere of secrecy that had for so long surrounded Irish politics, were anonymous even when they were most friendly. 'Let not the anonymity cause suspicion,' ran one such epistle of encouragement, carefully printed in block capitals throughout. 'I am a friend, I would be an admirer. Embrace your country's cause. Your education, your social position, and I hope your natural and national sentiments, lean in that direction. Sir H. G. Esmonde has done nobly. He is not better fitted for the position he seeks than you are to represent your native county. You love your country. You ought to. You ought to love and embrace the cause and the party that would raise up our wretched people and our enslaved land. Think for thirty minutes

what your address will be. Give it to Father Fahy,
V.G. or P.P., or both. He will propose you candidate for South Galway at next convention Athenry. No
time to be lost. Then the county will blaze with
bonfires.'

There was too much suggestion of an Abbey Theatre
play about invitations of that sort to leave Edward happy
in mind; and receiving such illiterate addresses, if more
responsible solicitations were not forthcoming, was
certain to antagonise him. A much more influential
invitation, however, soon reached him from a personal
friend whose opinion he regarded with real respect and
sympathy, Mr. R. J. Kelly, K.C., the editor and proprietor of the *Tuam Herald*. Mr. Kelly was not only an
admirer of Edward, but had a definite and highly attractive political programme of his own. 'I trust sincerely
you will agree with what I wrote about you and South
Galway,' he wrote privately to Edward after singing his
praises in the local newspaper, 'and that you will permit
yourself to be nominated and elected for that constituency at the coming election. I need not repeat some
of the arguments used in the *Herald* this week, but you
have a grand opportunity for doing good to your country,
your creed and your class. I wish I could get all classes
of Irishmen, particularly landlord and tenant, to combine
to better themselves, not at the cost of each other, as has
been our rulers' role and policy, but at the expense of the
British Exchequer, and I believe it to be quite feasible
by unity and combination. We went very near it on the
Financial question. Nothing like combination for John
Bull. It is the only argument he apprehends and appre-
ciates; all else is lost upon his dull intelligence. If men of

your stamp went into Parliament we would soon have a powerful and respected body of Irishmen of whom we might well feel proud, and who could do real and substantial good for the poor old country while yet there is time to save her.'

Even that blunt appeal, with its frank insistence upon the need for national unity as a preliminary to fleecing the British Exchequer could not overcome Edward's natural reluctance to enter public life. 'I wish most sincerely that I could induce you to reconsider your decision,' Mr. Kelly wrote again a month later. 'I assure you you underrate your own influence and importance, and you are mistaken in thinking you could do no good in that capacity for any of the causes you have at heart.' The language movement, for instance, would gain much by having a supporter of Edward's social status and intellectual abilities in Parliament. But above all Mr. Kelly looked for great results from the association of Edward, as a patriotic landlord, well known throughout the country, with the few other landlords who had entered Nationalist politics and who in that way could command the support of the tenants in an effort to seek an agrarian settlement. The land question seemed still as far as ever from solution. No one could have foreseen that within another three years a new era was to open, when Mr. George Wyndham, adopting the very policy which Mr. Kelly was urging upon Edward now, carried through Parliament the Land Purchase Act, which apparently satisfied both parties by the distribution of an immense bonus at the expense of the British Exchequer — (a liability which has since been taken over by the Irish Free State). For the time being it was not surprising that Edward could not see his way to enter politics to urge 'such a solution of this agrarian problem as, while satisfying the ends of justice, would at the cost of the British Exchequer be fair, if not generous.' 'It is in such a time of stress and difficulty,' Mr. Kelly pleaded, 'that such men are needed to steady the national movement by imparting to it a respectability and a reasonableness which otherwise it cannot possess. Men such as you may thereby be making sacrifices, but they are in a good cause and for a good end.'

Still more encouraging was a letter from the Archbishop of Tuam, not only regretting his refusal to stand for Parliament, but urging him to reconsider his decision: 'I am told you object to seek a seat in Parliament,' wrote the Archbishop. 'I must say I am sorry for it. I believe you would be without doubt elected for your own division, and that you might do much good in the House of Commons. So I venture to hope you will reconsider your decision, and get yourself put in nomination. You see what a fiasco the so-called Convention in Loughrea turned out to be. Is it not a pity to leave the representation of the country in the hands of such men?' He had even been approached also from North Tipperary, a county with which he had no connections, and where the Land League had always been specially powerful. A letter was sent to him on behalf of 'a very large meeting of the clergy of the North Tipperary constituency' to ask if he would agree to become the candidate at the next convention to be held a few days later. 'I may add,' wrote the priest who was instructed to approach him, 'that the Dean who is P.P. here takes an especial interest in the division in view of the fact that you may become the

candidate.' And it was flattering that the only question
raised concerning his political opinions was a postscript
suggesting modestly that 'in case you allow yourself to be
put forward, some expression of your political views would
be welcome.'

But though Edward wisely declined to become a
candidate for Parliament, he made public pronounce-
ments encouraging the Home Rulers, and he even caused
some embarrassment to Horace Plunkett by proclaiming
openly that Mr. Plunkett was obviously becoming
converted to Home Rule. The official Nationalist
leaders thought very much the opposite; and John
Dillon, who was the leader of the larger anti-Parnellite
group, had already formed his own life-long conviction
that Horace Plunkett, with his schemes for economic
development and his new Department of Agriculture
and Technical Instruction and its host of inspectors and
minor officials, had no other object than to 'kill Home
Rule by kindness,' so that he was in fact the most treacher-
ous and insidious enemy Irish Nationalism had ever
encountered. It was indeed a thankless position that Mr.
Plunkett had made for himself, and he was fiercely black-
guarded by both parties when he stood as a reforming
Unionist for South Dublin. In a vain effort to make his
own position clear, he antagonised the Nationalists, who
saw that he was in fact likely to undermine the Home
Rule movement by allaying discontent and creating
economic prosperity; while the Unionists of the old school
denounced him with ferocious wrath as a traitor in their
own camp. To Edward Martyn, after he had lost his
seat, he wrote a charmingly frank letter which throws
light on the whole period:

T

'My dear Martyn,

'Everything written to or about me was used by my despicable Tory opponents for my destruction. I suppose there is no one they hate more than they do yourself. But when you said I was becoming a Home Ruler, they made a Solomon of you. Your letter did me some harm. But I am grateful for it none the less. It was kindly meant. I have lost my seat, but I have gained in other ways. They are going to get up a testimonial to me and give me a substantial solace in the shape of a subscription to the I.A.O.S., I hear! In any case, although fearing that some Home Rulers would vote for me, imagining that I was what my Tory foes declared me to be, a Home Ruler in disguise, I came out strongly against Home Rule. I believe I have made friends throughout the country for my economic policy and educational ideas. I feel happier after my defeat than I did before.'

Horace Plunkett had few enough friends and supporters in those early years, and his unfailing courage made him welcome any ally who shared his own belief in the possibilities of Irish economic development and who was prepared to assist his schemes. Edward Martyn had in fact been one of his most generous supporters. A letter from R. A. Anderson, the devoted secretary of the Irish Agricultural Organisation Society, thanking Edward for a timely and unexpected donation, is one instance among many of how varied and how generous were his benefactions. Writing a year before Plunkett's defeat in South Dublin, Mr. Anderson had said: 'Let me thank you most sincerely on behalf of the Committee of the

I.A.O.S. for your very generous contribution to our funds. It could not have been more opportune, for as a matter of fact Russell and I were cudgelling our brains to know where we could scrape together enough money to pay our staff for September. I have written to tell Plunkett, and you may be sure that your public-spirited and kindly action will do him more good than all his surgeons put together.'

His connection with the co-operative movement had brought him in touch with the Jesuit Father Tom Finlay, who was much the most influential ally that Sir Horace Plunkett had found among his Catholic sympathisers. Father Tom's special line was the organisation of rural industries, technical education, and co-operative credit banks; and as a shrewd Ulsterman, he was expected to live up to the reputation of Ulster for hard-headed business methods. He did not hesitate in responding to the friendship of Edward, as one of the few prominent Catholics who were associated with Sir Horace's largely Protestant movement, and his first direct appeal to Edward for financial assistance was characteristically ambitious. 'I have for some time been working to extend the methods of co-operation beyond the farmer's industry,' wrote Father Tom. 'Their success as applied to agriculture has convinced me they can be applied successfully to the industries which are now disorganised and therefore unremunerative to the workers. Here in Dublin, with the assistance of a few capable ladies, I have succeeded in organising a society of needleworkers who manufacture articles of ladies' apparel, and sell them in a shop they have taken for the purpose. They thus secure for themselves the wages of the worker and the profits of

the trader, and this for many of them means a condition
of tolerable comfort. We have reached the end of the
first year of business and find that we have sold £1,400
of goods during this time. But we are sadly hampered for
want of a little capital. We have not been able to sub-
scribe more than £174, and this is not enough to enable
us to develop our business. Our security would not be
accepted by the banks, as we are all of us persons of very
limited means. My purpose in writing to you is to beg
you to make an investment of £500 in our business. It
would perhaps be much more in accordance with precedent to beg for a gift. But for the sake of our workers,
who are succeeding by business methods only, I should
prefer a loan. We would cheerfully undertake to pay
4 per cent. We can offer no security, only the character
and efforts of the members of the Society. But seeing
that our success so far has been what it is — these I hope
you will regard as trustworthy assets.'

George Moore, as readers of his trilogy will remember,
was fascinated by the enigmatical humour of Father Tom
— the little 'long-bodied' priest with the 'russet-coloured
face, withered like an apple, the small, bright, affectionate
eyes, the insignificant nose, the short grey hair.' It is
strange that he should make no mention of this surprising
venture, in which Edward and the Jesuit Professor of
Economics were to be allies in organising a Co-operative
shop to sell 'articles of ladies' apparel.' But Edward had
too much respect for the clergy to expose them to unnecessary ridicule at the hands of his shameless friend;
and he may well have decided to say nothing of it to
George Moore. Another surprising scheme was put up
to him about the same time by another of their mutual

acquaintances who wrote to congratulate Edward on his letters to Lord Clonbrock, and urging him and his friend George Moore to secure a regular organ of their own in the Press by buying the old *Farmers' Gazette*. 'All take it, irrespective of Creed,' he wrote, 'and with two such able writers it would be read widely and pay well.' The immediate cause that this particular correspondent had at heart was to uphold the rights of Irish landlords who had been so cruelly wronged by British Governments.

Whether at first or last, pretty nearly every national effort that required financing, however small, had to depend on Edward to some extent. Even when an enterprise had been set on foot by a few public-spirited men and women who felt that they could not in decency ask him to give his assistance in yet another direction, it was seldom that an appeal was not made to Edward in the last resort when finances began to run out. A typical letter of the kind, showing at once what small resources could achieve big results, and also how limited were the resources of those few people who were willing to attempt anything constructive, is one from professor Eoin MacNeill, the real originator of the Gaelic League. He and a few friends had between them guaranteed the necessary funds to start Cló-Cumann, the Irish printing-press, which was one of the very few printing-works in the country that as yet even possessed Gaelic type, or employed proof-readers or compositors capable of dealing with Irish manuscript. In time it had become the principal printing-works for all the many movements associated with 'Irish Ireland'; but inexperience had involved the guarantors in more expense than they had anticipated. The position was set out in a letter from Professor

MacNeill to Edward, who was already well accustomed
to such appeals, but seldom received any from a source
which commanded such genuine respect. 'Though I
think the interest on the Cló-Cumann debentures is
certain,' wrote Professor MacNeill, 'and that in any
event the principal is within the value of the Company's
property, I know that the concern cannot appeal to anyone as an investor merely. The case is this. The bank
loan is about to be terminated. The loan was guaranteed
by Dr. Boyd, Miss O'Farrelly, Mr. Cole, Mr. Geoghegan, and Mr. Hayden and myself. It is, therefore,
necessary for us either to pay off the loan ourselves, or to
replace it by debentures, and in the latter case it is certain
that we shall ourselves have to take up most of the
debentures. In my case, I have to raise a loan from the
bank to pay for my debentures. I may have to provide
£366 in this way, and the other guarantors in proportion.
Dr. Boyd is providing £1,000. We are asking others to
assist us. Up to the present we have had promises of
about £350. "Irish Ireland" in various forms owes the
Cló-Cumann about £1,200, on which the company has
had to pay abnormally heavy interest during the recent
period of dear money. Had this money been available,
the company would be in a position to command all it
requires. Of course we see now what temerity we had in
launching such an enterprise without experience. We
have had to pay dear in money, time and anxiety, but we
feel bound in honour to put the thing through. If we
were to drop it, it would be a severe blow to Gaelic
Leaguers all round. I ask you, not as an investment but
as a subscription, if you like to take up even a small
amount of the debentures. I am writing to you at the

request of my co-directors, and it is a very hateful task, for there seems to be always something poisonous in money matters between people whose interests in common are of another order.'

It pleased Edward to be so constantly appealed to, and he was well able to refuse the many solicitations for loans of money that reached him from acquaintances who thought that his resources were inexhaustible. Only in Ireland would a man with some two thousand a year be regarded as fabulously rich; but stories of his munificence spread far and wide, and Catholics in particular appeared to feel that they had a claim upon his purse. But Edward had inherited much of the financial sense that had built up the fortunes of his mother's father, old James Smith of Masonbrook: and as a young landlord in the west of Ireland, he had had the invaluable experience of direct dealings with horse-copers, until he had fancied himself as one who could buy or sell horses in any market without being fooled. He had long overcome the instinctive repugnance of a generous nature to refuse appeals for aid. His resources could not in any case have met more than a fraction of all the demands that were made upon him if he had wished to meet them all. Secure in the knowledge that he was well able to protect himself against begging letters, he made public a full catalogue of his chief interests in *Who's Who*, describing himself openly in his later years, as 'one of the original founders of the Irish Dramatic Movement in 1899; founder of the Palestrina Choir of men and boys at Dublin for the reform of liturgical music, in the same year, which in 1903 became the Schola Cantorum of that Arch-diocese; organised a reform of church architecture, stained glass,

etc., 1903; was President of Sinn Féin from 1904 until
he resigned in 1908; founded at Dublin, 1914, the Irish
Theatre, for the production of non-peasant plays, plays
in the Irish language, and translations of Continental
master-dramas; promoter of Gaelic League and other
educational improvements for Ireland; is a Governor of
the Galway College of the National University.'

It was no wonder if anyone who read that high-
sounding record of varied interests should assume that
Edward Martyn was a man who liked to be consulted
about new enterprises, and who realised the value of his
personal influence. It extended in many directions, and
all sorts of people were glad to invoke it if they could
gain his ear. At times Edward's close relations with the
clergy could be of direct importance to his neighbours,
and Lord Gough particularly was quite prepared to
make use of his good offices as a conciliator when trouble
arose. 'A regrettable incident has occurred,' Lord Gough
wrote on one such occasion, which suggests the many
difficulties of an Irish landlord in a changing age, 'which
may very likely come before you more or less in a business
way. To prevent you being embarrassed I give you my
version. If the matter does not come before you, so much
the better. My version is as follows. The trustees of
Caragh suggested that I should buy it. I asked them some
months ago about the price. They definitely laid down
twenty-five years' purchase of the non-judicial rent. I
accepted and sent the deed to be approved. They at once
served an ejectment for next April, giving no reason.
(The lease was thirty years, twenty-five years unexpired,
but with breaks in the lease.)

'Bishop O'Dea says that the farm has been turned into

a rabbit warren, greatly neglected, and furze encouraged. I am replying (*a*) I have done all I could to extirpate the rabbits, and employed two special experts last winter to destroy them; that I hate rabbits as destroying plantations, and that not one is there by my consent; (*b*) that I have not neglected the farm, but acted from a farmer's point of view; (*c*) that far from encouraging furze, I have spent a lot of money in putting it down, and burning it. Undoubtedly the furze and scrub are injuring the land, as also are the rabbits, which cannot properly be got at owing to the furze. This has been an increasing evil for years and has prevented the farm from paying. If any layman had accused me of encouraging furze and rabbits the accusation would be ridiculous, but from a Bishop, it is serious. Between ourselves, I expect that Father F. has produced this argument for want of a better one, without seriously reflecting on what he was doing, but merely wanting by hook or by crook to divide up the land. There is not a particle of foundation for it; it is absolutely untrue, but I do not resent Father F.'s action to promote a good cause, only it is terrible that the Bishop should have swallowed it without inquiry. Of course he is a new-comer, and so must be excused too, but I beg you not to believe a word of the accusations.

'Forgive my troubling you with what may be an unnecessary exculpation, but if the matter is brought before you, mind you say I have enough sins on my conscience without this additional one, of which I am innocent, being imputed to me, and do not let them pass on to other reasons for ejecting me. I don't dispute them. It is the unjustified accusations only that I resent.' Times had changed indeed, when a Lord Gough was

driven to seeking the influence of a Nationalist neighbour
to prevent the newly emancipated tenantry from ejecting
him!

He was full of activities during these years. He had
formed a close friendship with Arthur Griffith, and his
Presidency of the Sinn Féin movement gave him a
constant occupation. The triumph of the Liberals at the
general elections in 1906 seemed to have thrown back all
chance of obtaining Home Rule from a Parliament where
the Irish Nationalists could exercise no real influence
against an overwhelming majority. Sinn Féin even
undertook boldly to fight by-elections in Ireland; and
though it won no seats, the new policy of abstaining
altogether from Westminster and organising a new
political agitation in Ireland itself, while developing
Irish industries and economic resources by an intensive
campaign, began to make many converts. After long
preparation, it was even found possible to launch a small
evening newspaper in Dublin, which Edward and his
friend, John Sweetman, helped to finance and to subsidise. In politics and in the language revival, and in the
promotion of Irish arts, Edward found ample occupation
which compensated for his profound disappointment
with the development of the Abbey Theatre on its
restricted lines. Mr. George Moore, meditating upon the
multifarious activities of his friend, might well protest
that Edward left himself no time for original literary
work. So, Mr. Moore writes of him in *Vale*, 'On Monday
evening he presides at the Pipers' Club; on Tuesday he
goes to the theatre; on Wednesday he attends a meeting
of Sinn Féin; on Thursday he dozes through the proceedings of the Coisde Gnótha; on Friday there is choir

Arthur Griffith

From the painting by Miss L. Williams, A.R.H.A.

practice in the cathedral; on Saturday he speaks severely
to his disobedient choristers, tries new voices in his
rooms in Lincoln Place, and plans new programmes with
Vincent O'Brien, his choirmaster, chosen by him because
he believes in his talent and in his desire to give the
music in accordance with tradition and Edward's own
taste. On Sunday he is ever watchful in the cathedral,
sitting with his hand to his ear, noting the time and the
efficiency of the singers.'

But though he still continued to write plays, knowing
that they would never be acted unless some new attempt
were made to found another Irish theatre with the wider
aims he had always had in view himself, Edward was too
much preoccupied with his many enterprises. He found
an immense satisfaction in being so often consulted by all
sorts of people. The Gaelic League turned to him to
obtain his influence with Archbishop Walsh, and it had
delighted him that within a few months of his endowing
the Palestrina Choir he had been able to persuade the
Archbishop to lend its services for the funeral of Father
O'Growney. That shy, scholarly Irish-speaking priest
had compiled a series of simple text-books of the Irish
language, which had been adopted everywhere as the
only and the indispensable text-book of Irish studies for
the disciples of the Gaelic League. He had died when his
name was becoming a household word in 'Irish Ireland,'
and if he had lived, he would have been almost the most
famous Irishman of his day. But he lived only just long
enough to earn that 'great funeral,' which the old Fenian
John O'Leary, had so often said was the only hope of
recognition for an Irish leader. Edward, with his newly
founded Palestrina Choir, had been able to give a unique

distinction to his obsequies. Nor had it been altogether easy to gain his request, for Archbishop Walsh had quickly seen the danger of establishing awkward precedents. If the new choir at the pro-Cathedral were to be lent for every national celebration of the kind, the arrangements at the pro-Cathedral would be seriously upset. The decision, technically, at least, must rest with the Administrator. But the Archbishop's word was law, as Edward knew well; and he had gained his point when he received a letter from Dr. Walsh, expressly written so that it should be read to the other directors of the new Choir, which conveyed his personal hope that they would feel that this special occasion would justify an exception.

On artistic questions, Edward's authority was still more frequently invoked. He had had to deal with a prelate of most exceptional character, who happened to be an authority on Church music also, when he had been negotiating with Archbishop Walsh about the Palestrina Choir. But in his own county there was no one else with any pretentions whatever to understanding of ecclesiastical art. The arrival of a new bishop in Dr. O'Dea, who was a devoted admirer of Edward's, and a personal friend, gave him remarkable opportunities for furthering his own ideas of church decoration and architecture in Galway. 'I know no one but yourself except Jacky O'Connell (Sir John R. O'Connell), who has knowledge of such matters,' Bishop O'Dea wrote quite frankly concerning one important scheme when a considerable sum of money had to be spent. Even Lord Killanin had been delighted to invoke Edward's expert advice, and the result was the most remarkable church at Spiddal designed by his friend, Professor Scott. The sculptors

John Hughes and Oliver Shepherd, and Miss Sara
Purser's stained glass works in Dublin, could usually
count on obtaining interesting commissions if his advice
was being followed. From Cork, on another such
occasion, a frantic message reached him from his friend,
J. J. Horgan, imploring him to send a letter which would
avert a calamity in connection with the arrangements for
a new statue upon which £600 was to be spent. 'I want to
make an effort to save this statue from the Philistines,'
Mr. Horgan wrote. 'A strong letter from you would, I
believe, sway his reverence. I fear he will not listen to me.
He has seen some terrible statue in B—— by T——
which has completely captivated him. Surely something
fine can be done for £600. Executed is a good term to
describe what T—— would do. Let me have Shepherd's
address in the letter, and also any place where his work is
to be seen.'

But a controversy which produced one of the most
celebrated lawsuits in Dublin's history was to place a
severe check upon Edward's manifold activities. His
incursions into politics could never have made him a
serious leader of any party, even though he had accepted
the honorary position of President of Arthur Griffith's
Sinn Féin Movement. He had always been aloof from
the people and had led his own life as a country gentleman, whether at his castle in Tulira or in his rooms in
Dublin, while he made his headquarters at the Kildare
Street Club. And the preposterous contrast between his
extreme Nationalist views and the constant associations
of his private life brought about a collision between him
and his club, which was to absorb most of his energies
and a great deal of his resources for several years; at the

end of which he emerged with his spirit seriously impaired.

Like nearly every landowner of any importance in the country, Edward had been elected to the Kildare Street Club as a young man. He had found in its spacious rooms and comfortable arrangements an ideal solution of his own requirements as a bachelor in Dublin. Establishing himself in rooms almost across the road from the end of Kildare Street, he went to the Club constantly for his meals, and often for weeks on end he would use the club as a hotel, staying there for indefinite periods. The club was moreover the only place in Dublin where he could get really good food and drink of the expensive kind; and for a rich man whose only self-indulgence was eating and drinking and who trained himself to live on one enormous meal a day, food and drink were matters of some importance. At the Kildare Street Club also he could always count upon meeting any of his own friends from the West who were passing through Dublin. It was the recognised social headquarters of Irish landlordism; and Edward as a landlord with more means than most, and with an exceptionally strong inclination towards club life, soon came to regard it as a second home.

It was unfortunate, however, that membership of the Kildare Street Club involved a certain conformity to the political orthodoxy of Irish landlordism. Even the coy excursions of gifted and influential landlords like Lord Dunraven and Sir Horace Plunkett and their friends into such schemes as Devolution — which were in reality well calculated to kill the Home Rule agitation by taking the wind out of its sails — led to their being regarded with intense distrust as potential revolutionaries. Edward

himself as a young man had shared this inherited distrust of demagogues. He had looked upon Mr. Gladstone as a reckless and inflammatory agitator, even when
he was putting Parnell in gaol for what he called, in
Gladstonian language, an attempt at 'marching through
rapine to the dismemberment of the Empire.' But
Edward's politics had changed swiftly under the influence
of the Boer War; and his action in resigning his commission as a magistrate, and still more in resigning his
deputy-lieutenancy for the county, had scandalised the
squirearchy to such an extent that they had begun to
consider what means existed for expelling him from
membership of the Kildare Street Club.

So far back as April 1900, he had received the first
intimation of future trouble, in the shape of an anonymous
postcard written from the Club which asked: 'Had you
not better resign your membership here before you are
expelled?' But no serious step was taken in regard to his
obnoxious political views at the time, and the conclusion
of the Boer War removed the chief cause of friction.
Edward's unorthodox politics became a matter of more
serious concern to the Club not long afterwards, when
King Edward VII was preparing to visit Ireland. Edward
Martyn felt it incumbent upon him to write public
letters in the Nationalist *Freeman's Journal* to express his
own views on the proposed visitation. 'I understand from
your leading article in yesterday's *Freeman*,' he wrote at
the beginning of April 1903, 'that the British newspapers are already making capital out of the forthcoming
visit of the King to Ireland, whom they declare the Irish
people will receive as a welcome compensation for their
deprivation of Home Rule. By this means England has

once more thrown down the gauntlet to Nationalist
Ireland. It is for Nationalist Ireland to take it up and to
tell the Government with one voice that if they bring the
King here under any other guise than a restorer of our
stolen constitution they will regret their rashness.'

Some three weeks later the *Freeman's Journal* published
another letter of Edward's from Tulira, which began by
quoting in Gaelic an old Irish proverb, translated roughly
but inaccurately as 'The Irishman never understands his
advantage at the right time.' 'Its applicability came
vividly before me,' he wrote, 'when I read in the *Freeman's
Journal* of to-day the report of the Baltinglass Guardians'
expression of opinion on the King's visit to Ireland. It
was one of those deplorable exhibitions of incompetence
by which Irishmen every now and then make themselves
contemptible to foreign peoples. One would have thought
that, in a country which prides itself on its disloyalty,
there would be only one fate for a resolution of welcome.
But strange to say, that was not so. There was a discussion which developed into a wrangle. . . . The only
explanation I can find for all this absurdity is that such is
the pitiful spectacle to which a disloyal people are reduced
when their inherent passion for grovelling before visible
pomp had once been aroused. Some want to grovel for
the sake of grovelling itself. Some want to grovel for
filthy lucre. The best of them are paralysed and stand
aside. On the other hand I see the so-called Loyalists
of what Mr. Goulding,[1] of the manure, calls the English
Garrison in Ireland, united and determined to crush
Home Rule and the National spirit with their greatest

---

[1]Mr. Goulding, a prominent railway director, who also had a flourishing
fertiliser factory, was one of the pillars of Irish Unionist politics.

political trump card, the King of England. For this it is
impossible not to admire the determination of the
Unionists and to contrast that supreme quality of an
ascendency, viz., knowing its own mind, with the weak
shifty purpose of the Irish people.

'The policy of apathy or grovel, to which apathy will
eventually be turned, ought to be discovered by this,
with such previous experiences as the visits of George IV
and Victoria, to be the very worst of policies for obtaining
National self-government or any other advantage, while
the policy of giving a bad reception to the Sovereign
until he comes as a constitutional Sovereign to us should at
once appear the best of policies. Apart from the fact that
we have never got any of our rights from England except
by wringing them from her, would not the fact of the
King making his royal progress through a hissing
Ireland proclaim to the whole world the reality of Ireland's demand for Home Rule? Would it not at least
put the King in a somewhat ridiculous position? Was it
not thus that the Hungarians got their liberties? Has any
country ever got her liberties who fails at these turning
points of her destiny? . . .

'Neither King nor Government have promised Home
Rule. It is rumoured the King is in favour of it. I do not
believe he is. The Government have most publicly
denied their intention to grant it. If the King wants a
good reception here, he has only to declare for Home
Rule. If without this previous declaration he gets a good
reception, and Home Rule is repudiated, as it surely will
be when he leaves the country, I hope there will be no
complaints of English perfidy, or a renewal for an agitation for Home Rule. The farce had better be dropped,

U

and some practical work taken up instead. This is the way the situation strikes a person like me, who am in the somewhat odd position among my fellow-countrymen of always meaning what I say.'

In a landlord of Edward Martyn's standing, such an attitude was certain to embarrass the Government. The forcible commonsense of his argument — that the Home Rulers must either show their consistency by giving the King a bad reception, or else drop the pretence of being dissatisfied without Home Rule — was so obvious and direct that his letters could not fail to attract attention. That they should emanate from an Irish landlord was irritating enough to the loyal Unionists who had their principal stronghold in the Kildare Street Club. But that the author of such incitements to disloyalty to the King should be a member of the venerable club itself, and should constantly take advantage of his admission within its sacred precincts, was more than human nature could be expected to endure. The Committee of the Club were holding their weekly meeting immediately after the publication of this second letter, and they dispatched a protest to Edward Martyn at once, informing him that his letters 'in their opinion are derogatory to your station in society,' and desiring to know 'whether you have an explanation to offer to them or reason to adduce why your conduct in writing them such letters should not be referred to a general meeting of the Club as provided for under Rule XXV.'

Edward Martyn had arrived in Dublin when the Committee were actually sitting in judgment upon his letter in the *Freeman's Journal* of that morning, and he resumed his temporary residence in the Club that day.

The reprimand of the Committee was accordingly delivered to him in the Club itself, and he wrote his reply the same evening. His answer was direct and unambiguous. 'I beg to inform you,' he wrote, 'that I consider my political opinions as expressed in my various published letters or other works in no wise derogatory to my station in society or to that of any other Irishman. I have no explanation to offer, and retract nothing, and await with perfect equanimity the decision of a general meeting of the Club, should such be deemed advisable by the Committee to be called to decide a political matter in a club which is strictly non-political in its constitution.'

The Committee must have realised from the beginning that Edward Martyn was not a man who could be either bullied or frightened. No one was less impressed by social rank or by conventional regulations. They deferred further action until the next weekly meeting, and then they met his disclaimer with a considered argument. They were 'not concerned with the political opinion of any member of the Club,' they wrote. 'The matter in your published letters to which their attention has been called by many members of the Club, and which in their opinion called for explanation from you,' they went on, 'were not political opinions but suggestions that under certain circumstances disrespect should be manifested to His Majesty the King in the event of his visiting Ireland. It appears from the letter which you have addressed to the Committee that you have not realised the marked distinction which exists between political opinions and suggestions that disrespect should be manifested to the Sovereign. The Committee are very unwilling to take the serious step of bringing this matter before the Club, particularly as your letter leads them to believe that you have not realised the true bearing of some of the passages in your letter. At the same time they desire me to point out that suggestions that disrespect should be manifested to the Sovereign cannot be confounded with political opinions, and that the publication of such suggestions by a member of this Club, cannot fail to be in the highest degree distasteful and offensive to his fellow-members.'

Edward must have chuckled when he read this paternal lecture on the importance of verbal precision. But he had no intention of being drawn into an argument with the Committee, whose opinions he regarded with real contempt. Still less had he any thought of apologising for what he had written, and had every intention of writing again, if occasion should arise for him to do so. 'I quite realise,' he wrote in reply, 'the point of the Committee when they allude to "the marked distinction which exists between political opinions and suggestions that disrespect should be manifested to the Sovereign," only I do not agree with their estimate of the Sovereign. If a Sovereign who is unconstitutional in this country comes, in the guise of, and with the assumption of the authority of, a constitutional Sovereign, to this country, I believe I have a perfect right to show him disrespect, and I believe my action in so doing to be a political action, and consequently refuse to acknowledge the right of Kildare Street Club to dictate to me as to the propriety of such action.'

To this letter the Secretary sent only a formal reply, but it was considered by the Committee at their next meeting. How far the Club was in fact entitled to control the political eccentricities of Edward Martyn was indeed a problem, and after consulting the rules of the Club, and putting their heads together, they wrote to their solicitors to request advice upon a 'difficult and delicate matter.' The solicitor, when Lord Cloncurry and Mr. Bernard called upon him, decided that it was clearly a case for Counsel's opinion. It happened that the Master of the Rolls, Sir Andrew Porter, was a prominent member of the Club and of its Committee, and he had kindly gone over the rules himself. At his advice Counsel's assistance was secured; and within a few days a new and more carefully worded rule had been specially drafted to enable the Club to deal with any further indiscretions on Edward Martyn's part. By the end of June the customary procedure had been completed, and by a majority of one hundred and fifty-two votes against one, the amended Rules had been declared carried.

'Dear Edward' had been actually staying in the Club when the voting took place, and there could be little doubt as to the identity of the single voter who had opposed the amendment to the rules which the Committee had elaborated, with the object of taking power to deal with members whose conduct was not in accordance with its traditions. It had been an open secret that Edward's recent letters to the Press concerning the King's visit were under consideration by the Committee; and with the strengthening of their powers by the newly amended rules there was a general sense of relief in regard to Edward's future activities. Edward himself, however, had no intention of being muzzled by the rules of a social club, even though it provided him with his only

home in Dublin. The passing of the rule, in fact, determined him to a new defiance, and on July 2nd the
Freeman's Journal published a further manifesto emanat-
ing from him which could only be construed as a deliberate challenge to the Committee.

'The visit to Ireland of her unconstitutional King,' he
wrote to the *Freeman's Journal*, 'promises to be the
greatest of blows in recent years dealt to her hopes of
self-government and to that building up of character and
self-reliance without which self-government is impossible.
On next Friday the Nationalist Corporation of Dublin
will—unless Dublin Nationalists prevent them—vote an
address to King Edward, as the Paving Committee,
composed wholly of Nationalists, handed over the streets
of our capital to be decorated with the emblems of our
national extinction. This is what is being done by people
who were elected by Nationalists in order to oppose all
demonstrations of welcome to a Sovereign until such
time as he should come as the restorer of our stolen
rights.

'It is a strange and despairing spectacle and its significance may prove a profitable subject of meditation for
those Irishmen and women whose intellects have escaped
the anti-national distractions and drugs of the hour. For
in moments like the present crisis, the facts of a nation's
history come out clearer to the mind of the inquirer. At
the dramatic points of a nation's life, the inquirer can only
judge of that nation's character. What is the fact brought
home to him by the present attitude of Ireland? Is it not
that if we have hitherto failed to obtain Home Rule and
the other rights we claim, it is not because of the opposition of Orangemen, Unionists, and so forth, but because

of the inherent instability and want of purpose of the Nationalists themselves?

'The power of the Unionists as an ascendancy is fast going. They are, to those who really know them, but poor phantoms of what they once were. However, they possess two qualities which remain to them from their former habits of ascendancy and which serve to brace them up as a sort of substitute for self-respect, namely, a faculty of acting together when it is a question of being anti-National, and a lofty, if somewhat absurd, contempt for every Nationalist in Ireland. With so many Nationalists astray, such qualities in their opponents are a danger. But if Ireland were really true to herself, these Unionists, or Ascendancy, or whatever else they may be called, would be of no avail to retard her regeneration. It is because she is ineffective that this grotesque minority is now leading her.'

There could be no mistake as to the intention of that passing reference to the 'grotesque minority,' who entertained that 'lofty, if somewhat absurd, contempt for every Nationalist in Ireland.' But the Club was not yet in a position to enforce its new rules, and the time would have been extremely inopportune for advertising Edward's protest against the King's visit, even if they had desired to prove their own loyalty by expelling him from the Club because of his political views. In any case he could claim that he had never identified the Club in any way with his own political activities; and that was more than all members of the Club who belonged to the opposite camp in politics could claim.

The year passed without further action being taken by the Club, and in the following October it was Edward who took the offensive, when he wrote to expostulate against the political activities of one of its most prominent members. 'I beg to call your attention to the by-law on Page 20 of the Rules of the Kildare Street Club, dated 1904,' he wrote to the Secretary. 'You will agree with the old proverb: "What's sauce for the goose is sauce for the gander"? You may remember that we had some correspondence in which I was unjustly accused of breaking the above by-law. May I ask you to read at the top of Column 8, Page 5 of the *Freeman's Journal*, of Monday, September 26th, 1904, a communication to the Press and dated from Kildare Street Club, which I think should be brought to the notice of the Committee.' The enemy had in fact played into his hands. Colonel Hutcheson Poe had sent a circular letter to the Press in connection with a report of the Irish Reform Association; and two of the newspapers had published the covering letter, injudiciously addressed from the Kildare Street Club, as well as the report which it enclosed. Edward's letter of complaint was duly laid before the next meeting of the Committee, and they were obliged to instruct the Secretary to reply that Colonel Poe had written them 'a very handsome apology' on the day after the two newspapers had 'inadvertently' printed his covering letter.

So the feud smouldered through another year, until a really blazing provocation on Edward's part brought matters to a crisis. Sinn Féin had come into existence and grown active in the interval since the King's visit in 1903, and Edward had become one of its most prominent supporters. At the National Councils Convention, meeting in the Rotunda in Dublin on November 28th, he had even taken the chair and delivered himself of characteristically provocative speeches. Full reports of the proceedings were published in the *United Irishman*, a newspaper edited by the founder of the Sinn Féin movement, Mr. Arthur Griffith, and a copy of this highly inflammatory journal was quickly brought to the notice of the Kildare Street Club. It was in due course laid before the weekly meeting of the Committee, and a letter was dispatched that evening to Edward Martyn, which enclosed a copy of the newspaper that most members of the Club would probably not have touched without tongs.

'I am directed by the Committee to ask,' wrote Mr. Bailey, the Secretary, 'if the speeches made by you upon those occasions are correctly reported in that paper and more especially the following statement attributed to you, viz., "The Irishman who enters the Army or Navy of England deserves to be flogged." I am further to add that in the event of your not denying the accuracy of these reports of your speeches, the Committee will assume that they are correctly reported in the paper.'

Edward had by this time retired to Tulira, and a week before Christmas he replied curtly to acknowledge receipt of the *United Irishman* (which was in enjoyment of a subsidy from his own generous purse) and to state that the reports of his two speeches 'are on the whole correct.' The challenge had this time been thrown down in earnest and Edward could only expect that the matter would have to be fought out. Just before Christmas, matters were carried a step further by Mr. Bailey's reply, stating that his own acceptance of the reports had been reported to the Committee and that 'the Committee regard the matter as one very seriously affecting the character and interests of the Club. Before, however, sending you an official notification of their intention to proceed further in the matter,' he went on, 'they will be anxious to know whether there is any statement or explanation which you would wish to put before them.' By return of post Edward answered that he had 'no statement or explanation to lay before the Committee of the Kildare Street Club. I refuse to acknowledge their right in this matter.' That was the attitude which he adopted throughout, and he announced his intention now of persevering in it.

Immediately after Christmas the Committee decided to take action at once. A resolution demanding Edward's expulsion from the Club was drafted for submission to a general meeting under the amended rules of the Club, and as a prudent precaution they submitted the draft resolution to Mr. Matheson, K.C., for his approval. Before the end of the month, Mr. Bailey had issued the ultimàtum to Edward, announcing that the Committee, having considered the reports of his speeches and his own replies concerning them, 'had no alternative consistent with their duty to the Club but to carry out the provisions of Rule XXV of the Club rules, and call a General Meeting to deal with the matter as therein provided.'

Open war had thus been declared between them, and Edward — partly from a genuine affection for the Club and its associations, and still more to assert his own right to express whatever political views he might think fit — determined to fight the matter out to the end. He had been out-voted by the whole Club once before, when there had been a question of altering the rules, especially to provide powers for expelling him in such a contingency as he had now actually produced. No man in his senses, it might be supposed, would have the least desire to remain a member of a club which was overwhelmingly anxious to expel him. And his own *obiter dictum*, even though it was obviously in joke, in declaring that any Irishman joining either the British Army or Navy deserved to be flogged, was not only a deliberate insult to the great majority of the Club's members, but apparently an indication that he had no desire to be associated with them.

Nevertheless he determined to fight the Committee as a matter of principle. He replied at once to the Secretary's letter by insisting that he must be given due notice of any meeting called to expel him. Meanwhile he wished to have all his letters forwarded to his rooms across the road at 4 Leinster Street. On January 8th, the circular letter was issued to all members of the Club, informing them that a ballot to decide upon Edward's expulsion was to be held.

Three days before the circular was issued, Edward's old friend, Lord Gough, at the British Legation in Dresden, had seen reports in the newspapers of his withdrawal from the Club, and of the fact that Edward had decided to contest the matter and had already briefed Mr. Tim Healy to conduct his case. It was sad news; for Lord Gough was stirred not only by the trouble of his old friend, but by personal qualms of conscience because he had himself prevailed upon Edward to refrain from resigning his membership some years before. He took up his pen and wrote a singularly charming letter of remonstrance: 'Some few years ago,' he wrote, 'when remonstrating with you at your intended resignation of the J.P.-ship, I urged you at least to stick to the Club and to the County Galway Hunt, etc., so that I feel rather responsible for you. All I want to do now it to persuade you, though I daresay it is unnecessary, that even whilst proceeding against the Club you should try to think as gently as you can of the members. For I can well fancy that your action, in just one single respect, has hurt their feelings. I mean, of course, your action as to the King and the Irish regiments. The 87th Regiment is the one in which I am specially interested, and I daresay your brother was in some Irish regiment. Yesterday (Sunday) morning I could not help thinking of you in Church, as the psalm happened to be sung which contains the *Domine salvum fac regem et exaudi nos in die quo invocaverimus te.*

'I am not bothering you to concur, I am only explaining the position, or what I suppose is the position of our fellow members generally, which was yours till twenty years ago, that is, considering loyalty to the Sovereign as part of religion. You should not think too bitterly, therefore, even in the midst of your lawsuit, of people whom, however correct you may be, and however wrong we may be, you have grievously injured in a religious matter. To my mind a parallel would be a Club frequented by 500 Gaelic League friends of various religions and politics. Supposing that one of them, an extreme Protestant, went to public meetings and wrote to papers and devoted his talents to attacks upon His Holiness, that would be a matter with which the Club, as such, would be in no way concerned, just as little as the Kildare Street Club is with the Royal Supremacy. Who can, however, doubt that the members would resent it, as too excessively distressing to many of them.

'I cannot think of anything more to say but fully trust to your supplying the deficiency. It will be very interesting for you to be confabulating with Mr. T. Healy,' he continued. 'If he comes down to Tulira next summer, you must not fail to invite me to lunch to meet him. What fun if you bring him over to the next garden party at Lough Cutra: a bombshell for the Archdeacon and the Miss O'Haras of Raheen.' Little did Lord Gough — or for that matter did Edward himself — foresee that within some fifteen years Mr. Tim Healy's appearance at a county garden party would be no longer a 'bombshell for archdeacons,' and that persons even more eminent than they would be glad to accept his official invitations to his own garden parties as the King's representative at the Viceregal Lodge. For the time being the Ascendancy had only one thought — to purge the Club from the presence of so thoroughly undesirable a member.

Almost at the same time that Edward received that kindly letter of rebuke from his old friend in the Embassy at Dresden, he received the official notification from Mr Bailey that a resolution was to be proposed at a specially convened General Meeting, declaring the opinion that his conduct had been injurious to its character and interests. Should Edward desire to submit to the meeting a statement in writing on his own behalf, it must be received before the commencement of the ballot, and would be posted in the morning-room beside the notice setting forth the cause of complaint. Member after member wrote in during the first weeks of January, enclosing cheques for their annual subscriptions and announcing their intention of coming up to Dublin in time to take part in the meeting called for Edward's expulsion, or promising to come if there was any fear of the resolution not being passed. Edward himself replied indignantly that he had 'no statement in writing to lay before such a meeting, which I consider convened for a purpose beyond its rights or its powers.' He wished for fuller information concerning the meeting itself. Was there to be a meeting at all or only a ballot? If there was to be a proper meeting, what exactly was to take place, and where would it be held? Meanwhile he enclosed his subscription for the new year, in evidence of his determination to assert his rights. He did not know that he had already seized upon the weak spot in the defences of the Committee. And although Mr. Bailey had already consulted the Master of the Rolls as a member of the Committee, and obtained his approval, he had already delivered himself into Edward's hands when he wrote in reply that there would be no discussion and that the ballot would merely be held in the Strangers' Room, commencing at 2 and closing at 5.

On what ground Edward could hope to base his case against the Club, it was certainly not easy to see. The Committee had actually taken the necessary steps, by amending their rules in 1903, to obtain further powers of expulsion against any member whose conduct might be such that the Club as a whole would resent it. And within the scope of the rule adopted for this very purpose, or indeed within the scope of any ordinary club rules, Edward had given more than sufficient provocation. The Club's membership consisted chiefly of men who had held the King's commission either in the Army or in the Navy, or who held important positions under the Crown; and it was ridiculous, on the face of things, that anyone who proclaimed that Irishmen joining the Army or Navy deserved to be flogged, should desire to continue his membership of a club which in its whole character was intensely loyal to the Crown. But Edward had resolved to contest the action of the Committee so long as he had the slightest ground for going into court, and no matter how remote was the chance of winning his case. He was bent upon upholding two principles: that a member of the club was perfectly entitled to express his own political opinions, whether they agreed with those of the majority or not; and, secondly, that an Irish Nationalist was entitled to denounce the established order of politics without being treated as a social outcast. Only his extraordinary indifference to public opinion and his contempt for those who looked down upon him as a Catholic, could have enabled him to persevere in such an utterly invidious contest, by attempting to force his own society upon a club who had declared quite plainly that they did not want him.

The trial added to the gaiety of Dublin as few trials have ever done; and by the fifth day, the issue had been narrowed down to a perfectly simple question of whether or not the Club had complied with the necessary implications of its own rules. The chances of success for Edward seemed extremely remote. Why he should wish to remain in the Club was more than anyone could say; and the pretext on which his lawyer was trying to upset the Committee's decision seemed the merest quibble. Sir Andrew Porter's retirement had simplified matters, and the new Master of the Rolls had thoroughly enjoyed his own position in the case. The Committee, he declared (with a generous compliment to his predecessor), were intelligent and honourable men. Had they, he asked, sufficient evidence to justify them in holding that Edward's conduct was 'injurious to the character and interests of the Club?' His own opinion was that it would be 'a mockery' to pretend that they had not ample justification. With admirable dexterity he managed to evade the tangled controversy as to whether or not the question of loyalty to the Crown was a political matter. What did matter, from the judicial point of view, was that Edward's words in defamation of the Army and Navy were a direct insult to the majority of members of the Club. So far, at any rate, his decision was quite definitely against Edward. But the Master of the Rolls approached the question of the procedure in his expulsion with a tantalising open-mindedness. A 'meeting' was, according to the Club's own rules, indispensable for the purpose of expelling an obnoxious member. But the whole history of the Club showed that at such 'meetings' nothing ever happened beyond the holding of a ballot. Was that a reasonable procedure? asked the Master of the Rolls. 'I think,' he said deliberately, 'that view is wrong. I decide that, though the defendants, the Committee of the Club, acted in a manner which cannot be assailed by any right-minded person, though their integrity and honesty can never be called in question, yet the rules, or the particular rule under which they purported to act, did not give them the jurisdiction they assumed in this particular case, and the plaintiff must succeed in his action.'

It would be hard to imagine a more ridiculous conclusion to a ridiculous lawsuit. The Club had unquestionably expressed its overwhelming desire to have no more to say to Edward Martyn; and he himself had proclaimed

his opinion of the great majority of its members by his
absurd declaration that any Irishman who entered the
Army or Navy deserved to be flogged. What conceivable
satisfaction he could derive from asserting his right to
belong to the Club, in spite of their desire to throw him
out, and his own publicly expressed contempt for them,
was more than most people could attempt to understand.
It had certainly been a very costly lawsuit for both parties.
The Club had employed a whole panel of distinguished
lawyers, including three King's Counsel, Mr. Ronan,
Mr. J. H. Campbell, and Mr. Walker, in addition to
Mr. Matheson, who had already earned a series of fees
before the case ever came into court by his opinions on the
interpretation of the rules.   Edward himself had been
obliged to confront this imposing array of pleaders with
a no less formidable list of counsel, and he had briefed
not only his friend, Serjeant O'Connor, and the redoubt-
able Mr. Tim Healy, but Mr. Henry, K.C., and Mr.
A. M. Sullivan.

With the possibility that he would have to pay most
of the Club's costs as well as all his own, and the certainty that he would have to pay much of his own even if
the Master of the Rolls gave judgment in his favour in
regard to costs, even Edward must have wondered
whether his resources might not have been spent to better
advantage. The legal arguments had done much to
clarify the issue in which he had become involved; and
it was painfully apparent — as the Master of the Rolls
had insisted in his summing up — that the Club had
wished to expel him, not because of his politics, but
because he had deliberately insulted the great majority
of its members. And now even those who had sym-

x

pathised with his stand for independence of political
opinion were asking whether or not he would continue
his active membership of the Club which was so anxious
to see the last of him. One of his few friends in the Club
met him after the decision had been given in court, and
asked him at once whether he intended to frequent it as
before. His answer was unhesitating and characteristic.
'Of course, I will,' he replied. 'It's the only place in
Dublin where I can get caviare.'

For Edward indeed to frequent the Club meant to
make more use of it than almost any other member. He
had been for years one of its most familiar and conspicuous figures. In the lawsuit it had been proved in evidence
that he had made much more use of the Club's residential
facilities than any other member over a long period of
years. The devoted secretary, Mr. Bailey, had even
provided a special desk for him in one of the club rooms,
where he could write standing instead of sitting down.
And though he mixed little with most of his fellow-
members, he was so familiar a figure in the building that
his presence had been missed as a long-established
institution during the months when he had been obliged
to absent himself. He certainly could not hope now for a
friendly reception when he returned. But Edward was
completely indifferent to what others thought of him,
and the prospect of humiliating the Committee pleased
him. They had shut the doors of the Club against him
for the past two years, and he decided to take the very
first opportunity of coming back to it. That evening he
dined festively in his own place in the Club dining-room;
and it was a pleasant surprise to find that the public
quarrel had not left him entirely without friends. It was

a source of astonished gratification to him that when he had mounted the old steps and passed through the big hall door, where for so long the Club servants had been under orders to refuse him admission, more than one of the old members whom he had expected to scowl at his reappearance had come to shake his hand and congratulate him on his courage in fighting and winning his case. 'Handy Andyism,' Edward would have said, could scarcely have shown itself more unmistakably than in this greeting of him as a long-lost brother by men who had probably voted for his expulsion and subscribed to the expenses of the lawsuit which he had won.

Not for the first time was Edward in the unique position in Ireland of meaning what he said. And the Club was to know it more than ever in the following years, when he made use of it as freely and as constantly as before, bringing all sorts of unusual visitors within its sacred portals, whose appearance even more than their politics was a sacrilege and a profanation. It was not only Sinn Féiners whom he brought to dine with him and to enjoy the good cooking of the only place in Dublin where Edward could find caviare. From time to time he would bring guileless long-bearded Franciscans, and ascetic-faced priests and monks to meet him there, who could only guess what exquisite pleasure their company was giving to their host in his absurdly incongruous surroundings. And there were occasions, if he found that his fellow-members were denouncing him with more than usual violence, when 'dear Edward' had gone down on his knees in the smoking-room and produced an ostentatious rosary, on which he recited his prayers for their edification.

Edward had won his lawsuit, but the strain and the suspense had told heavily upon him. His resignation of the Presidency of Sinn Féin in 1908 was symptomatic of the relaxation that followed upon the subsequent reaction from a long anxiety. The sudden revival of Home Rule as a practical issue, when Mr. Redmond obtained the 'balance of power' between the English parties at Westminster, destroyed all hopes of winning support for the Sinn Féin policy in the following years. And during the period of political uncertainty and the playing off of one party against another, Edward realised that his personal views were of no importance. It was not till the Home Rule crisis was already at hand, and all public interest was focussed upon the outcome of a swiftly developing conflict between Redmond and Sir Edward Carson, that a new small group of very young men, who took no interest in Home Rule, brought him the opportunity he had sought so long of creating an Irish Theatre which would act his own plays and carry on the tradition of Ibsen that still haunted him as a dream.

In the intervening years time had slipped by quickly, and he had done very little that was new. But in 1911, his friendship with D. P. Moran, the editor of the weekly *Leader*, which had been the truculent organ of 'Irish Ireland' when it was founded in the excitement of the Boer War's aftermath, had induced him to publish, in a series of issues, a number of the poems he had composed at various times and which were still awaiting publication. More than twenty years had passed since, in a mood of fierce scrupulosity, he had destroyed the work of his youth and burned the long classical poem upon which he had once counted for the attainment of literary fame.

It was so long ago, and all dreams of fame as a poet were now so remote, that he could afford to publish his occasional verses as literary curiosities. He could now see as well as anyone else how laboured they were, and how hopelessly unsuited his own slow, deliberate mentality was for finding expression in verse. Yet there was a real poignancy in those clumsy, laboured verses, apparently begun as a sonnet, which could not fit the restrictions of a difficult metre, in which he had lifted part of the veil upon his own unhappy youth:

'Oft in the sad and wayward youth of man
    Come moments full of pure unearthly peace,
Like frankincense in stillness sweet! Who can
    Describe its short, yet exquisite release
From mental anguish luring to despair
    The heart for all the troubles that attend
    Toiling youth thwarted from each wished-for end,
And make it loathe this fair earth, sea and air?

'It is as if some all-defying charm,
    Seizing possession of the human soul,
Strips it stark naked of this writhing swarm
    Of cares, then calmeth anger's fierce control,
And leaveth longing for some lonely life,
    Mayhap by peak or cave or fragrant shore,
    Where thunders of the sea through mountains roar,
And Nature healeth souls in spirit strife.'

As he published, week after week, with scarcely any interval, these memories of early moments of passion and of inspiration, he could feel glad that all the world should know how much his religious life meant to him. It had inspired the only verses in all the lot which were worth remembering. Had he not been wise, as well as justified, in destroying that long early poem, which had seemed to him to reflect the vanity of desire and to be a distraction from the life of the spirit? He could be proud of the crabbed sonnet that he had composed on Piero della Francesca's picture of 'The Singing Angels of the Nativity' in the National Gallery in London:

'You choristers of God, who welcome in
    The Child Redeemer's meek nativity—
    Him who thus feeble 'neath the starry sky
Comes to deliver us from weight of sin—

'How strange, unearthly, are your charms, akin
    To graces supernatural that lie,
    At touch of old Italian mastery
In work whose thoughts our soul's obeisance win.

'What carol hymn'd you on that hallowed night
    Unto your lutes and viol jubilant
Vouchsafed for lowly shepherd swains' delight?
    Gloria in excelsis — thus you chant
With mystic chord and voice in dove-like flight,
    While-as I watch you tuneful, ministrant.'

There was that other sonnet, too, on *The Death of Saint Francis Xavier*:

'On desert shores beneath a shed of reeds,
    Xavier, I see thee breathe thy soul away!
    Thy Lord now sendeth thee this long'd-for day
When He would crown thy life and wondrous deeds.

›Oh, thou wer't like a seraph! For thy needs
　　Perplex us, little men with hearts of clay.
　　O'er thee thy spirit ruled with rapturous sway,
Through thee commanded credence from old creeds.

'And thou wer't like thy Indies too, where sweet
　　Aromas from spice islands load the air!
Thou had'st their kings and nations at thy feet
　　When, lonely in thy ecstasy of prayer,
The scented breeze bore to the judgment seat
　　Thy soul more sweet than Orient incense rare!'

And there was another, inspired by some vision of
A White Thurifer, which gives a wistful glimpse of his
intense love of boyhood, and of his abhorrence of the
disillusionments of youth:

'He passes, like an apparition, white,
　　And stepless through the sanctuary's space,
　　As if he came from statelier spheres. Such grace
Of shape and movement haunts this acolyte.
　　And while he wafts the thurible, its bright
　　Embers alight and colour his pale face
　　Pink, as a flaming angel's limners trace
In minster lancet jewelled to joy our sight.

'Child of the earth or heaven, mysterious child,
　　Oh would thou could'st live on undefiled!
Gross manhood with such angel genius wars.
　　Thou'lt change — alas! Yet thy boy memory
　　Fair-haired and white, will flutter to the sky —
A beauty among the children of the stars!'

But the verses which probably pleased him most were the rhetorical lines addressed to Philip the Second of Spain, as the champion of Catholic tradition against the Reformation:

'Hail, brooding Cheops of the Escorial,
    Thy pyramid with primal strength devised
    For a world wonder! hugeness solemnised
By art ascetic clouding like a pall
In grandiose reserve thy genius, all
    Thy artists, councillors, thy monks — here prized,
    What time were priests and orders civilised
Who dower the Church with art majestical!

'Great Catholic! strong king o'er home, o'er clime
    Afar from thy bare cell where thou could'st hear
    Dream organ gusts mid liturgy severe,
Or sad Vittoria weave voice chords sublime,
Hail! Thou did'st keep, with Culture's cold disdain,
The vulgar Reformation out of Spain!'

His eccentric habits of life had begun to tell heavily upon his constitution. For years he had accustomed himself to live upon only one meal a day. Even the breakfasts to which Mr. George Moore devotes so much ludicrous attention in his trilogy had long ago ceased to be part of his daily routine. His natural obesity demanded a rigid discipline in regard to eating, and Edward solved the problem by abstaining entirely from food until the evening. But his appetite had always been excessive, and the result of restricting himself to one solid meal a day was to make him eat much too heavily at the only meal which he allowed himself. Food and drink had been the only appetite that he had ever indulged, and his generous hospitality towards his friends had constantly encouraged him to strain the intolerable limits he had imposed upon himself. His constitution had suffered in consequence; and he had fiercely aggravated a natural tendency to rheumatism by his persistence in sleeping in the cold, flagged room in his tower at Tulira, and by his disregard for all reasonable comfort in his miserable lodgings in Dublin. He had always been acutely sensitive to draughts, liable to severe colds in inclement weather; and he had brought crippling rheumatic troubles upon himself by insisting, as a measure of self-discipline and mortification, that he should sleep in extreme discomfort, although his house gave every luxury to his guests. His vitality, as well as his health, began to fail; and he was already much older than his years, when a new lease of life had apparently opened before him with the foundation of the Irish Theatre just before the war.

'Living such a detached life, his visitors were very rare,' writes Mr. John MacDonagh, who was closely associated with him as his manager when he founded the new Irish Theatre. 'He showed a child-like pleasure in having someone to talk to. "I thought you weren't coming," he would say, "Sit down, and let us talk," and so the hours passed pleasantly. Pipe after pipe he would smoke in his long churchwarden, and midnight often found me still there, held by the magnetism of his words. One would be dull indeed who did not catch some spark from that mind stored with culture and experience, and it would be a nature bereft of sympathy that did not expand in that kindly and genial presence.' Describing him at rehearsals in the large old hall at Hardwicke Street, which Edward had rented for his experiment, Mr. MacDonagh continues: 'He sat long hours in our cold and draughty hall, interfering little, but glad when any problem of interpretation came up, so that he felt he was being useful. On such occasions he was a pathetic figure, sitting hunched up, near a radiator, but we all knew the keen enjoyment he experienced as he saw the play taking shape, and his interest was always reflected in greater efforts by the actors.'

'The tragedies of late years saddened him beyond expression,' writes the same friend of his closing years. 'One after another he saw his friends and associates pass away, and the hopes and ideals of his life pushed into unfulfilment. After Easter Week, 1916, he wrote to me to Knutsford Prison, "I'm glad of the prospect of seeing you again. Alas for your poor brother and the others! It was an awful shock to me, such great talents and high ideals, only the jobbers and place-hunters left. Everything is in ruins in Ireland. I am trying to carry on the theatre, but what can I do without your brother?"' He had been deeply grieved by the death of so many of his friends through the insurrection of Easter Week, 1916. It had taken him, as it took most people, completely by surprise. He had known Patrick Pearse well for many years, since the days when Pearse, as little more than a boy, had edited the Gaelic League's organ the *Claidheamh Soluis* with rare distinction and literary ability. But Pearse's lieutenants, in the re-birth of Fenianism, had been his close friends in the years immediately before the war. Thomas MacDonagh, who had had several plays produced at the Abbey Theatre, had joined eagerly with Joseph

Plunkett — they both married sisters soon afterwards —
in organising the Literary Theatre, which Edward had
enabled them to bring into being for the production of
plays that broke new ground. And Thomas MacDonagh's
brother had been the chief producer of all the plays in
Edward's venture with them. He had built great hopes
upon the future of the little theatre he had provided for
his young friends. They were constantly with him, though
he knew nothing of their political conspiracies; and on the
very evening before the rising of Easter Sunday, 1916,
Thomas MacDonagh had called at his rooms for the last
time, and found him there, sitting behind the big shabby
screen that kept out draughts, with Vincent O'Brien.
They had even spent their last hour together discussing
the possibilities of a rising, which Edward was still convinced could never materialise. Thomas MacDonagh
had left him without revealing the secret in his own
possession, and the next morning he was engaged with
Pearse and Connolly in starting the revolution.

No man felt more overwhelmed by the sanguinary
suppression of the rising which his young friends had so
recklessly undertaken. And the increasing chaos and
turmoil of the following years afflicted him sorely. Time
passed, and his old friend Arthur Griffith, who had succeeded him in the Presidency of Sinn Féin, when no one
could have foreseen what immense forces the new movement would let loose, came suddenly into power after the
'midnight treaty' of 1921, as the chairman of the Pro-
visional Government of the Irish Free State. But Griffith
died suddenly from sheer exhaustion when the new era
was just about to begin; and the civil strife that followed
threw all Ireland into a state of anarchy and chaos. In the

West, lawlessness was rampant and almost unchecked. Most of the great mansions among which Edward had grown up, and which in his own boyhood had been the centres of undisputed power and wealth, were now burned down by incendiaries, determined to cast out the last remnants of the ascendancy whom Edward had denounced through so many years for their blindness to the signs of the times. Destruction became utterly indiscriminate. The few public-spirited landowners who had shared Edward's own enthusiasms in different ways seemed before long to become a special target for the revolutionaries. Lord Killanin, his neighbour and close friend, was to have his house burned down. Lord Mayo was to be turned out of his own mansion, after the carpets had been soaked in petrol till the beautiful rooms where he had accumulated unique treasures of French art became a blazing furnace. Plunkett—for the same reason, being a member of the new Free State Senate, and a patriotic gentleman whose example was likely to create sympathy with his own class—was to have his house burned down also; and on the following day, when it was found that his library and pictures had escaped the fire, the incendiaries returned deliberately to complete their destruction.

It became more and more probable that Tulira also would be made a smoky ruin like the rest; and Edward, alone and crippled with rheumatism, could only wait from day to day to see what fate would bring, to him who had been the first distinguished supporter of Sinn Féin. But even at its worst he could still discern a more hopeful side to the vast transformation that was taking place. Armed fanatics might make life intolerable for all who desired the quiet peaceful life of the old days, but their operations were not everywhere unchecked. The new Government, mustering what forces it could to restore order from the chaos that had emerged from two years' of Black-and-Tan regime, was slowly mastering the situation. New men, unheard of until the revolution, many of them little more than university students who had thrown in their lot with Sinn Féin in its guerilla warfare against Sir Hamar Greenwood's Black and Tans, were suddenly given positions of great responsibility; and the vitality and earnestness of a new generation began to grapple fiercely with the chaos that disgraced the birth of a new Ireland. And as the months passed the success of their determined efforts began to show promise of a real reconstruction.

All over the country, while the Black and Tans were still running amok, the administration of justice had been gradually passing into the hands of the popular movement; and the newly constituted, unauthorised, Sinn Féin courts had begun to administer the law on the spot, with a rapidity and a sense of impartial justice that restored confidence and won unmeasured praises from people of all classes who were sick alike of politicians, of Black and Tans, and of revolutionaries. Edward himself had found it necessary to invoke one of the Sinn Féin courts in 1919, when some of his former tenants, taking advantage of the prevailing unrest and of the strong prejudice against landowners, had sought to encroach upon his property. He had written without hesitation to tell them in vigorous language what he thought of their menaces, telling them that since they had bought their properties from him they had no more claims upon him than he had upon them. He had concluded by assuring them that if their demands

were to prevail, he would have no more to do with any of
them; that he was very happy where he was in Dublin,
and that he would never set foot in Tulira again if his
rights were infringed. Their case was heard publicly
before one of the Sinn Féin arbitration courts at Gort,
in August 1919, and it attracted wide notice because of
Edward's own former prominence in the Sinn Féin
movement as its earliest President. The fact stood him
in good stead, and the court decided in his favour after
investigating the case. His letter to the court was characteristic: 'I have certainly no objection to submit my case
to an impartial arbitration such as Sinn Féin would
appoint,' he wrote, 'because my experience of Sinn Féiners
is that they are superior and fair-minded. . . . Any
judgment that would put me in a different position as
regards the management of my domain from the position
of my former tenants, now proprietors in regard to the
management of theirs, I would consider not an impartial
judgment. Grant me this equality of rights with them,
and the whole case of my persecutors falls to the ground.
I claim their right not to be forced to do business with
anyone in whom I have no confidence. I do not see how
there can be a compromise without injustice. You will
be only acting like the British Government in the case
of Carson v. the Sinn Féin Volunteers if you give greater
rights to one of us beyond the other.'

That threat was thus overcome, and he was glad to feel
that his own vigorous protest had set an example of
courage in face of intimidation. But matters had grown
worse as the Black and Tan regime developed, and even
the signing of the Treaty brought no more than a
momentary lessening of the strain. He felt sadly forlorn

and lonely in the state of chaos that resulted in the West, and it was a source of immense joy to him when occasionally some old friend would write him news. 'My dear Sweetman,' he wrote at once in reply to a letter from one of his closest allies in the birth of the Sinn Féin movement — another Catholic landowner like himself, who had been almost alone in his complete sympathy with Edward Martyn in most of his political adventures. 'Your letter was like a breeze from the outer world to a captive. I am practically imprisoned here, for although the railways are open off and on, it is practically impossible to go to Dublin by road, so many are the obstacles and uncertainties. I want very much to return, but dare not risk the journey and be deprived of my motor, as I very nearly was when coming down last May. Barring all this, they leave me here altogether in peace. They all say that they do not wish to disturb me at all, although they are always prowling about the place. I hope they may continue in this mind. I'm afraid it's going to be a long business.

'We suffer in Eire from a plague of *minorities*. There is the Unionist minority, the Protestant minority, the Ascendancy minority, the Carson minority, and what not — waiting to impose their will on the *majority* of the Irish, who are fairly decent and reasonable; and now that they have made a treaty with England and confirmed it by Parliament, lo and behold, true to the country's native instincts, another minority leaps into national life and seeks to impose its murderous tyranny on the majority. I think this is probably the reason we have the reputation of not being fit to govern ourselves. We have now certainly made as great a mess of government as before. It's all along of our mania for minorities!

'When I stopped to say farewell to you last May,' he continued, in a parenthesis that reveals the helplessness of those closing years, 'I wondered at the effect I seemed to produce in your household. I seemed to throw all into confusion. It never occurred to me until some time afterwards that when I arrived at your house with motor and baggage so unexpectedly, you must evidently have thought that I came to throw myself on your hospitality in my pitiable condition. You must have felt relieved when I departed. In the days of the saints,' he concluded, reverting to political questions, ' one might confess one's self in the wrong. To do so nowadays is political extinction. No — de Valera won't go to China — worse luck — but after all I don't think he was a free agent.'

His health showed little sign of improvement, and though his doctor persisted in encouraging him to hope for recovery, he became fully aware that he could not live much longer. Nor did he want to live, compelled to be pushed about in a bath chair. The tall, bulky figure that had for so long been a familiar sight in the Dublin streets was seen there no more. The red, fat face was now partly hidden by a short beard that was rapidly turning from grey to white; and his former cheerfulness could no longer bear up against the constant agony of rheumatic pains that crippled him completely. It was the result of his self-imposed Spartan ways of life, and he had no regrets as he faced the end. His life's work was done, and he could feel, in spite of all the temporary discouragements of a period of chaotic transition, that he had shown how much could be accomplished, if only a few more rich men with a generosity like his own would make the small contribution that was required to give youth its chance in Ireland.

Edward Martyn

From a painting by Norman French McLachlan, in Joseph Holloway's Collection.

And as the last years closed in, he could derive much satisfaction from the thought of what great assistance it was still in his power to give to many causes dear to him, by the fulfilment of his will. The will in its main provisions was made in February 1909, nearly fifteen years before Edward's death; and it was not modified in any important respect by the three codicils subsequently attached to it. For Edward, everything connected with death had always had a peculiar significance and intimacy, and his will gives a remarkably close expression to the trend of his aims and affections throughout his life. He had much to leave. The whole family property which he had inherited was now at his disposal; and there was not even a nephew or niece, or any near relative, to whom it could be left. But it was not of Tulira that Edward thought first in the elaborate provisions of his will. His first legacy was to be the collection of pictures that he had himself got together, and his next thoughts were for the private library to which he had added with affectionate diligence, and with so much anxiety lest he might be acquiring books forbidden by the Sacred Congregation of the Index. He had decided that it must be entrusted to safe hands; and the first sections of his will accordingly bequeathed 'to the Provincial for the time being of the Discalced Carmelites at Clarendon Street in the City of Dublin, as a legacy to him personally and not otherwise, all the printed books and manuscripts, photographs, engravings, and statues of which I shall be possessed at the time of my decease.' With the library was to go another gift — a painting by A. E. entitled 'The Enchanted Sea,' which Edward cherished with a paternal affection. That picture was expressly excluded from the main

Y

donation of all his pictures, oil paintings, water colours, pastels and drawings, which were to be offered to the Municipal Gallery of Modern Art, that Sir Hugh Lane had founded in Dublin, for a selection to be made. In the event of the Modern Art Gallery not wanting them, they were to be offered for acceptance as a complete collection to the National Gallery of Ireland. There were some of them which any Gallery in Europe would desire—a lovely Corot, a Claude Monet, two pictures of Degas, a vivid landscape by Brabazon, and portraits of Mr. Yeats by William Rothenstein and of Robert Louis Stevenson by William Strang.

His books and his pictures had come first in his thoughts, before he turned to the disposal of the inherited castle and estate. A reminiscence of *Morgante* rings through the Homeric catalogue of all his effects which he bequeathed to his cousin the Honourable Mrs. Fitzroy Hemphill and her son. To her and to him he bequeathed 'all my estate and interest in the demesne lands of Tulira, with the Mansion House thereon called Tulira Castle, together with the household furniture, plate, linen, china, glass, and articles of household use and ornament, musical instruments, wines, provisions, and other household effects, in, upon, or about the said Mansion House . . . save and except . . . and also my carriages, with the horses and other appendages thereto respectively belonging, also all the implements and utensils, stock of hay, corn, and straw and of other moveable effects which shall at my death be used or employed in or about my coach house or other houses, stables and buildings at Tulira aforesaid. Also the gardening implements and utensils, greenhouse and outhouse furniture, pots, plants in pots, and other moveable effects, which shall be used or employed in or about my garden and pleasure grounds at Tulira at the time of my death. And also the plot of land with the gate lodge thereon opposite to the gate known as the Gort Gate, adjoining the said demesne lands of Tulira.'

All real and personal property belonging to him at his death was similarly bequeathed to his cousin, subject to whatever other provisions might be contained in the will. The excepting clause was indeed a formidable matter; for the string of Edward's charitable donations was to fill many pages of the legal document. Even the possibility of any flaw arising in the disposition of any of the charitable bequests, was expressly provided for, and the catalogue of his charitable legacies opened with a stipution that, in the event of any funds destined for some such purpose being inapplicable for the purpose outlined, then the surplus so available should be bequeathed to the Catholic Archbishop of Dublin, 'for his absolute use, as a personal legacy to him absolutely, freed and discharged from obligation at law or trust in equity of any nature or kind whatsoever.'

The donations then follow in an imposing series. First to the Provincial of the Discalced Carmelites in Clarendon Street he left £300, to have twelve hundred Masses 'publicly celebrated in Ireland for the repose of his soul.' Then to the President of the diocesan college of the Holy Cross at Clonliffe, £500; and to the President of All Hallows College at Drumcondra also £500. To the Bishop of Galway, 'for such charitable purposes within the diocese of Kilmacduagh as he may think fit,' the handsome legacy of £5,000; and to the same bishop a further £3,000 'for application towards the erection of a new Roman Catholic Cathedral in Galway.' To the Archbishop of Dublin there was a further special legacy of £1,000, to be invested in trustee securities so that the income from it should be applied 'towards providing annually two entertainments, one at Christmas and the other in the summer of each year, for the members of the Roman Catholic Cathedral Choir of Dublin, so long as my endowment of the said choir is preserved.' To the Saint Vincent de Paul Society of Dublin, for the benefit of any of its charitable purposes, he left £2,000, the only restriction being that the charitable purposes must be in Ireland.

Among these religious legacies another was surprisingly inserted, giving £2,000 to the Gaelic League 'to be expended in promoting and sustaining the cultivation of the Irish language in the Irish-speaking districts,' and leaving to the Coisde Gnótha or 'Governing Body' of the Gaelic League the decision as to what were the Irish-speaking districts. The series of religious legacies is then resumed with a donation of £1,000 as 'a personal legacy' to the Provincial for the time being of the Discalced Carmelites at Clarendon Street, and a gift of £2,000, also as a 'personal legacy,' to the Superior-General for the time being of the Christian Brothers in Ireland. A curious legacy follows for the benefit of each of his former tenants in counties Galway or Roscommon who had bought their estates from him under the Land Purchase Acts. They were to receive a gift of three pounds for each holding that had been so bought from him as their former landlord.

Personal legacies to friends and relatives then followed. The principal legacy was £16,000 to his cousin Robert

Smyth or his children. He gave £5,000 to his friend Mr. Vincent O'Brien, and £1,000 each to his two godsons, Joseph Smyth Pigott, and Francis, son of his old school friend the Duke de Stackpoole, and also to his cousin Mrs. Lucy Burke, and to his steward James Acton. To his housekeeper at Tulira he left £300, and £100 to be divided between the servants in his employment at the time of his death. The combined total of these many legacies had made enormous inroads upon his personal estate; but if there should be any residue still remaining, Edward stipulated that it should go to the Archbishop of Dublin, to be applied towards the building of a new Catholic Cathedral in Dublin, 'respectfully recommending, though not imposing any trust or obligation in that behalf,' that before adopting the designs and plans for such cathedral, 'the Archbishop shall consult with, and have the advice of, and assistance of, some Irish artists of eminence and distinction in their Art or profession.'

Ten years passed before Edward made any alteration in this remarkable document; and the first codicil, made in the summer of 1919, added only two bequests, of £500 each, to his chauffeur and to his housekeeper at Tulira. To Mr. George Moore the same codicil bequeathed 'any right, title or interest which I may have at my death in the two plays of which I am the author and which are respectively called *The Heather Field* and *Maeve*.' This special bequest seems surprising at first sight in view of the fact that the two old friends had long been estranged by Mr. Moore's caricature of Edward in his trilogy of Irish reminiscences. Mr. Moore was also considerably senior to Edward and scarcely likely to benefit by any such provision. But the object of inserting the codicil presumably was that it gave Edward an opportunity to make a solemn declaration that the two plays were his own work, and not — as had been freely said since the publication of Mr. Moore's books — a collaboration in which Mr. Moore was the principal author.

Another year passed and Edward, with infirmity encroaching fast upon his strength, again added a codicil. This time it was to make a legacy of £300 to his male nurse, who had been attending him for some time, and to increase the legacy to his chauffeur to £1,000. There was a new legacy also to Father Carr, the Parish Priest of Ardrahan, leaving him £300 to buy a monstrance for use in the church. He revised also the earlier disposition of his collection of pictures, now leaving them to the National Gallery of Ireland instead of the Municipal Gallery of Modern Art. He was so infirm that already he was obliged to sign with a mark, instead of with his name, in the presence of his solicitor. But his illness abated, and it was three years more before he added yet another codicil, a few months before his death. Once again the legacies to his personal attendants were increased; his nurse, Laurence Burke, was now to receive £1,000 instead of £300 'for the purpose of enabling him to continue and complete his medical studies and become a fully qualified Physician or Surgeon, and to enable him to buy all necessary books and up-to-date surgical appliances.' A special stipulation was now entered also, that these two increased legacies, payable to his chauffeur and to his nurse, should, notwithstanding anything to the contrary in his will, be payable in priority to any other pecuniary bequests. Realising also that the long list of separate legacies and additional donations made in the codicils had exhausted his personal estate, Edward now made express provision that the main legacy to his cousin and his prospective heir, her son, should be charged with any deficiency.

One other provision in his will was to make a sensation when it became known. He had placed it before all the rest, and it represented a wish that had haunted him all through his life. Long before, in the first early will that had been made before his mother died, when he had bequeathed all his property to her, he had insisted under pain of revoking the entire bequest that his body was to be dissected, so that the cause of his death might be ascertained. But after her death he had evidently felt greater freedom in following upon his own most intimate wishes; and he now made express provision for an arrangement which he had described in the chapter of *Morgante* that represented his own view of the ideal state. 'When a citizen falls sick,' Edward had written in that fantastic description of 'the ideal commonwealth of uncloistered monks' — 'he is immediately taken to one of the many State hospitals, which are under the management of the various religious orders. There he is tenderly nursed, and receives every spiritual and bodily comfort from those pious and gentle brethren who have devoted their noble lives to the alleviation of human suffering. Should he die, his body is first dissected in the medical school attached to the hospital, and afterwards buried in consecrated ground according to the Christian rite. This compulsory dissection of the bodies of all our citizens without respect of persons is the oldest among our existing laws, and, instead of being viewed with the aversion of those who are enslaved by the concupiscence of the flesh and the pride of life, is by us esteemed to be most just and salutary, in that it mortifies carnal vainness, and affords a more ample supply of subjects for our medical schools, which are consequently for the curing of most ailments the first in the world.'

So now at the very outset of his own will — re-made after his mother's death — which was to bring so much relief and assistance to the poor and to the promotion of his own Church in Ireland, he laid down the one condition that he had longed to have fulfilled. To the Cecilia Street School of Medicine or any other School of Medicine that might afterwards be formed within the recently constituted National University of Ireland, he left a legacy of £1,000 on condition that its doctors undertook the strange task that he imposed. 'After my death and before the cover of the coffin in which my corpse may have been placed shall have been screwed down or otherwise affixed to said coffin preparatory to interment, the proper authorities of the said Cecilia Street School of Medicine or of other said School of Medicine aforesaid, shall take my body (as they respectively are hereby authorised to do, and my executors are hereby directed to permit) and as soon as, but not before decomposition thereof shall have set in, cause the same to be dissected in the dissecting room or rooms of the said School, in the same manner in all respects as a subject acquired in the ordinary course for dissection therein would then be dissected; and, when same shall have been fully so dissected, cause my remains to be gathered and interred with Christian burial, and simply as the remains of paupers and other bodies, for the time being dissected in the said dissecting room or rooms, are then usually interred.'

It was a strange wish indeed, but it had been for years the most cherished desire of all his life, that his body in its decomposition might yet serve some useful purpose. It was his supreme gesture of indifference to the vanities of human life, the last act of relentless discipline over his body which he had rigorously controlled. He had cared nothing for the fact that the Martyn family were to be extinguished by his own refusal to marry, yet he had loved his old home, and had been genuinely and deeply proud of his family tradition. He might at least have allowed his own body to lie in peace among his fathers in the old vault at Loughrea Abbey. But his own preoccupation with death had been too strong for any compromise with sentiment. He had determined that his last action, even after death, should bring his body into absolute subjection. He had brooded over death so long that it had no terrors for him; and he was resolved that in the last contest his own mastery should be unqualified.

Many years before, he had discovered somewhere the poetic epitaph that was engraved on the tomb on the Black Prince according to the directions in his will; and among the papers written when Edward's handwriting was still that of a young man, and preserved until his death, was the transcript he had made of the Black Prince's epitaph, with the original old French in its archaic spelling carefully copied out on one side of the page, and Edward's own translation opposite to it. The translation ran:

I

'Who passeth here with closed lips, near to where this body reposeth, let him hear what I shall say, saying only what I know. Even as thou art so once was I: and as I am so thou shalt be.

2

'On death I never thought whilst I had life, though having great riches, which I dispensed with great state and nobleness. Land had I, great treasure, rich robes, houses, and gold and silver.

3

'But now I am mean and poor, deep in the earth I lie. Great beauty is departed and my flesh is withered away.

4

'Very narrow is my house; and of me, of a truth, there is nothing left; and if any one saw me, I doubt whether he would say that I was once a man, so greatly am I changed.

5

'In God's name pray to the celestial King to have mercy on my soul. All who shall pray for me, or make my peace with God, may God place them in His paradise, where none can be wretched.'

He had no fear of death, but as the end came near, old scruples that had always haunted him at times, began to torment him again. In his early manhood he had felt it necessary to write to his bishop for a personal dispensation to read books that had been placed on the Index. The bishop had enabled him to get a special dispensation direct from Rome, and that had appeased his conscience in those early years of vague ambitions and morbid fears. But now as he felt death approaching, he began to have new qualms of conscience, lest any of the books which he had obtained permission, at such trouble, to read and to possess, might perhaps fall into the hands of those who might be scandalised. Long ago, he had bequeathed his entire library to the Carmelites in Clarendon Street, Dublin, and now he became impatient to have all his books removed to that safe custody. A pathetic eagerness to have matters settled appears in one of his last letters to his friend the Carmelite Father Cyril Ryan. 'I write to ask you to be so kind as to come here as soon as you can,' he wrote in a dictated letter, 'as I have some very important business to communicate with you. I hope you will not be absent or away giving retreats anywhere, as I have weighty matters to discuss with you. Could you kindly come at once? The doctor seems confident of me although I am improving very slowly. Will you kindly come at once?' It was an immense relief to his mind when he had arranged for their dispatch to Dublin. 'My dear Father Cyril,' he had written in answer to Father Ryan's reluctance to presume that he was about to die, 'I do not see why you should not have the Library as it is quite useless to me and might get dispersed. So I would be very much obliged if you would remove it at once. Send down a man who can pack the books carefully and get them out of the place. You should also provide the necessary cases to put them in. If anything else occurs to me I shall let you know from time to time. They are now perfect, having been uninterfered with.' A week later he had written again to expostulate. 'I do not see your difficulty, and cannot understand why I cannot do what I like with my own property. So please arrange to have the books removed at once. I should like altogether to be free of the Index, etc. On the other hand, if the books were pillaged, I should never forgive myself.'

A note of immense relief runs through the next letter, after they had been safely taken away. 'I have kept some books — a few dozen or so,' he wrote after Tulira had been stripped of the magnificent library, which had given him so much happiness through years of lonely study. A historic interest had already become attached to many of the volumes which he had helped to get published, or which had been written by his own friends and associates. 'Owen has also kept *Sinn Féin Policy* by Griffith,' he wrote. 'The others I have let nearly all go. The former chiefly on account of its convenience of being easily destroyed and for other reasons rendering it more easy of destruction. You can judge of it, and some of the books of an unpleasant nature, etc., you can do with them what you like. You are at perfect liberty to accept them or not. The same applies to the whole collection, destroying or keeping whatever you wish.'

He had been ill for so long that Dublin no longer knew him, and only a few old friends continued to write to him. A charming letter from Colonel Maurice Moore a few months before the end, remains among his papers: 'I have been hoping these few months that you would be in Dublin soon, so that I could see you and talk to you. There is so much we could discuss, but I heard from the Stackpooles you are not well enough. It is a pity, and I fear you must be lonely in Tulira with none of your old friends to talk to. You remember the days when we used to go hunting together? I can see you now jumping a coped wall that I avoided, and everyone else too. Well, I am nearly as lame as you; I went to London and found there is no cure for osteo-arthritis (which is my form) but a splint. I am getting one. I wish you were in the Senate, it would just suit you. I rather prefer it to the Dáil, though it looks rather like the last refuge of the old régime.' A postscript, referring to the memorial to Arthur Griffith and Michael Collins erected at the back of the Parliament buildings, adds: 'We have just unveiled a monument to your friend Arthur Griffith. It is hideous. M.M.'

He lingered on through the autumn, a helpless invalid, scarcely able to emerge from his house at Tulira; and with the approach of winter it was evident that his sufferings were nearly over. His closest friend, Father Cyril Ryan, who had met him first when he was at Loughrea as a young Carmelite priest, and who had been his unfailing counsellor and ally in all his enterprises, was with him when the end came on December 15th, and gave him the last sacraments of his Church. Edward had left no loophole by which the wishes concerning his burial expressed in his will might be evaded, and they were faithfully carried out. His body was duly taken to Cecilia Street for dissection by the medical students, among the other corpses that are provided from the workhouse infirmaries. The remains were conveyed afterwards in the workhouse mortuary van, together with the six other bodies that were being interred by the public authorities. The coffin, which was only a plain box, was exactly like the others. The customary Mass was celebrated in the cemetery chapel for him and for the six

paupers who shared his grave, and the only ceremonial
was the singing of the *Benedictus* by the Palestrina Choir
which he had endowed, and for whose benefit in his last
testament he had bequeathed a further thousand pounds,
to provide them with two annual entertainments in the
winter and summer of each year.

The philosophy of life that he had evolved for himself
as a young man had stood him in good stead, throughout
a lonely and at all times an unhappy life; and with a
strange but noble gesture he had proclaimed himself an
impenitent eccentric to the end. It fell to one of his
oldest friends, Father Tom Finlay, who had worked with
him in many good causes, and who as a priest with his
own Jesuit vows of poverty, chastity and obedience could
sympathise most intimately with the austere life Edward
had always led, to write the most notable of the obituary
notices that surveyed his life's work and ambitions.
'To the public,' wrote Father Finlay, in the *Belvederian*,
the magazine of his old preparatory school in Dublin,
'Mr. Martyn was a politician, a connoisseur in art, and a
playwright; those who knew him more intimately found
something higher and more estimable to admire in him.
Before all else he was profoundly and practically religious.
For him religion was the supreme interest of life; it
entered in and influenced all his pursuits. He had in him
much of that spirit which has impelled many followers of
Christ to practise in the midst of wealth, and behind the
pomp of high station, the austerities of asceticism. He
was master of a lordly mansion; in it he selected for his
own use an apartment which a hermit would not have
deemed too sumptuous. He was bearer of an ancient
name, the last of a line in which social rank had been for

centuries a family inheritance; he chose to be buried in a
pauper's grave, side by side with the unclaimed workhouse dead, for whom public charity provides a resting
place. Eccentricities these, it may be said. Possibly; but
in such eccentricities the lives of the Saints abound.'
There were others among his friends who were profoundly impressed by the last gesture of his will. And
among them especially his old friend, Mr. R. J. Kelly,
K.C., who wrote a long obituary notice in the *Tuam
Herald*. 'No man had a greater reverence for the memory
of his ancestors, and particularly his mother,' wrote Mr.
Kelly, who knew the whole family history of the Martyns
by heart; 'and one would have thought he would like to
rest in the old family tomb in the Abbey at Loughrea,
where so many of the Martyns lie in peace, but it was not
so. His dismembered body was brought and thrown into
an unknown grave in the pauper part of Glasnevin, and
there he rests, and may God have mercy on his soul — for
a kinder friend, a finer soul, full of charity and sympathy
and compassion, never breathed.'